I'LL TAKE YOU THERE

DEAR JAKE!

IT HAS BEEN SUCH A JOYFU
EXPERIENCE TO LEARN ABOUT
YOUR PASSION FOR FOOD AND
JUSTICE. THIS YEAR, AND TO SEE IT
IN ACTION IN THE FOOD BANK!

MARTHA O'BRYAN CENTER IS GRATEFUL
TO YOU!

GOOD LUCK IN CALI AND
BEYOND!

NATE KERN
AMERICORPS 20-21

I'LL TAKE YOU THERE

EXPLORING NASHVILLE'S SOCIAL JUSTICE SITES

EDITED BY
AMIE THURBER AND LEAROTHA WILLIAMS JR.

VANDERBILT UNIVERSITY PRESS
NASHVILLE, TENNESSEE

Library of Congress Cataloging-in-Publication Data
Names: Thurber, Amie, editor. | Williams, Learotha, Jr., editor.
Title: I'll take you there : Nashville stories of place, power, and the
   struggle for social justice / Amie Thurber, Learotha Williams Jr.
Description: Nashville : Vanderbilt University Press, [2021] | Includes
   bibliographical references.
Identifiers: LCCN 2021000001 (print) | LCCN 2021000002 (ebook) | ISBN
   9780826501530 (paperback) | ISBN 9780826501547 (epub) | ISBN
   9780826501561 (pdf)
Subjects: LCSH: Social justice—Tennessee—Nashville. | Nashville
   (Tenn.)—Guidebooks. | LCGFT: Guidebooks.
Classification: LCC F444.N23 I44 2021 (print) | LCC F444.N23 (ebook) |
   DDC 976.8/55—dc23
LC record available at https://lccn.loc.gov/2021000001
LC ebook record available at https://lccn.loc.gov/2021000002

We dedicate this work to the life and memory of **Kwame Lillard**. When we first began this project there was no doubt among those that gathered that if we were going to attempt a work that explored sites of social justice, we would have to include his voice. For much of his adult life, Kwame fought for justice. Kwame was our gladiator; our dashiki-clad champion, and the Music City was his coliseum.

He walked, he sat, he rode, he swam, he shouted, and he wrote for the cause of freedom. He added to our understanding of the past and how it informed the present, and he demonstrated how his love for his community was the strongest weapon in his arsenal.

When Kwame raised his fist to the heavens, striking a pose that those of us who knew him recognized and adored, he became a symbol of power and a commitment to justice and equality. With him on our side, anything seemed possible, and all enemies—despite how formidable they appeared—could be vanquished.

We miss our dear friend and colleague and dedicate this book to his memory as one of Nashville's most outstanding and heroic citizens.

Lea Williams and Amie Thurber
Spring 2021

CONTENTS

ACKNOWLEDGMENTS   XI

INTRODUCTION   1

---

1. DOWNTOWN

AN INTRODUCTION TO DOWNTOWN   23

1.1 Nunna-daul-Tsuny (Trail Where They Cried)   29

1.2 Public Square   31

1.3 Maxwell House Hotel   33

1.4 Juanita's   34

1.5 Ryman Auditorium   36

1.6 Tara Cole Memorial Bench   38

1.7 Black Bottom (Country Music Hall of Fame)   40

1.8 Downtown Incinerator / Ascend Amphitheatre   42

1.9 Tent City / 2010 Flood   44

1.10 James Robertson Apartments   45

1.11 Nashville Public Library Civil Rights Room   47

1.12 Walgreens Lunch Counter   49

1.13 Tennessee State Capitol   52

1.14 The Hermitage Hotel   54

1.15 Legislative Plaza   56

1.16 Music City Central Bus Station Bathroom   59

1.17 The *Nashville Globe*   60

1.18 Duncan Hotel   62

1.19 The Nashville Farmers' Market   63

1.20 First Baptist Church, Capitol Hill   66

2.   NORTHWEST

AN INTRODUCTION TO NORTHWEST NASHVILLE   73

2.1   Gateway to Heritage / I-40   77
2.2   American Baptist College   81
2.3   Clark Memorial Methodist Church   82
2.4   Fisk University   84
2.5   Jubilee Hall   86
2.6   Tennessee State University   88
2.7   Hadley Park   90
2.8   Meharry Medical College   93
2.9   Nashville Greenlands   94
2.10 Pearl High School   96
2.11 Planned Parenthood   98
2.12 The Tennessee State Penitentiary   100
2.13 William Edmondson Park   102
2.14 John Henry Hale Apartments   104
2.15 Z. Alexander Looby's home   105
2.16 Bordeaux Landfill   108
2.17 Southern Publishing Association   109
2.18 Beaman Park / Bells Bend   111

3.   NORTHEAST

AN INTRODUCTION TO NORTHEAST NASHVILLE   119

3.1   John Seigenthaler Pedestrian Bridge   122
3.2   Greenwood Cemetery   124
3.3   Edgefield House   125
3.4   Sunday Night Soul at the 5 Spot   127
3.5   QDP   129
3.6   Hattie Cotton Elementary   130
3.7   First Baptist Church of East Nashville   132
3.8   Winfrey's Barber Shop   134
3.9   Stratford High School   135
3.10 Cornelia Fort Park   137
3.11 Nashville National Cemetery / US Colored Troops National Monument   139
3.12 Mansker Station   141
3.13 Gass's Store / Cinco de Mayo Mexican Restaurant   143

4. SOUTHEAST

AN INTRODUCTION TO SOUTHEAST NASHVILLE   151

4.1 Nashville International Airport / Nashville Metro Taxi Drivers Alliance   154
4.2 The Camps of Saint Cloud Hill   156
4.3 Wilson Park   158
4.4 Nashville Fairgrounds   160
4.5 Casa Azafrán   163
4.6 Clairmont Apartments   165
4.7 The Buddhist Temple   167
4.8 La Hacienda Taqueria y SuperMercado   168
4.9 Workers' Dignity   171
4.10 Global Mall at the Crossings   172
4.11 Hands On Nashville Urban Farm   174
4.12 Salahadeen Center   175
4.13 Nashville Zoo at Grassmere   177

5. SOUTHWEST

AN INTRODUCTION TO SOUTHWEST NASHVILLE   185

5.1 Capers Memorial Christian Methodist Episcopal Church   188
5.2 Local 257 American Federation of Musicians   190
5.3 Nashville Songwriters Association International   192
5.4 Music Row / Quonset Hut   194
5.5 Edgehill United Methodist Church   196
5.6 Edgehill Village   198
5.7 Scarritt Bennett Center   199
5.8 Roger Williams University   201
5.9 Vanderbilt Divinity School   202
5.10 Confederate Memorial Hall   205
5.11 Memorial Gymnasium   207
5.12 Vanderbilt Kirkland Hall / Occupy Vanderbilt   209
5.13 Centennial Park   211
5.14 The Parthenon   213
5.15 Fannie Mae Dees Park   215
5.16 International Market and Restaurant   217
5.17 Carver Food Park   218
5.18 CCA/CoreCivic   220
5.19 Glendale Baptist Church   222
5.20 Radnor Lake   224
5.21 Gordon Jewish Community Center   226
5.22 Aaittafama' Archeological Park   228

6. ON THE ROAD

INTRODUCTION   235

6.1   Promise Land   237

6.2   Wessyngton Plantation   239

6.3   Coal Creek Miners Museum   241

6.4   Highlander Research and Education Center   243

6.5   Islamic Center of Murfreesboro   245

6.6   The Town of Old Jefferson   247

6.7   The Farm   249

6.8   Giles County Trail of Tears Interpretive Center   251

6.9   Walnut Street Bridge, Chattanooga   253

6.10   Mound Bottom   254

6.11   Fayette County Courthouse   256

7. THEMATIC TOURS

7.1   "It City"   264

7.2   Athens of the South   270

7.3   Music City   276

7.4   Southern Hospitality   280

RECOMMENDED READING   283

ACKNOWLEDGMENTS

WE SET OUT TO create an alternative guide to Nashville, written by those who intimately know the city, and we have incredible appreciation for the more than one hundred people who co-authored this guide. We are indebted to the contributions from our students, thankful for the participation of our academic colleagues, and are particularly grateful to the fifty-nine community members—community organizers, small-business owners, neighborhood leaders, civil servants, and more—who shared histories of Nashville that might not otherwise be documented, in their own words. In the course of collecting and editing these stories, three contributing authors were laid to rest, underscoring the significance of this project.

This project was inspired by the *People's Guide to Los Angeles*, and we are honored to have had coaching and support from its authors: Laura Barraclough, Laura Pulido, and Wendy Cheng. Your work elevates the importance of counter-stories in animating more just relationships with our past, present, and future. We are indebted to the Advisory Committee members who helped envision this book, including Joe Bandy, Tristan Call, Daniel B. Cornfield, K. T. Ewing, Kelly Frances Fenelon, Jyoti Gupta, Rogers Hall, Mike Hodge, Elizabeth Meadows, Reavis Mitchell, Hasina Mohyuddin, Wayne Moore, David Padgett, Sarah Passino, Doug Perkins, Leah Roberts, Sharon Shields, Loraine Segovia-Paz, Paul Speer, Kimberly Tripplett, Janet Walsh, and Linda Wynn. You collectively held us to our commitment to democratize the telling of place-stories and helped operationalize that intention by recruiting prospective authors and submitting entries yourselves. Tristan deserves particular credit for offering a guiding vision at one of our first meetings: "Once this comes out, I want a hundred people in Nashville to be able to pick up this guide and say, 'Yeah, I helped write that.'" Eight years later, that vision is now realized.

In many ways, the engine for collecting entries for this guide became a graduate course in Vanderbilt University's Community Development and Action program. Over two years, students were charged with building relationships with community partners to collectively document sites of significance in Nashville's struggle for social justice. We are grateful to Sarah Suiter, the program director, for believing in this project and integrating it so fully into the program. Coordinating and completing this project would not have been possible without the dedicated work of student research assistants Hannah Collins, Katie Goodman, Joseph Guttierez, Ryan Schooly, Quinntana Slaughter, Mike Thompson, and Bailey Via. These students solicited and co-authored entries, conducted archival research, maintained a public presence for the project, and created systems to manage and track all entries. The editorial team acknowledges the contributions of Tristan Call, Jyoti Gupta, and Sarah Passino to the introduction, and the contributions of Katie Goodman and Mike Thompson to the thematic tours.

While not a history text, this guide is historical in nature, and there were many people who helped ensure this guide was historically robust. Special thanks to Deirdre Duker for assistance in identifying sites of significance to early Nashville feminists and LGBTQ communities and to Pat Cummings for providing expertise related to the Indigenous peoples of Middle Tennessee. We are incredibly thankful to the Nashville Public Library for becoming an early partner, and we extend our appreciation to Andrea Blackman, who opened the archives to our authors, and to the many archivists who saw us through the life of the project. We received editorial assistance from Dr. Reavis L. Mitchell Jr. and are particularly indebted to Davidson County Historian Dr. Carole Bucy for her detailed review and invaluable recommendations.

The maps and images in the following pages bring this text to life. Thank you to Joseph Speer for generously providing your time and talent to serve as the project's cartographer, and to all who shared photographs to this project. We are particularly grateful to the Nashville Public Library archives for helping identify and share historical images, to the *Tennessean* for providing access to several important images, and to Hillary Barsky for photo repair assistance.

We appreciate our home institutions, Portland State University and Tennessee State University, who supported our time and effort on this project, and especially to Vanderbilt University's Peabody College of Education, who championed the project from conception to completion. We are grateful to Vanderbilt University Press for believing that the people of Nashville had stories worth telling and for their commitment to bringing these stories into print. The deep historical knowledge of VUP's editorial team enriched this project. This project was also made possible by support from The Frist

Foundation; the Vanderbilt Curb Center for Art, Enterprise, and Public Policy; and the Vanderbilt Office for Equity, Diversity, and Research. Finally, we extend our gratitude to our friends and family members; your sustained enthusiasm and support—not to mention editing—kept us inspired to do our best work over the life of this project.

Despite the incredible investment of so many people to the creation of this guide, we know it is necessarily and inevitably incomplete. We shoulder responsibility for any omissions and mistakes and hope this is only a beginning of people's projects in Nashville, and beyond.

INTRODUCTION

YOU HAVE IN YOUR hands a different sort of guidebook, both in terms of what you will be guided to see and experience and who is doing the guiding. A typical guidebook might introduce key moments in Nashville's history, such as the area's settlement in the 1700s and the city's charter in 1806, and ignore the Paleo-Indian and Indigenous history of the region that stretches back more than ten thousand years, and the more than one hundred years of Indigenous resistance to colonization. It might emphasize Nashville's reputation as a river trade depot, manufacturing site, and political center in the 1800s and omit the city's role in establishing slavery throughout the Deep South. Such a rendering of history might highlight the social and economic ruptures caused by the 1862 Union takeover of Nashville during the Civil War and overlook the industry of Black Nashvillians who—in the years following the war—created the complex social, cultural, spiritual, and economic foundation needed to uplift future generations. It might give nod to the Nashville sit-ins and neglect the community-organizing infrastructure that made both historic and contemporary movements for social justice possible. It might highlight the disasters that have reshaped the city—such as the 2010 flood and 2020 tornado—and fail to tease apart the intersections of poverty, race, and place that make some communities particularly vulnerable to harm during, and displacement after, such events.

A typical guidebook might emphasize the city's function as a hub. Indeed, Nashvillians frequently describe the city's geography as a wagon wheel, which is an apt metaphor for newcomers trying to make sense of the city. Nashville's primary freeways form a central hub enclosing downtown before branching into four prominent spokes that divide the city's inner-ring neighborhoods into quadrants. A pair of beltways enclose the central metropolitan area, forming something of a wheel. Beyond the physical likeness, the city also operates as a

Figure 1. Titled *Jazz*, this mural was painted in 2016 by artist Bryan Deese to represent historic clubs on North Nashville's Jefferson Street. It was painted over in 2018. Photo courtesy of Learotha Williams Jr.

hub, with direct interstate connections to Birmingham, Alabama; Charlotte, North Carolina; Louisville, Kentucky; St. Louis, Missouri; and Little Rock, Arkansas— all within a few hours' drive. Indeed, for thousands of years before European contact, the Cumberland River Valley functioned in much the same way. Indigenous people in this region formed complex trade networks from the Great Lakes region to the Florida coast. But while this area has long drawn in those in search of better opportunities, the thousands of Cherokee who were marched through Nashville along the Trail of Tears offer a stark reminder that forced removal and dispossession are equally part of the state's heritage. And as much as the freeways that bifurcate the city create pathways for some, they also have served to annex and isolate others.

Nashville is indeed a hub—but one full of contradictions.

A typical guidebook would feature a singular voice (most likely that of a professional travel writer) and perspective, wherein sites of conflict, struggle, and resistance are tidied up in the interest of marketing commercialized "main attractions." These attractions generally align with the four common tropes of the city: Nashville is portrayed as an "It City" driven by booming financial and housing markets, and visitors are invited to experience the various professional sports arenas and commercial centers. Nashville is cast as the "Music City," and tourists are encouraged to explore downtown's country music venues and museums. It is lauded as the "Athens of the South," and travelers are invited to appreciate the abundance of elite educational institutions.

It is elevated as the epitome of "Southern Hospitality," renowned for a generous and charitable spirit, and sightseers are guided to the latest "best" neighborhoods and newest restaurants and bars.

As you may have already gathered, this is not a typical guidebook. Rather than signposting the most well-documented historical events, we follow Howard Zinn, American historian and author of the classic book *A People's History of the United States* (1980), in foregrounding the struggles and achievements of people's movements toward social justice. Instead of uncritically emphasizing the connection afforded by Nashville's hub-like qualities, the entries herein explore the contradictions of this place that has drawn people in and pushed people out, a place that fosters rich social justice organizing and reproduces deep social inequalities, a place where some people are experiencing the benefits of rapid economic growth and others are living the consequences of low wages and lost affordable housing. Perhaps most significantly, in place of offering a single voice and perspective on the city, we offer a multitude, and intentionally privilege the perspectives of those most directly impacted by injustice in the city.

Supported by a diverse Advisory Committee, the editorial team adopted the organizing credo "Nada sobre nosotros, sin nosotros / Nothing about us, without us." As such, we endeavored to create a people's guide that would be written by and with the people who most intimately know the city. In doing so, we are indebted to Civil Rights leader Ella Baker, who reminds us that "Oppressed people, whatever their level of formal education, have the ability to understand and interpret the world around them, to see the world for what it is, and move to transform it." We set three broad criteria for entries: sites that challenge missing or misinformation; sites that reveal privilege or dominance; and/or sites that celebrate cultural resistance, resilience, and creativity. We collected entries for more than three years, soliciting contributions through formal and informal community networks. In total, the entries herein come from more than one hundred Nashvillians: community organizers, neighborhood leaders, lay historians, local scholars, and college students who worked with community members to co-author sites. As a result, this is truly a people's project, grounded in the voices of the people of Nashville. The book's title reflects the spirit of this effort: Before there were guidebooks there were just guides. The colloquial use of "I'll take you there" has long been a response to the call of a stranger: for recommendations of safe passage through unfamiliar territory, a decent meal and place to lay one's head, or perhaps a watering hole or juke joint. In the pages that follow, more than one hundred Nashvillians answer this call; it is they who "take us there," guiding us to places we might not otherwise encounter. Their collective entries bear witness to the ways that power has been used by social, political, and economic elites to tell or omit certain stories, while celebrating the power of counternarratives as a tool to resist injustice. Indeed, each entry is simultaneously a story about place, power, and the historic and ongoing struggle toward a more just city for all. We hope the result is akin to the experience of arriving in an unfamiliar place and asking directions, and rather than simply getting pointed in the right direction, receiving a warm offer from a local to lead us on, accompanied by a tale or two.

We began knowing this would be an incomplete project. All place-stories are partial, political, and contested. This is particularly true of guidebooks; they offer a particular way of seeing, experiencing, and relating to the environment. As such, the entries herein inform *and* editorialize. Authors chose sites of significance to them personally, and to their communities. We encouraged authors to represent their particular perspectives and insights, knowing that different authors would have chosen different sites or different stories to tell about these sites, or may have told the same stories differently. We encourage readers to consider these differences and seek out alternative perspectives just as you have sought out this collection. Furthermore, while many voices are included in this guide, there are undoubtedly perspectives that are absent, and some places undoubtedly worthy of investigation that have been left out. For readers familiar with Nashville, we imagine you will both delight in learning new things about this city and puzzle over sites that appear neglected. A consequence of our commitment to telling

stories *with* and not *for* or *about* others is that some stories are missing because those who lived and/or are descendants of that place-story are no longer living, or their stories are so underground we did not surface them, or simply that the authors who participated in this project chose to highlight other places.

Ultimately, we had problems of abundance, receiving many more entries than we had room to include. As editors, we focused on selecting a multiplicity of perspectives on the city, both historic and contemporary, hoping to expose readers to places they may not otherwise encounter, or to lesser-known stories of well-known sites. We conducted background research on each entry while seeking to preserve the voice and perspective of each author. Taken together, the entries in *I'll Take You There: Nashville Stories of Place, Power, and the Struggle for Social Justice* re-explore and recast the dominant narratives of Nashville against the lived experiences of those who call this place home. To further contextualize the need for these counter-stories, we return to the four common storylines, that of the It City, Music City, Athens of the South, and Southern Hospitality.

The "It City"?

In 2013, the *New York Times* declared Nashville, Tennessee, the nation's "It City."[1] Nashville had risen to prominence on a variety of "best city" lists for economic growth, cultural amenities, population growth, tourism, and overall as one of America's "best places to live." Many

Figure 2. Cranes over the "It City." Lower Broadway at night. Photo © Bruce Cain - Elevated Lens Photography

entries in this guide interrogate these claims, asking, Whom is the "It City" for?

Despite the recent acclaim, there is evidence that Nashville has been something of a destination city since the Mississippian people (often referred to as mound builders for the large earthen mounds they left behind) populated the region between 800 and 1500 CE. Likely attracted by the valley's fertile soils, ample game, and abundant natural salt licks, one of the largest known Mississippian societies in the United States was located minutes from downtown Nashville. Later, the Cherokee, Chickasaw, and Shawnee all had seasonal camps in the region, and the Creek and Iroquois also hunted in the area. The valley's ample natural resources also made it attractive to French fur traders, who built a trading post near what is now Bicentennial Mall as early as the 1690s. While many groups traded with the French, once Europeans settlers made their intentions clear—to claim the land and resources for their exclusive use—Indigenous people fought for their continued right to exist in the region. Despite treaties that guaranteed tribal land rights, after the Land Grab Act of 1783, settlers flooded the region. The next fifty years were marked by violent resistance as Indigenous peoples fought to maintain access to hunting, gathering, and burial grounds.

Chief Dragging Canoe (1738–1792) is among the most storied examples of Indigenous resistance to European settlement. For nineteen years, Dragging Canoe led the Chickamauga Cherokee—a multiracial group of Creeks, Cherokee, disaffected Whites, and Blacks—in attacks on colonists throughout Eastern and Middle Tennessee. Although the written and oral records of this period from the perspective of these groups remain elusive or have disappeared from public memory, recent scholarship suggests that this conflict was a common feature of Nashville's territorial period.[2] Ultimately, one of Nashville's elite, President Andrew Jackson, made it clear that the future "It City"—and indeed the entire southeastern United States— was not intended for Indigenous people.

The Indian Removal Act (1830) led to the expulsion of tens of thousands of Indigenous people from their homelands. Today, though there are an estimated nineteen thousand Indigenous people living in Tennessee, the US government recognizes no tribes in the state. While the Indigenous presence on the landscape is not always easy to see, a number of entries in the guide explore indigeneity during prehistoric times and colonization and the contemporary struggles of Indigenous activists to preserve sacred sites.

Just as Nashville's growth was predicated on the exploitation of land taken from Indigenous people, so too was it built on the exploited labor of enslaved Africans. In 1795, nearly a third of all residents of what is now Davidson County were enslaved, and much of the city's early wealth was generated by their labor on cotton and tobacco farms. The city's geography took shape over the next hundred years, with the commercial and industrial center growing up along the banks of the Cumberland, and the city's White elites settling beyond the fray of downtown, to the southwest and east of the Cumberland. These outer-ring pockets of wealth extended with the development of the streetcar in the 1880s, and as explored in this guide, many of these areas remain concentrations of wealth and power today.

There were also free Blacks in Nashville's early years, and as the city grew through the 1800s, Black and working-class White neighborhoods formed vibrant retail and residential areas within and adjacent to the industrial downtown. Nashville's Black population increased dramatically during and after the Civil War, when many of the state's 275,000 enslaved Africans fled to Nashville to escape the bonds of slavery. As news of the 1862 Union takeover of Nashville spread, the African American population in the city nearly tripled, growing from four thousand in 1860 to twelve thousand by 1865. The Union Army offered conditional sanctuary to these refugees, who were considered contraband property by the US government, in three "contraband camps" around the city, one at Fort Negley in the Southeast, one in North Nashville near Fisk University, and one in East Nashville in the Edgefield neighborhood.[3] Following the war, these campsites evolved into Black neighborhoods and centers of commerce. Though subject to flooding and extremely substandard housing, and exposed to environmental hazards, Nashville's Black neighborhoods also provided spaces of cultural resilience and generativity. Beginning in the 1950s, racial justice organizers convened in neighborhood schools and churches to develop strategies to advance the Civil Rights Movement. After staging some of the first student-led sit-ins in downtown Nashville, their tactics of nonviolent protest quickly spread throughout the South. Yet the same neighborhoods that seeded the Movement later proved vulnerable to government-led disinvestment and demolition.

During the mid-twentieth century, urban renewal programs designed to stimulate economic growth through

Figure 3. Building the city. Lower Broadway at night. Photo © Bruce Cain - Elevated Lens Photography

large-scale highway and infrastructure development razed thousands of homes in the name of progress. Nashville's Black communities were hit the hardest. The large-scale demolition cut swaths through neighborhoods, physically separating historically Black institutions of higher education, playgrounds, and public schools from each other and the residents they served. Concurrently, much of the city's less desirable infrastructure—such as incinerators and dumps—were also sited in or adjacent to communities of color, who disproportionately bore the negative health consequences of these industries. Many entries in the guide explore the legacies of urban development, and how residents fought and are fighting to maintain their place and well-being in the city.

During the current era, Nashville's landscape continues to change dramatically. With construction at an all-time high, cranes perch over the downtown skyline, and the city is also investing heavily in its cultural life by sponsoring mural projects, expanding greenways, and creating arts districts and new music venues. While these investments are attracting new residents and tourists, Nashville's celebrated "vibrancy" has been built upon the backs of hospitality workers, municipal government employees, day laborers, and artists. Yet their wages are not increasing with the city's rising cost of living. Nashville is in the midst of an affordable housing crisis: half of the city's renters spend more than 30 percent of their monthly income on housing, and the rising rents have pushed growing numbers of people out of homes and onto the streets. While Nashville continues to be lauded as a boomtown, ranking high on indexes measuring economic and population growth, the city falls to seventy-third out of one hundred for measures of inclusion and equity, based on the median wage, poverty levels, and rates of unemployment. This guide offers counter-stories to the typical "It City" narrative, documenting displacement, wage theft, and worker exploitation, as well as alternative models of housing, worker centers, and sites of labor struggle where residents organize for a city that truly serves us all.

The Music City?

Nashville opened its $623 million, 1.2 million square-foot Music City Center to both fanfare and voices of dissent in May 2013. Its boosters call it a shining monument to the hopes of all who came to the Music City with guitars on their backs and dreams in their hearts. This often-told story of the Music City's past is one that celebrates tales of smoke-filled honky-tonks, crushed and realized dreams, record stores, dynamic disc jockeys, and the creation of a billion-dollar country music industry. This narrative, though, obscures the fact that historically, Nashville's diverse musical culture rivaled that of any city in America. Indeed, although there has long been the presence of great musicians in Nashville, it is only since the mid-twentieth century that the city has cultivated its popular image as the center of the country music recording industry. And though Nashville has sparked cultural movements—drawing in and supporting musicians from around the country—it has also nearly extinguished them—burying one of the nation's most prominent Black music centers beneath a freeway.

I'll Take You There presents an opportunity to redefine what is meant by the "Music City" moniker in both historical and contemporary times and to explore the often open and contentious conflicts of race and class in the American South. As Nashville gained its reputation as the Music City, two genres of music—both with roots in gospel and Negro spirituals—contested and complimented each other on the Nashville airwaves: Country Music, which was defined by music industry elites as largely as White and conservative, and "Race Music," the musical forms associated with African Americans.

Interestingly, at a time when *hillbilly* was synonymous for poor, rural, White Southerners, Nashville's elites initially scorned the sounds that earned the city the mantle of the "Hillbilly Music Capitol of the World." Nashville's reputation for "hillbilly music" was eschewed until the music began to gain larger audiences as a result of recordings made during the 1920s. During the 1940s and '50s, programs such as the Grand Ole Opry helped rebrand and popularize the sound as "Country Music." Concurrently, Nashville saw the development of "Race Music" rooted in the musical traditions of descendants of enslaved Africans, who numbered among the earliest settlers in Nashville. The banjo, an instrument created in Africa and one that recent scholarship demonstrates is a common signifier of the transatlantic experience and Blackness, became a centerpiece of twentieth-century folk, hillbilly, and bluegrass music—all forms that gained acclaim in Music City.[4]

Despite the segregation of musical forms, artists undeniably influenced one another, and the rise of the city's most celebrated music genre coincided with the growing popularity of rhythm and blues in the South. Nashville's historic WLAC, whose nighttime fifty-thousand-watt broadcasts during the 1950s did

Figure 4. Inside the Country Music Hall of Fame. Photo courtesy of Dev Bahvsar

much to increase R&B's popularity, convinced many in the music industry that they could increase their profits by signing, recording, and producing both country and R&B artists. Music performed by African Americans sometimes resonated in these country spaces, and while most Black artists never succeeded in gaining a foothold in the almost exclusively White genre, as background musicians, they nevertheless contributed to its continuing development and to the cultural life of the city.

Indeed, although Nashville's celebrated status as "Music City, USA"—a term many credit to local WSM-AM radio personality David Cobb—has made the city's name synonymous with country music, this guide offers insight into the many places and organizations that contributed to its earning this title: from the Fisk Jubilee Singers to the acclaimed Ryman Auditorium, and from the honky-tonks that line Broadway today to the many clubs on Jefferson Street that were destroyed during succeeding

waves of so-called urban renewal. Some of America's greatest songwriters and musicians of all genres have at times called Nashville home, including Bob Dylan, Jimi Hendrix, Joan Baez, DeFord Bailey, Gillian Welch, Béla Fleck, and Chris Stapleton. Although the city increasingly celebrates many of the genres that laid the foundation for Country Music, the contributions of Black musicians to this and other genres are often marginalized.[5] Within the last half of the twentieth century, individuals have challenged the geographical boundaries of what many have defined as the Music City, as evidenced by the eclectic sounds that emanated from the Woodland Sound Studio in East Nashville after 1967, a space that provided an opportunity for Nashboro and Excello Records to produce gospel and R&B records.

There is no doubt that Nashville has earned its musical acclaim. And yet, equating "music city" with Nashville has functioned to overshadow musical hubs across Tennessee, most notably Memphis, home to Stax Records, one of the most influential soul music record labels in American history. The title of this guide—in addition to reflecting the participatory nature of this text—is a nod to the hit single by the same name. Recorded at Stax and written by Al Bell, originally of Little Rock and later co-owner of Stax, "I'll Take You There" was made famous by the Staple Singers of Chicago. Musicians recording and performing in Nashville were no doubt influenced by Memphis artists to the west and Chicago artists to the north, much as they were by Appalachian music to the east and the Delta Blues further south. Such geographic and cross-genre connections were on full display in 2019, when Mavis Staples celebrated her eightieth birthday with a concert at Nashville's Ryman auditorium, sharing the stage with country and soul singers. This guide explores the intersection of music, artists, and audiences with attention to the complexities of race relations in Nashville and in the South.

Athens of the South?

Philip Lindsley—a Presbyterian minister, educator, and early abolitionist—is credited as the first person to openly compare Nashville to the ancient capital of Greece, calling it the "Athens of the West." The Tennessee State Capitol, sitting atop a grand hill overlooking the Cumberland River, stood as a visible statement of the city's indebtedness to Greek civilization. However, it was the founders' commitment to education that most influenced Lindsley to make the grand comparison. This guide offers an opportunity to explore this point of pride in the city.

As early as 1785, just one year after the founding of this frontier settlement, James Robertson secured land for what would eventually be known as the

University of Nashville. Nashville's early years brought a proliferation of institutions of higher learning, including the Nashville Female Academy, Ward's Seminary, Buford College, Radnor College, St. Bernard's Academy, St. Cecelia's Academy, Peabody School for Teachers, Belmont College, Nashville College for Women, and Vanderbilt University. Many of these educational institutions continue to this day, serving as intellectual leaders of the region.[6] Yet during the first eighty-one years of Nashville's existence, the city did not extend educational opportunities to its Black population, whom law and custom defined as both human and chattel. Although the existence of many of Nashville's universities depended upon the wealth that uncompensated, compulsory African American labor produced, it was not until the mid-twentieth century that a Black resident of Nashville could attend one of these institutions. In spite of the intense effort to restrict African American education, historian Crystal de Gregory's pioneering work provides evidence of a "Black Athens of the South." Beginning with clandestine schools that operated illicitly under slavery and continuing with the establishment of free schools after the Civil War, these educational spaces are a testament to the determination of Nashville's Black residents to educate their community, often at great risk. Many of these schools exist to this day and are featured in this guide; they are the brick and mortar legacies of Black liberation, teaching, and learning that ring the city.[7]

Figure 5. Tennessee State University's Walter S. Davis Humanities Building. Photo courtesy of Learotha Williams Jr.

While Nashville's earliest Black educational institutions were hard-won, hopes for increased educational access for Nashville's African American population eroded following the 1870 Tennessee gubernatorial election of ex-confederate and known Klansman John C. Brown. The state constitution, adopted that year, barred state funding to any school which would "allow white and negro children to be received as scholars together in the same school." By the turn of the twentieth century, Nashville boasted twenty-one high schools for Whites, only eleven high schools for Blacks, and one accessible public library, the Colored Carnegie Library located at Twelfth Avenue North. African Americans seeking higher education had even fewer options. The city's resistance to Black education endured well past the 1954 *Brown* decision that outlawed the segregation of public schools. Its persistence was such that the 1970 mayoral race hinged on a single issue: maintaining school segregation.[8]

Despite the legal architecture upholding White supremacy in the city's educational system, the institutions that composed the Black Athens of the South continued to grow. Within the African American community, the students and faculty of Fisk University led the way, joined by Meharry Medical College, the first medical school in the United States to accept Blacks, and what would become Tennessee State University. These institutions had a notable influence on the struggle for Black liberation in the South. Student leaders from the city's historically Black colleges led the movement to protest lynching in the United States, raise awareness of police brutality in Nashville, and dismantle segregation in education and other social spaces in the city and throughout the region. Tennessee State University's Avon Williams Campus, named after a prominent attorney who was introduced to the city as the Apostle of Civil Rights, Avon N. Williams Jr., stands today as a monument to the city's post-sixties struggle for equality in higher education. Today, student leaders are again on the forefront of many social justice efforts in the city, from Black Lives Matter to organizing for immigrant and refugee rights.

I'll Take You There provides a deeper exploration of Nashville's historic reputation as the Athens of the South, by highlighting the varied influences its educational institutions have had on those living here and how Nashville has simultaneously assisted and hindered educational access. It also explores the role of student activists and popular education—historically and in the current era—in shaping the city.

Southern Hospitality?

Nashville boosters cherish the city's reputation for Southern hospitality. Yet the very notion of hospitality raises questions of power and delineates lines of inclusion and exclusion. In Nashville, a city built from the displacement of Indigenous groups, on the backs of enslaved labor, and on the continued exploitation of a low-wage workforce, the legacy of hospitality has been highly racialized and drawn along lines of class and gender. This guide explores the changing ideas of hospitality, with

Figure 6. Anti-integration protesters. Photo courtesy of Nashville Metro Archives

particular attention to the role of faith communities, places of cultural organizing, and sites of protest.

Since Reconstruction, many Nashville churches have nurtured the struggle for equality by providing places of refuge and restoration for marginalized populations. In particular, independent Black churches provided a moral foundation upon which Black communities could challenge racism and the hypocrisy of Southern hospitality. It was no accident that James Lawson, Bernard Lafayette, James Bevel, John Lewis, and other icons of the Civil Rights Movement emerged out of the minister class.[9] At the same time, other Nashville churches have functioned as a base for anti-integration and anti-immigration organizing. And the failure of many faith communities—even those that have led the city toward racial justice—to welcome LGBTQ community members demonstrates how hospitality remains contested in the current era.

Figure 7. July 2017 housekeepers' truth march through downtown convention and tourism district. Photo courtesy of Workers' Dignity

I'll Take You There also explores hospitality in relation to struggles for immigrant rights. With one of the fastest growing immigrant populations in the country, Nashville is quickly becoming a global city. The most sizable immigrant group is comprised of Hispanics/Latinos, and Nashville is home to the largest Kurdish population outside of the Middle East, as well as one of the most substantial Somali populations in the United States. A full third of all children in Nashville public schools live in homes where English is not their first language, and more than 120 languages are represented in the city's public school system. While many welcome the region's increasing diversity, others have exploited the anxieties and fears of US-born Tennesseans to create a climate of fear and hostility toward immigrants and refugees.

Over the past fifteen years, immigrant and refugee rights organizations have defeated 150 anti-immigrant and anti-refugee bills, including a 2008 referendum that would have made English the official and only language of city government. Despite these successes, fierce battles remain, particularly given the degree that racism and xenophobia became more visible during—and were often legitimized by—the administration of President Donald J. Trump. This guide explores sites of significance for immigrants and refugees who struggle to defend their rights, maintain cultural ties, and resist discrimination and workplace exploitation.

In addition, the guide also considers issues of Southern hospitality from the perspective of others too often marginalized in the city: unhoused people subject

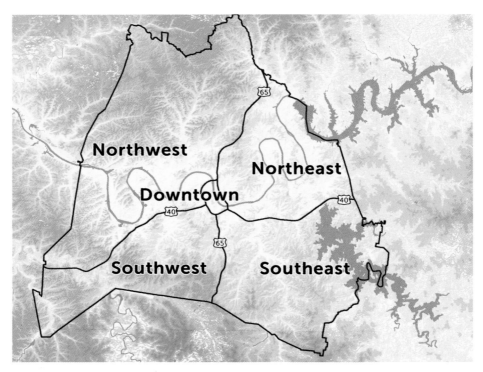

Map 1. Davidson County overview. Courtesy of Joseph Speer

to street violence and slashed safety nets, people with disabilities evicted from housing and fighting institutionalization, and LGBTQ residents who continue to face overt and state-sanctioned discrimination. As recently as 2016, the Tennessee legislature passed a bill that allows counselors to refuse mental health services to LGBTQ clients, and another bill in 2019 that bars transgender people the use of school bathrooms that align with their gender identities.[10] In light of these continued struggles, this guide also celebrates the spaces of inclusion, transformation, and justice co-created by those who have been marginalized, be they within places of worship, at protest sites, or in nightclubs.

How the Book Is Organized

We invite you to trace and turn over these four Nashville storylines—It City, Music City, Athens of the South, and Southern Hospitality—as you explore the city. *I'll Take You There* is organized geographically. Five chapters contain sites within Davidson County: Downtown, Northwest, Northeast, Southeast, and Southwest. These regions are demarcated by the interstate and road system that has had a profound and lasting impact on the demographic, social, economic, and political experience of the city.

While the freeways play a profound role in shaping the city, we note that communities—as all living things—are beautifully messy and wily, and the best

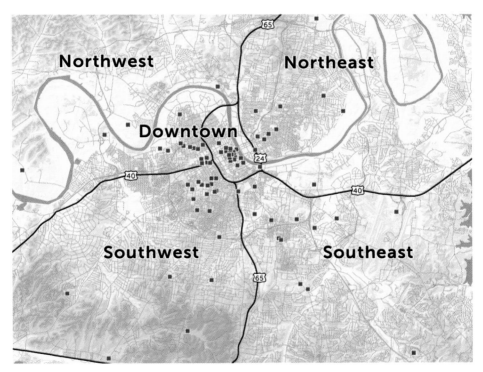

Map 2. Davidson County with squares indicating site locations. Courtesy of Joseph Speer

ones trespass across false boundaries, refusing to be contained. For example, though the Northwest region is generally viewed as the heart of Black Nashville, Capers CME Church, a keystone institution to the North Nashville Black community, is located in the southwest region of this guide. And while the Southeast region is known as the city's international district, immigrant residents are not confined to one geographic area and you will find sites of significance related to Nashville's immigrant and refugee communities throughout the book.

Each chapter begins with a brief orientation to the region and then offers a collection of entries featuring significant sites in the region. In some cases, entries are also accompanied by personal reflections presenting a more intimate account of the significance of the site. Each entry includes a brief byline introducing the author, and most are followed by "Nearby Sites of Interest," a section that features other stops of historical and/or cultural significance. In some cases, additional site-specific reading is suggested.

Given the role of Nashville as a hub connecting people and places, an additional chapter offers sites within driving distance of the city. Time and again, events that have taken place in this valley have radiated out to affect other places just as external regional, national, and international forces sent ripples—and shock waves—through Nashville. With this "On the Road" collection of entries, the guide draws local connections with seemingly extra-local events and locations. A final chapter is organized thematically, offering day tours for those interested in more intentionally tracing the guiding themes through their exploration of the city.

Importantly, we offer this project, necessarily modest in scope, not as an exhaustive list of places worth visiting, but rather as a broad invitation to engage with cities as sites of struggle. As readers, may this guide sharpen our collective understanding of Nashville's political, economic, and social movements and inspire us toward new ways of hearing and sharing stories of social struggle. And as residents, may this guide quicken our steps toward re-imagining how we might live better together in this city. May the omissions in this book be viewed as openings for more people's projects to document historic and contemporary sites of significance. And may the end of the book be the beginning of new conversations, new journeys, and new struggles for freedom.

NOTES

1.   "Nashville's Latest Big Hit Could Be the City Itself," *New York Times*, January 8, 2013.

2.   For more information on the history of Tennessee and the complex relationship between African Americans, Native Americans, and Whites living in the state during the territorial period, see Cynthia Cumfer, *Separate Peoples, One Land: The Minds of Cherokees, Blacks, and Whites on the Tennessee Frontier* (Chapel Hill: University of North Carolina Press, 2012).

3.   For a detailed account of this period, see Bobby L. Lovett, *The African-American History of Nashville, Tennessee: 1780–1930* (Fayetteville: University of Arkansas Press, 1999).

4.   For more insight into the political and cultural evolution of music in Nashville, see Peter La Chapelle, *I'd Fight the World: A Political History of Old-Time, Hillbilly, and Country Music* (Chicago: University of Chicago Press, 2019); and Laurent Dubois, *The Banjo: America's African Instrument* (Cambridge, MA: Harvard University Press, 2016).

5.   See Charles L. Hughes, *Country Soul: Making Music and Making Race in the American South* (Chapel Hill: University of North Carolina Press, 2017).

6.   Mary Ellen Pethel, *Athens of the New South: College Life and the Making of Modern Nashville* (Knoxville: University of Tennessee Press, 2017).

7.   Crystal A. deGregory, "We Built Black Athens: How Black Determination Secured Black Education in Antebellum Nashville," *Tennessee Historical Quarterly* 69, no. 2 (Summer 2010): 124–45.

8.   For more on education in Nashville and an astute analysis of the city's struggle to integrate public schools, see Ansley T. Erickson, *Making the Unequal Metropolis: School Desegregation and Its Limits* (Chicago: University of Chicago Press, 2017).

9.   David Halberstam, *The Children* (New York: Random House, 1998), 50–53; Benjamin Houston, *The Nashville Way: Racial Etiquette and the Struggle for Social Justice in a Southern City* (Athens: University of Georgia Press, 2012), 80–84; John Lewis with Michael D'Orso, *Walking with the Wind: A Memoir of the Movement* (1998; reissue ed., New York: Simon and Shuster, 2017).

10. "Indecent Exposure Legislation Criticized by Opponents as 'Bathroom Bill' Passes Tennessee House," *Tennessean*, April 8, 2019.

A Letter to Nashville   Kwame Lillard

Those of us who participated in the 1960 sit-in movement that desegregated the city's down-town corridor, the 1961 Freedom Rides that attacked segregated interstate transportation and commercial activities, and other racial/social justice and civil rights struggles in the 1960s believed that Nashville really wanted to change. Yet we underestimated the resilience of institutional racism and White supremacy, which continue to cause great injury to Black Nashvillians in the twenty-first century.

While my generation exposed the naked truths of US racial apartheid and the racial caste system in Nashville, the city's political and economic elites undermined our efforts by initiating policies that harmed the Black community's highly developed cultural politics, economic vitality, educational institutions, and neighborhoods. Sadly, fifty years after Nash-ville experienced some of the most important civil rights and social justice campaigns in US history, most residents cannot accurately name the dates, places, or targets, the activities of historically Black colleges and universities (HBCUs), or the legal strategies that defined and augmented the sit-ins, "stand-ins," "sleep-ins," and freedom rides of my generation. Moreover, the gains of using desegregated bathrooms and restaurants must be measured against the pains of the last fifty years. These include urban renewal initiatives that razed Black neighborhoods; the building of Interstate 40 through North Nashville's Jefferson Street corridor; the 1963 creation of the Metropolitan Nashville and Davidson County consolidated government, which diluted Black political and cultural influence in Nashville; the continued segregation of city-owned swimming pools throughout the 1960s; the closures of thriving Black neighborhood schools; the demolition or closure of lunch counters, theaters, hotels, and transportation depots that were successfully desegregated by civil rights activists; and contemporary land-use, housing, and zoning policies that have led to the gentrification of many historically Black neighborhoods and dispersed poor, working class, and other people of color to neighboring suburban communities.

Despite these pains, the Civil Rights Movement of the 1960s, and specifically our efforts in Nashville, helped inspire new movements. The women's rights movement, anti-Vietnam War protests, the environmental and consumer advocacy movements, the organizing activi-ties of disability rights activists and senior citizens, the expansion of the 1964 Civil Rights Act's Title VI and VII provisions to non-Blacks and women, the tenant rights movement, the immigrant rights movement, and the adoption of regulatory protections for nursing homes, day-care, and child care centers were all influenced by the Civil Rights, social justice, and Black student movements of the 1960s.

Nashville was and is central to this narrative of justice. Our protest movement ignited a spark in middle Tennessee that fanned the flames of social change throughout the country. Since then, a few of us have continued to stay the course and remain committed to justice and freedom despite the pitfalls, drug epidemics, racial hostilities, and economic cutbacks that harmed our communities during the past few decades. But still, with God's help, our determination and steadfast commitment demonstrate the force of the rallying cry by South African freedom fighters: "Amandla Nawethu—We Have the Power."

Kwame Lillard *was the Director of the African American Cultural Alliance and Co-Founder of the Nashville Student Movement Legacy Foundation. The former Metro Councilman was a well-known leader in the sit-in and freedom ride movements of the 1960s. A version of this letter was published in* The State of Blacks in Middle Tennessee *(2010).*

1. DOWNTOWN

1.1   Nunna-daul-Tsuny (Trail Where They Cried)   29

1.2   Public Square   31

1.3   Maxwell House Hotel   33

1.4   Juanita's   34

1.5   Ryman Auditorium   36

1.6   Tara Cole Memorial Bench   38

1.7   Black Bottom (Country Music Hall of Fame)   40

1.8   Downtown Incinerator / Ascend Amphitheatre   42

1.9   Tent City / 2010 Flood   44

1.10   James Robertson Apartments   45

1.11   Nashville Public Library Civil Rights Room   47

1.12   Walgreens Lunch Counter   49

1.13   Tennessee State Capitol   52

1.14   The Hermitage Hotel   54

1.15   Legislative Plaza   56

1.16   Music City Central Bus Station Bathroom   59

1.17   The *Nashville Globe*   60

1.18   Duncan Hotel   62

1.19   The Nashville Farmer's Market   63

1.20   First Baptist Church, Capitol Hill   66

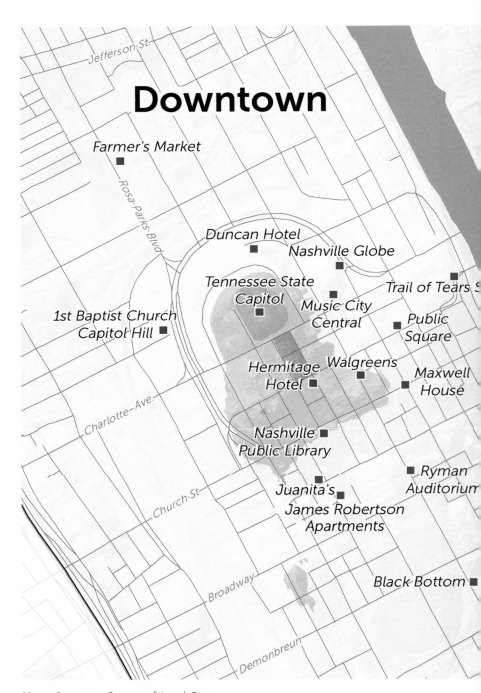

Map 3. Downtown. Courtesy of Joseph Speer

Main St

Tara Cole
Memorial Bench

1st Ave S

Downtown
Incinerator

Cumberland River

Tent City

AN INTRODUCTION TO DOWNTOWN

DOWNTOWN NASHVILLE HAS LONG been a gathering place. Although there is no visible sign of it now, Mississippian people (800–1500 CE) built a mound thirty yards across and ten feet high in the area of Centennial Park. Later, the Cherokee, Chickasaw, and Shawnee all had camps in the same vicinity. In 1691, a French trader named Martin Chartier established a trading post on top of a Mississippian mound in the area that would become known as the French Lick. Jean de Charleville would open another post at the site in 1710 and engage in trade with local Indigenous groups until 1714. In 1780, James Robertson and John Donelson, a land speculator and slaveholder, led two groups of settlers (including at least one free Black man named Jack Civil) to the Cumberland River Valley. The settlers and the enslaved Africans they brought with them built Fort Nashborough—an encampment of twenty log cabins and the precursor to the city of Nashville. Ever since, the downtown region has been shaped by questions of power and belonging: who has claims to exist on this land, and who has the power to enforce those claims?

For twelve years, the Cherokee conducted frequent attacks on Fort Nashborough, seeking to slow further encroachment on their hunting grounds. But fifty-one years after James Robertson arrived and made claims to the land, President Andrew Jackson ushered the passage of a much more expansive claim through the Indian Removal Act of 1830. As you will read in this chapter, the Trail of Tears, known as Nunnadaul-Tsuny— "trail where they cried"—in Cherokee, passed through the heart of downtown Nashville.

Figure 1.1. Protestors at the Women's March on January 21, 2017. Photo courtesy of Dev Bahvsar

Since these early days, Nashville's downtown has been shaped into an area of commerce, residence, political activity, and protest. The Public Square was created in 1783, flanked by a courthouse, jail, stores, and taverns. Until the mid-nineteenth century, the Public Square was the site of slave auctions, and today it serves as an important place of remembrance of the transcontinental slave trade. In 1843, the Tennessee General Assembly named Nashville the state's permanent capital, and the Tennessee State Capitol was soon built downtown. Over the course of its history, Public Square has also represented Nashville's struggle to reconcile its antebellum past with its emerging presence as a modern, twentieth-century Southern city. One of the clearest examples of this public struggle was the Great Depression–era proposal to allow the old courthouse to escape demolition and continue to stand next to the planned state-of-the-art, two-million-dollar courthouse in the Public Square. Many in the city argued against modernizing the square, believing that the improvements would destroy the space's public character. As entries in this chapter attest, it is at these city and state seats of political power that some of the most punishing policies and liberatory reforms were enacted, and where residents converged to fight for freedom from injustice.

As the city grew, an industrial ring of railroad and commercial facilities formed along the river and around the business district, and working-class neighborhoods populated by White immigrant laborers and Blacks, both free and enslaved, emerged between the two. As reflected in the popular names of these neighborhoods—Smokey Row (the red-light district), Hell's Half Acre, and Black

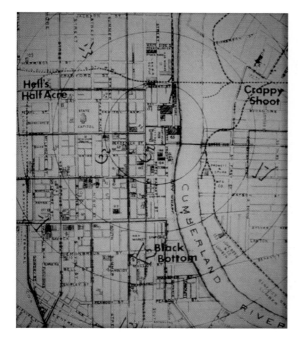

Figure 1.2. (left) Map of Downtown and South Nashville (circa 1900), with Black Bottom indicated. From Don Harrison Doyle, *Nashville in the New South, 1880–1930*. Knoxville: University of Tennessee Press, 1985.

Figure 1.3. (below) Union Street, circa 1920. Photo courtesy of Nashville Metro Archives

When most people think of downtown Nashville, honky-tonks and country music come to mind … and rightfully so. Nashville is the headquarters for country music, an industry that employs many of the good people who live here, including yours truly (I sing backup for Zac Brown Band). Nashville isn't just country music though. There's rock, soul, jazz, hip-hop, and every other genre you can think of. However, Lower Broadway isn't always the easiest place to get booked as a soul artist. It can be discouraging to see downtown—the area that in many people's eyes defines Nashville—offer a one-dimensional representation of all the good music that is being made in the city.

There are some important exceptions. At the end of honky-tonk row, across the street from the river, you'll find ACME Feed and Seed. ACME is one of the rare downtown venues that offers the thousands of tourists who pour into Lower Broadway every week the opportunity to experience Nashville's diverse music scene. On any night of the week, you can walk in and hear funk, soul, jazz, rock, or country. For years, Bourbon Street Blues and Boogie Bar (Printers Alley) and BB King's Blues Club (Second Avenue) have also provided soul, funk, and blues artists a place to spread their musical wings. So, enjoy the honky-tonks when you are downtown, but don't forget that this city has a wide range of music for you to experience, and support those venues that create opportunities for musicians of all stripes to share their talent. Speaking of BB King's, I actually got to shake the hand of B.B. King himself when I opened for him there a few years back … that's an experience I'll never forget.

Jason Eskridge, Nashville musician

Bottom—for many years, these parts of downtown were the only places that the people and businesses deemed "undesirable" were allowed to exist.

In the 1920s, downtown also became home to Nashville's emergent service industry, including banks, insurance agencies, and publishing houses along with department stores and movie houses. As downtown commerce developed, the area was characterized by what historian Benjamin Houston has called a "tangled racial etiquette." Black customers could order food from the back door but could not eat in restaurants or at lunch counters like White customers. Though Nashville was a majority White city, by 1930, people of color made up 55 percent of the downtown population. Within twenty years, the Nashville Housing Authority targeted the

city's downtown Black residents for eviction. Indeed, the Bijou Theater, a space created in 1903 that quickly grew to be one of the most impressive African American theaters in the South, was demolished in 1957 to make way for the city's Municipal Auditorium. Other than the majestic Morris Memorial Building—built by the Black architectural firm McKissack and McKissack in 1926 to house the National Baptist Publishing Board—there are few if any monuments to the presence of Blacks in downtown spaces. As you will read in this chapter, one of the United States' first urban renewal projects demolished the Black neighborhoods known as Hell's Half Acre and Black Bottom, destroying homes and churches and displacing communities. Given that downtown had been a site of both Black community building

Figure 1.4. Lower Broadway at night. Photo © Bruce Cain - Elevated Lens Photography

and rampant racism under Jim Crow, it is unsurprising that it also became a key area for civil rights training and protest. By the 1950s, leaders in the Black community organized workshops at downtown churches on nonviolent direct actions, and led protests at downtown businesses, many of which are featured in this chapter.

Downtown—particularly the area including and surrounding Lower Broadway (the four blocks on Broadway closest to the river)—has also long been a site of cultural generativity. The Grand Old Opry—a weekly, country-music, radio-broadcast concert that began in Nashville in 1925—moved to the Ryman Auditorium in 1943. As the number of music recording studios increased in Nashville, so too did the venues to hear music, many of which popped up on Lower Broadway. In this earlier era of the "music city," people of means might visit Lower Broad to hear music, though the area remained a place where the city's "undesirables" lived and worked—including poor people, sex workers, LGBTQ people, street performers, gamblers, and aspiring musicians of all varieties.

Over the last fifty years, the completion of two interstate highways and a number of large-scale investments have contributed to downtown Nashville's evolution into a tourist destination. These include building the Bridgestone Arena, a large capacity event venue and home of the Nashville Predators hockey team, and the Music City Center, a 1,200,000-square-foot convention complex flanked by the Country Music Hall of Fame and the twenty-one-story Omni Hotel. The city also now hosts the Country Music Awards Festival, an annual event attended by more than 250,000 people. In 2003, the city opened the John Seigenthaler Pedestrian Bridge, connecting downtown to the Tennessee Titan's stadium on the city's east side. And at the heart of the downtown tourist experience is the Honky-Tonk Highway, several blocks of bars playing live country music all day, every day.

Investments to rebrand and "clean up" downtown have kept—and attracted— a rowdy crowd of country fans, while pushing remnants of the red-light district, including adult stores and gay bars, further from the urban center. At the same time, much of downtown's affordable housing has been transformed into luxury condominiums, hotels, and office buildings. According to Census data, between 2000 and 2010 there was a 30 percent jump in median income downtown, and the area is also becoming more White.

As you travel through downtown Nashville, we encourage you to explore sites of injustice—from the Trail of Tears to the James Robertson Apartments—as well as sites of resistance—from the Walgreens Lunch Counter to the Downtown Incinerator. We hope the entries in this section encourage reflection on questions of who the city is built for, whose stories are visible in the landscape, and whose stories have been erased.

ABOUT THE AUTHORS

Vanderbilt graduate students **Lauren Baer, Nicole Escobedo, Joseph Gutierrez, Allie Mikels, Chris Shefelton, Mike Thompson,** and **Ashley Vega** contributed to this section.

1.1 NUNNA-DAUL-TSUNY (TRAIL WHERE THEY CRIED)

100 Union St.,
Nashville, TN 37201

Figure 1.5. 1823 Nashville Toll Bridge Abutment, as seen from Gay Street Connector. Photo courtesy of Amie Thurber

It was a cold rainy Monday in 1838 when Nashvillians gathered in the public square. As they looked around, they saw hundreds of Cherokee, including pregnant women, young children, and elderly people, as well as members of wealthy land- and slave-owning families, all waiting their turn to cross the bridge and leave their ancestral lands behind. These were among the seventeen thousand Cherokee dispossessed of their land and sovereignty and forced to relocate from Tennessee, Georgia, North Carolina, and Alabama to Oklahoma. An estimated four thousand Cherokee lost their lives on Nunna-daul-Tsuny (Trail where they cried).

In the 1700s, European settlers began encroaching on lands inhabited by Indigenous people in the Tennessee region. Although a number of tribes had ties to the region, the Cherokees and the Chickasaws were the only tribes recognized by the US government as landowners within the future state boundaries. Indeed, when the state entered the Union in 1796, these two tribes claimed nearly 75 percent of the territory of Tennessee. In the first years of Andrew Jackson's presidency, settlers discovered gold in Monroe County, and prospectors flooded the region, disregarding treaties recognizing Indigenous claims to the land.

The US government incited violence against Indigenous people and negotiated a series of new treaties that dramatically reduced—and ultimately erased—any Cherokee land claims in the state. In 1830, President Andrew Jackson pushed Congress to pass the Indian Removal Act, which led to the forceful removal of five Native American tribes—the Cherokee, Choctaws, Creek, Chickasaws, and Seminoles—from their land in Southern states. This removal opened up thousands of square miles of land to settlers, a significant portion of which had been under cultivation by Cherokee farmers.

After being temporarily held in stockades, the US military split the Cherokees into detachments of approximately one thousand people and forced tribal members to make a grueling one-thousand-mile journey to Oklahoma by foot. These groups traversed by three routes; the northernmost route passed through Nashville. On October 22, 1838, the second detachment assembled in Nashville's Public Square, and many Nashville residents gathered to bear witness. Two days later, the *Nashville Whig* wrote, "Barefooted and badly clad, they cannot all hope to withstand the fatigues of travel and the inclemency of the season." Some local residents, including church elders and Nashville's women of charity, offered assistance. Many others, perhaps overwhelmed by the magnitude of need, stood by and did nothing.

It was only in 2013 that the exact location of the trail's Cumberland crossing in Nashville was discovered. Through archival research and scouring the Cumberland River area, Patrick Cummins, president of the Native History Association, and fellow Indigenous historian Toye Heape discovered a partial bridge foundation on the western bank of the river. The National Park Service validated this finding as the first bridge to cross the Cumberland River and the only documented surviving bridge structure related to Nunna-daul-Tsuny. The Trail of Tears National Historic Trail continues across the river, through northeast Nashville, and it eventually parallels Interstate-24 as it approaches Kentucky. The Cherokee who survived the journey emerged to build a unified Nation in Oklahoma. Today, they are 190,000 tribal members strong.

Through a partnership with the National Park Service and local Indigenous groups, visitors today can travel the route which the Cherokees journeyed on the Trail of Tears National Historic Trail. To honor those that journeyed the Trail, walk north through Nashville's Public Square Park, and down the stairs to the Gay Street Connector, where you can view the top of the original abutment. As you overlook the Cumberland River, listen for the whisper in the rustling trees and the river below reminding us of those who were forced to leave their homes, those who lost their lives along the way, and those that survived.

ABOUT THE AUTHORS

Dawn Harris is a graduate of Vanderbilt University's Community Development and Action program. **Patrick Cummins** is the president of the Native History Association.

ADDITIONAL READING

M. R. Foreman. "Reverend Stephen Foreman, Chronicles of Oklahoma." *Oklahoma Historical Society* 18, no. 3 (1940): 229–41.

NEARBY SITES OF INTEREST

Fort Nashborough Replica (170 1st Avenue North): This replica of the original stockade is free and open to the public. An interpretive plaza includes information about the area's Indigenous history, as well as experiences of early settlers.

Figure 1.6. Walter Hood, *Witness Walls*, 2017, commissioned by the Metro Nashville Arts Commission. © 2017 Stacey Irvin

1.2   PUBLIC SQUARE

350 Deaderick St.,
Nashville, TN 37201

Though today Public Square Park is home to the Civil Rights–inspired public artwork *Witness Walls*, for most of Nashville's history, the square was the central place of commodification and devaluing of Black life. There are few remaining places that provide a glimpse into the lives of Nashville's enslaved population—the brokerage houses where Blacks were bought, sold, and traded no longer exist, and the narratives that describe their existence have been sanitized, muted, or erased. Yet the history of Public Square reveals a relationship with this "peculiar institution" that was intimate and ubiquitous.

Historically, Nashville's Public Square Park was a place where White Nashvillians met to shop, mingle, conduct business, and celebrate events. On Saturday afternoons, it became a space where the horrors of slavery were laid bare for the world to see. In a 1918 interview with the *Nashville Globe*, James Harding, a formerly enslaved city resident, remembered the square as a place where slave brokers and the county clerk "would auction off slaves as if they were cattle." Fear, uncertainty, and psychological trauma became the defining features of the Public Square for generations of Nashville's enslaved Africans.

Yet as the power center of the city, the Public Square later became a place

Figure 1.7. Diane Nash leading marchers to confront Mayor West. Photo courtesy of Special Collections Division, Nashville Public Library

of protest, resistance, and resilience. After the April 19, 1960, bombing of the home of civil rights attorney Z. Alexander Looby (who believed he was targeted for representing student protesters involved in lunch counter sit-ins), three thousand Nashville residents marched from Tennessee State and Fisk Universities to the Public Square. There, on the steps of City Hall, Fisk student Diane Nash asked Mayor Ben West pointed questions about the unfairness of segregation. Before the crowd of thousands, West finally publicly agreed that Nashville lunch counters must desegregate, and downtown stores began to integrate within the month.

The Public Square remains a powerful gathering space for social justice movements. In 2007, the Nashville Homeless Power Project set up a tent city in the Public Square just days before the Mayor's budget address. Upward of one hundred homeless people, joined by students and community allies, pledged to camp until there was safe, affordable housing for all. Fourteen people were arrested the first day. Later that week, the Metro-Davidson budget passed with the first sizable allocation of funds for affordable housing in the city's history. More recently, after the horrific 2016 shootings at Pulse, a gay nightclub in Orlando, Florida, a record-breaking eighteen-thousand-plus people filled the Public Square in a vigil to show love and support for the LGBT community locally and abroad.

While the square is a frequent site for community vigils and protests, it is also a site of cultural celebration, including the annual Nashville Pride Festival. In June 2015, festival goers celebrated together on the heels of the Supreme Court ruling that legalized same-sex marriages that same weekend and joined in roaring cheers after the first legal same-sex wedding in Tennessee kicked off the event.

If there are no events in the Public Square today, take time to explore *Witness Walls* between the sidewalk on Third Avenue North and the courthouse. This installation honors the events and people who fought for racial equality in Nashville, educates the public about this history, and encourages Nashvillians to continue the conversation about social justice in our city.

ABOUT THE AUTHORS

Historian **Learotha Williams Jr.** and community organizers **Matt Leber, Kwame Lillard, Joey Leslie,** and **Barbara Clinton** contributed to this entry.

ADDITIONAL READING

Homeless Power: The Road Home Campaign. Nashville, TN: Nashville Homeless Power Project, 2007.

Benjamin Houston. *The Nashville Way: Racial Etiquette and the Struggle for Social Justice in a Southern City.* Athens: University of Georgia Press, 2012.

NEARBY SITES OF INTEREST

Citizen (located in Public Square Park): While you are here, visit these interactive sculptures of two thirty-foot figures. The crank device allows visitors to point the figures' outstretched arms.

Figure 1.8. Maxwell House Hotel. Photo courtesy of Special Collections Division, Nashville Public Library

1.3 MAXWELL HOUSE HOTEL

201 4th Ave. N., Nashville, TN 37219

The Maxwell House Hotel was at the center of much of Nashville's early history. The massive construction project was initiated in 1859 by a wealthy Tennessean, John Overton, and the hotel was named for his wife, Harriet Maxwell Overton. Located at Fourth Avenue and Church Street downtown, the hotel was perhaps best known for its connection with Maxwell House Coffee, which was first blended in Nashville. Throughout its tenure, the hotel welcomed various United States presidents, famous actors, and musicians. It served as a barracks, a prison, and a hospital during the Civil War, and it was the setting of O. Henry's renowned short story "A Municipal Report." As the site of regular social and political activities, the Maxwell House Hotel also became the venue for the first national convention of the Ku Klux Klan.

The Grand Cyclops of the Pulaski den of the Ku Klux Klan invited delegates from other dens to gather at the Maxwell House Hotel in April 1867. The recorded goal of the convention was to reorganize the Klan and ensure unity of purpose, and the primary agenda item was the adoption of an official constitution. Known as "The Prescript," the document emphasized secrecy, contained an organizational plan, and laid out administrative duties. It is thought that this gathering at the Maxwell House Hotel marked the Klan's political rebirth as a partisan organization, and that the convention was instrumental in transforming the Ku Klux Klan from a social club into a terrorist movement. A sinister, powerful force with an official philosophy of White supremacy emerged, and the Klan's now-familiar violent tactics date to this period. In the years following the convention, Klan activity spread throughout the South, wreaking havoc and imposing fear with threats, night raids, mass demonstrations, mutilations, floggings, and lynchings; it is difficult to comprehend the full consequences of the Ku Klux Klan's terror.

In addition to hosting the Klan's convention, Maxwell House Hotel was also the location of the Democratic Party's 1922 State Convention, and John F. Kennedy campaigned here in 1959. Throughout its lifetime, the Maxwell House Hotel was visited by seven presidents and many dignitaries, making it a significant political site in Nashville. It was also a highly gendered space, with a separate entrance for women on Fifth Avenue. A fire devastated the Maxwell House Hotel on Christmas Day in 1961, but the landmark's name and legacy—one that unfortunately includes a history of intense racial and gender discrimination—live on through Millennium Maxwell House Nashville in MetroCenter, which opened in the late 1970s. The SunTrust Building now stands where the original Maxwell House Hotel once held court in downtown Nashville.

ABOUT THE AUTHOR

Lauren Baer is a graduate of Vanderbilt University's Community Development and Action program.

ADDITIONAL READING

Stanley F. Horn. *Invisible Empire: The Story of the Ku Klux Klan, 1866–1871.* Cambridge: Riverside Press, 1939.

"Maxwell House, Connected with Social, Political History of City, to Get New Lease on Life through Rehabilitation." *Nashville Tennessean* (Nashville, TN), April 24, 1941.

Allen Trelease. *White Terror: The Ku Klux Klan Conspiracy and Southern Reconstruction.* New York: Harper & Row, 1971.

1.4 JUANITA'S

713 Commerce St.,
Nashville, TN 37203

Juanita's may be closed now, but the bar's impact lingers in Nashville. The bar and lounge opened in 1953, originally intended for straight customers. It soon became a haven—and over the years an institution—for gay men. Located on

Figure 1.9. For many years, Juanita's was located next to The Jungle, which was Nashville's longest operating gay bar. Photo courtesy of Special Collections Division, Nashville Public Library

Commerce Street near what was formerly the red-light district of Nashville, Juanita's was known for many years as Nashville's oldest gay bar. The bar was open for Whites only until desegregation in the 1960s, and served generations of LGBTQ patrons until it burned down in 1995.

Juanita Braizer, a diminutive woman with bright red hair, opened and ran the bar. Both her vivacious personality and the sanctuary she provided led to a fierce sense of loyalty from her regular customers. A welcoming gathering spot for newcomers, gay men would travel by bus from all over the South to visit Juanita's. Always one to lend a helping hand, Juanita would often give new arrivals money to stay in a hotel once they came to town. Juanita had a larger than life personality and was known to keep the party going

after closing time, hitting local nightclubs with the nicknamed "Juanita's boys." Juanita's was known for its rousing New Year's Eve and Halloween parties, and was said to be the first place in town a man could safely appear in a dress and wig, even if only on Halloween. The jukebox was filled with show tunes, and the booth nearby was known as a place for picking people up. At a time when homophobia was at a terrifying level for LGBTQ people, inside Juanita's, many found comfort, and even joy.

While Juanita provided a rare space of sanctuary, she could not guarantee safety. Police video-surveilled and raided the bar often, arresting customers for offenses as slight as touching another man's knee. On each occasion, Juanita would head down to jail and bail the customers out, sometimes several times a night. Nonetheless, many customers have said that some of the best days of their lives were spent at Juanita's.

Over the years, other gay bars opened in the area, including the Watch Your Hat and Coat Saloon, which opened in 1971 as the city's first drag bar. The Cabaret, the Jungle, Connection of Nashville, Stirrup, TC's Triangle, and Purple Heys followed, providing spaces of solidarity for Nashville's LGBTQ community, though many of these venues were short-lived. Even as additional gay bars opened, and Juanita's moved locations, Juanita's remained an anchor for the LGBTQ community in Nashville.

With the impacts of the HIV/AIDS crisis on a generation of the LGBTQ community and Juanita's own failing health, the bar was sold in the late 1980s. It moved several more times, and eventually burned down in 1995. In fact, a number of Nashville's downtown gay bars burned down between the 1970s and 1990s. While not suspected to be arson, the cumulative effect of these losses were significant. It was not until the early 2000s that gay bars made a return to Nashville. The 700 block of Commerce Street—once home to gay bars and music shops—is now primarily parking lots. Today, the heart of queer nightlife in the city is on Church Street, featuring numerous queer-friendly bars, clubs, and restaurants, including Tribe, Play, Canvas, Suzy Wong's House of Yum, and Vibe. Following Juanita's example, Church Street has become a safe haven for members of the queer community.

ABOUT THE AUTHORS

Hannah Nell and **Bailey Via** are queer women and graduates of Vanderbilt University's Community Development and Action program.

ADDITIONAL READING

Hollis Hollywood. "The Kings and Queens of Tennessee." *Out and About Nashville* (Nashville, TN), May 5, 2012.

Jim Ridley. "Last Call at Juanita's." *Nashville Scene* (Nashville, TN), Oct. 19, 1995.

1.5 RYMAN AUDITORIUM

116 5th Ave. N.,
Nashville, TN 37219
(615) 889-3060

Renowned as the "Mother Church of Country Music" for the innumerable country stars that have performed there, the Ryman Auditorium is also a site of intrigue for the other events it has hosted over the years, and the woman who managed the venue for nearly half a century. Located on Fifth Avenue just north of Broadway, the Ryman was built in 1882 by steamboat captain Tom Ryman and originally known as the Union Gospel Tabernacle. As legend has it, while attending a Christian revival he intended to heckle, Captain Ryman was instead converted and committed himself to constructing a permanent site for revivals in Nashville. The Tabernacle quickly gained popularity for its acoustics and soon began hosting a range of preachers, musicians, performers, and speakers. After Captain Ryman's funeral in 1904, the Tabernacle's name was changed in his honor.

Though the Ryman is known today as a music venue, over the years it has hosted a wide variety of events. On July 4, 1910, the Ryman opened its doors for a live reading of the telegram description of the Johnson versus Jefferies boxing match, known as the fight of the

Figure 1.10. The historic Ryman Auditorium. Photo courtesy of Nashville Metro Archives

century. After Jack Johnson became the first African American heavyweight boxing champion, former undefeated heavyweight champion James J. Jeffries came out of retirement to challenge him in a racially charged match, saying, "*I am going into this fight for the sole purpose of proving that a White man is better than a Negro.*" The Ryman opened its doors to a "for colored only" crowd that night, and spectators listened to the local announcers as they read round by round telegraphs of the fight, ultimately celebrating Johnson's defeat of "the Great White Hope."

The Ryman's ascent to the national spotlight was due largely to the hard work and dedication of Lula C. Naff. A single working mother, Naff was hired by the Ryman in 1914 and soon promoted to manager, where she remained until her retirement in 1955. During Naff's reign, she brought in famous performers (including Harry Houdini and Katherine Hepburn), as well as the national radio program the Grand Ole Opry, which broadcast live from the Ryman from 1943 to 1974. Significantly, Naff championed women's rights and racial equality and brought in many African American performers where they were welcomed by racially integrated audiences, which was considered radical during the Jim Crow era in Nashville. Still, the Ryman sent mixed messages to its African American audiences and performers as its Confederate Gallery—arguably the most conspicuous feature of the auditorium—honored participants in a war fought to keep their ancestors enslaved.

After Naff's retirement, however, the new owners invested little into the quickly deteriorating building. The high cost for the building's much-needed renovations stalled progress, and the Ryman faced multiple demolition threats. Preservation efforts led to the building being listed on the National Register of Historic Places in 1971, and in 1989—as a result of ongoing pressure from preservationists, musicians, and journalists across the country—the current owners, in conjunction with larger development throughout downtown, invested significant funds to finally renovate the Ryman to its former glory. Deemed the "Carnegie Hall of the South," the Ryman today sets the standard for all music venues across the South and remains a critical cultural icon to the people of Nashville.

Figure 1.11. Tara Cole Memorial Bench. Photo courtesy of Joseph Gutierrez

ABOUT THE AUTHORS

Kate Goodman and **Mike Thompson** are graduates of Vanderbilt University's Community Development and Action program.

ADDITIONAL READING

Jerry Henderson. "Nashville's Ryman Auditorium." *Tennessee Historical Quarterly* 27, no. 4 (1968): 305–28.

Don H. Doyle. *Nashville in the New South, 1880–1930.* Knoxville: University of Tennessee Press, 1985.

NEARBY SITES OF INTEREST:

Historical Marker 92 (500 block, 2nd Ave. S.): While you are in the area, visit the site of the original home of Captain Thomas Green Ryman.

1.6 TARA COLE MEMORIAL BENCH

Located at Riverfront Park near 106 1st Ave. S., Nashville, TN 37201 (near the circular drive and the flags)

A park bench in downtown Nashville stands as an ever-present reminder of many people who have died on the streets without housing. On August 11, 2006, Tara Cole was sleeping on a pier at Riverfront Park with several others. Police came through around 10:00 p.m. that night and told everyone to leave. While most people moved out of sight, Tara, who suffered from mental health issues and was too tired to move, stayed on the pier. She reportedly told the police, "I'm not leaving! There is no-where else to go." The thirty-two-year-old woman was more vulnerable without her friends around her, and around 3:00 a.m., two White men in their twenties stumbled down to where Tara was sleeping. According to the *Tennessean*, their friends reported that they had been drinking and went downtown to have some fun and to "rough up" people who were homeless. They kicked and rolled Tara, who was wrapped in her army blanket, into the Cumberland River. Some people who were unhoused and sleeping nearby heard her scream and ran to help. A couple jumped in after her, but were unable to save her. Despite public pleas from the Search and Rescue Unit, and a nightly vigil held by homeless advocates and local faith leaders, it took officials ten days to recover her body.

Seven years later, on August 7, 2013, the Tara Cole Memorial Bench was unveiled at Riverfront Park. Local homeless advocate Howard Allen had known Tara and participated in the vigils after her death. He worked with council members to sponsor "a resolution recognizing the installation of a bench in Riverfront Park in memory of Tara Cole as a reminder of the senseless violent acts against homeless persons in Nashville."

According to her family, Tara loved music and writing plays and poetry. She was known by others as quiet and kind. She wrote to her mother and described herself as "a strong willed, extremely warm and open hearted, intelligent human being. Unfortunately," Tara continued, "I'm a victim of this unchanging world.

So, I have to struggle just to be myself." Tara's memory lives on and her friends and family continue to work for housing and mental health care for all people, especially those experiencing homelessness. Numerous plays, poetry, and films have been made about Tara, including the 2007 documentary *Angel Unaware: The Tara Cole Story*. Homeless advocate Cathie Buckner says, "The fact is that she could have been any of us. We would not leave until we found her and we will never forget her. We hope everyone will sit on her bench and remember her."

ABOUT THE AUTHORS

Rev. Lindsey Krinks is a street chaplain, homeless-outreach worker, and housing advocate with Open Table Nashville. **Cathie Buckner** is a homeless advocate who worked with the Nashville Homeless Power Project, knew Tara Cole, and was formerly homeless.

ADDITIONAL RESOURCES

Angel Unaware: The Tara Cole Story (film). Leo Hall, dir. Antioch, TN: Leo Hall Productions, 2007.
Homeless Power: The Road Home Campaign. Nashville, TN: Nashville Homeless Power Project, 2007.

NEARBY SITES OF INTEREST

Riverfront Park (170 1st Ave. N.): The park runs along 1st Ave. and the Cumberland River.

1.7 BLACK BOTTOM (COUNTRY MUSIC HALL OF FAME)

277–299 4th Ave. S.,
Nashville, TN 37201

The area now known as South Broadway, or "SoBro," is famously home to the Country Music Hall of Fame and nearby bars, sports arenas, and a growing number of luxury hotels and restaurants. However, here at the corner of Fourth Avenue South (formerly Cherry Street) and Molloy Street was once the slums of Black Bottom, a community with a proud and painful history that influenced what has become the heart of Nashville.

Formally known as the Sixth Ward, "Black Bottom" referenced the dark color of the soil unique to the low-lying area as well as the predominantly Black population who lived there. Throughout the nineteenth century, residents of Black Bottom worked in shipping, milling, construction, and local industry, and created a vibrant community. For many years, the neighborhood was a center of African American education, culture, and business in Nashville. It was the original home of Pearl School (1883–1915), the University of Nashville (later Peabody College), and Meharry Medical College. St. Paul's African Methodist Episcopal (AME) Church was a cultural cornerstone for the community and much of Black Nashville. The area also was home to a bottling company, the Gerst Brewery, a clothing store, an ice cream factory, a city market, and an iron foundry, as well as many Black-owned businesses, doctor's offices, and funeral homes. Novelist Zora Neale Hurston, who lived on the edge of Black Bottom for several years, compared it to Memphis's Beale Street, seeing it as "a place where Black urban and rural life merged in colorful and folk ways."

Unfortunately, during a time of institutional racism in housing and labor markets, residents isolated in Black Bottom also suffered from overcrowding, high rates of unemployment, and unhealthy environmental conditions. According to Randal Brown, who represented the Sixth Ward on the Nashville Council in 1869, "the death rate for Negroes per one thousand persons from diseases was nearly twice that for White Nashvillians. There was inadequate ventilation, dusty streets, and a proliferation of outdoor toilet facilities. . . . Residents held menial jobs, and unemployment was twice as high for Blacks."

During Reconstruction, Black Bottom became a target for White fears of urban decay and paternalistic interests in redevelopment. According to historian Don Doyle, Black Bottom's lively saloons, pawnshops, brothels, and desegregated dance halls became a symbol of "all that threatened the physical, moral, and economic health of the 'decent' White community." Over time, city leaders and citizen's groups successfully prevented the sale of liquor, harming the Sixth Ward economy, and sought to raze parts of the neighborhood for "beautification." The 1920s saw the Sixth Ward decline further when Pearl School and later, in 1931, Meharry Medical College moved to North Nashville and much of Black Bottom's

Figure 1.12. Country Music Hall of Fame, during construction of the Music City Center. This area was once known as Black Bottom. Photo © Bruce Cain - Elevated Lens Photography

Black middle class followed. By the mid-twentieth century, Black Bottom once again was subject to redevelopment, this time in the form of "urban renewal." This spelled the end of Black Bottom's community. The area was incorporated into the Central Business District through a combination of rezoning, large commercial investments, and highway development, and ultimately bulldozers destroyed many of the community's institutions. The slums of Black Bottom existed on the very spot where the Country Music Hall of Fame now stands.

Although the name Black Bottom is unknown to most of Nashville's citizens and visitors, its history is relevant to us all. It represents both the beginning of downtown's raucous nightlife, and a warning about the human costs associated with development, particularly for those with little power.

ABOUT THE AUTHORS

Joe Bandy is a professor of sociology at Vanderbilt University, and **Chloe Herzog** and **Basil Dababneh** studied environmental justice at Vanderbilt University.

ADDITIONAL READING

Tennessee Encyclopedia 3.0, s.v. "Black Bottom," by Bobby L. Lovett. Last updated March 1, 2018. https://tennesseeencyclopedia.net/entries/black-bottom.

Bobby L. Lovett. *The African-American History of Nashville, Tennessee, 1780–1930: Elites and Dilemmas.* Fayetteville: University of Arkansas Press, 1999.

James Summerville. "The City and Slum: 'Black Bottom' in the Development of South Nashville." *Tennessean Historical Quarterly* 40, no. 2 (1981): 182–92.

Don H. Doyle. *New Men, New Cities, New South: Atlanta, Nashville, Charleston, Mobile, 1860–1910.* Chapel Hill: University of North Carolina Press, 1990.

NEARBY SITES OF INTEREST

Country Music Hall of Fame and Museum
(222 5th Ave. S.): The museum has one of the
largest collections of country music albums in
the world and interactive exhibits exploring folk,
Americana, and blues roots of country music.

Hatch Show Print (224 5th Ave. S.): A historical print shop with a gallery and guided tours.

1.8 DOWNTOWN INCINERATOR / ASCEND AMPHITHEATRE

301 1st Ave. S.,
Nashville, TN 37201

Figure 1.13. Downtown Incinerator. Photo courtesy
of Special Collections Division, Nashville Public Library

These days, local residents and tourists
attend concerts and festivals at the riverfront Ascend Amphitheatre. But very
few revelers are aware that without fourteen years of intensive volunteer citizen
action, this beautiful music venue would
still be home to a smelly, dangerous, and
polluting garbage incinerator.

When proposed in 1969, the incinerator's advocates praised its ability to
turn solid waste into a useful commod-
ity: energy that would heat and cool downtown buildings. Support for the incinerator was so widely shared in the business
and government communities that when
an expansion of the plant was proposed
in 1988, it was expected to pass easily. But
by then, the Nashville Thermal Transfer Plant's neighbors had become all too
familiar with the fumes and toxic ash spill-
ing out of the incinerator. Depending on

the weather and the wind, the people who
lived in public housing across the river,
or in any of Nashville's other inner-ring
neighborhoods, found themselves smell-
ing and breathing in the incinerator's
waste. From this diverse group of residents
came the activists who worked with local
environmentalists to create BURNT (Bring
Urban Recycling to Nashville Today), a
non-profit organization working to stop
the burning of recyclables, heavy metals,
toxic materials, and other garbage in Nashville. BURNT forged coalitions with the
Cumberland Greens, the Tennessee Environmental Council, the Sierra Club, Green-
peace, and many other neighborhood
groups and organizations. For fourteen
years, BURNT members attended Metro
Council and state meetings, held public

Figure 1.14. Ascend Amphitheater. Photo courtesy of Mike Thompson

hearings and community gatherings, and sponsored petitions and rallies to bring the facts about garbage incineration to the city.

When a 2001 operational failure at the incinerator prompted the EPA to ask why the incinerator should continue to operate while it violated pollution standards, Metro Council voted to switch the incinerator from burning garbage to natural gas by 2004. Five months later a fire destroyed the twenty-five-year-old incinerator, and the shift to natural gas was immediate. By then, however, BURNT's activism had successfully eroded public support for the incinerator. Consequently, the facility was demolished the following December.

The former incinerator site has since become an attractive waterfront park and music venue. Built with taxpayer dollars, the intention was for the park to be open for residents and visitors to walk, picnic, and people-watch except during concert events when gates would be closed

to ticketed patrons only. However, residents have had to fight to keep the gates open, even when there are no events taking place. The absence of the Nashville Thermal Transfer Plant from the banks of the Cumberland River serves as a testament to the power coalitions of hardworking volunteers can have in improving the health of their city. At the same time, the continued struggle to preserve public access is a reminder of the vigilance required to preserve social justice gains.

ABOUT THE AUTHORS

Jim Selin and **Joyce Vaughn** are former presidents of BURNT. **Barbara Clinton** was a founding member.

NEARBY SITES OF INTEREST

Stix (in the roundabout at Korean Veterans' Blvd. and 8th Ave.): This seventy-foot-tall art installation was constructed by Christian Moeller and is meant to be viewed from all 360 degrees of the roundabout.

Figure 1.15. Tent City, before the flood. Photo courtesy of Justin Wright

1.9 TENT CITY /
2010 FLOOD

185 Athens Way,
Nashville, TN 37228

Beneath the Silliman Evans Bridge once stood an encampment known as Tent City, which provided shelter to more than one hundred people experiencing homelessness. The camp was tragically flooded in 2010. For over twenty years leading up to the flood, this area along the banks of the Cumberland River was a site of semi-permanent camping. In 2008, Metro police threatened to close the camp, then home to about fifty individuals. Tent City residents included many who could not access or afford permanent housing and who faced barriers to accessing homeless shelters—people who were pet owners, couples, members of the LGBQTI community, refugees, and/or who worked non-traditional hours. After local homeless advocates and residents petitioned and protested, former Mayor Karl Dean gave the camp a reprieve. Local congregations and individuals helped residents clean the camp and provided dumpsters, portable toilets, and a shower.

Throughout its existence, the residents of Tent City evolved into a community and demonstrated solidarity, resilience, and resistance. They looked out for one another, enduring the daily struggles and trauma of homelessness by providing support and sharing resources. In collaboration with advocates, residents developed a self-governing community council in 2009 that helped allocate donations and oversee camp security. After the economic recession, the population grew. When the 2010 flood came, approximately 140 people called Tent City home.

Beginning Saturday, May 1, Nashville experienced thirty-six continuous hours of rain. Fearing the Old Hickory or Percy Priest dams would give way due to the record-breaking 13.5 inches of rainfall, Nashville officials of the US Army Corps of Engineers released 5.4 billion gallons of water from the dams into the Cumberland River. Days later, the release of water caused the river to crest at 51.86 feet, and massive flooding ensued. Nearly ten thousand people in the Nashville area were displaced, and among the most vulnerable were residents of Tent City, which was awash in floodwater and diesel fuel. Tent City residents lost everything. Most were evacuated into a temporary Red Cross shelter, and when the shelter closed, city officials capitalized on the environmental disaster and labeled Tent City "condemned," rather than "contaminated." With this designation, Tent City was ineligible for public assistance for cleanup.

In coordination with advocates, Lee Beaman, owner of Beaman Toyota, allowed nearly two dozen Tent City residents to temporarily camp on a two-acre tract of land he owned in the Southeastern corner of Davidson County. Some residents of the nearby Antioch neighborhood, however, campaigned to have this temporary camp closed, and within forty days, displaced Tent City residents were forced to move again. While some received transitional and permanent housing, others are still fighting for their right to exist in the margins of our society.

Organizations like Open Table Nashville and people experiencing homelessness continue to advocate for affordable housing and an end to the criminalization of poverty. The story of Tent City and the 2010 flood is featured in the documentary *Tent City, U.S.A.*, available online.

ABOUT THE AUTHORS

Wendell Segroves is a former resident of Tent City and a homeless advocate. **Rev. Lindsey Krinks** is a street chaplain, homeless outreach worker, and housing advocate with Open Table Nashville. **Laurel Hattix** is a graduate of Vanderbilt University.

NEARBY SITES OF INTEREST

Green Street Church (146 Green St.): Curious about how microhouses might help address the housing crisis? Visit the tiny-house village at Green Street, now a national model for providing sanctuary to people experiencing homelessness.

1.10 JAMES ROBERTSON APARTMENTS

118 7th Ave. N.,
Nashville, TN 37203
(615) 255-0402

Listed on the National Register of Historic Places, the James Robertson Apartments is a striking twelve-story, art deco, brick building located in the heart of downtown Nashville. Proximal

Figure 1.16. James Robertson Apartments, 1978. Photo courtesy of Special Collections Division, Nashville Public Library

to public transit, the downtown library, and other amenities, this apartment building served for years as an ideal location for its residents. But in April 2015, the sale of the building resulted in the eviction of over one hundred tenants, all of whom were at least sixty-two years of age and low-income, and many of whom lived with disabilities. Prior to the sale, the 125-unit apartment operated on a project-based Section-8 contract with the federal government. Under this contract, the owners were required to make units available to renters with Section-8 vouchers, which subsidizes the cost of rent for qualifying low-income residents.

Project-based Section 8 contracts run for a fixed period of time. Upon expiration, the owners have a choice of whether to renew their participation in the program or to opt-out, returning the building to market-rate rents. Across the nation, owners of apartment buildings in hot housing markets are increasingly opting out, displacing low-income residents at a time when finding affordable alternatives is most difficult. Following this trend, the owners of the James Robertson did not renew their Section 8 contract and instead executed the sale of the building without a re-housing plan, demonstrating a blatant disregard for the well-being of Nashville's most vulnerable residents.

As news of the sale broke, concerned citizens came together to prevent residents from becoming homeless. With coordination through Open Table Nashville and Metro Social Services, hundreds of volunteers assisted in cleaning, packing, and moving residents, and donated money for deposits, moving trucks, and other necessities. Open Table Nashville contacted the new buyer, Covenant Capitol, and secured a $15,000 gift to help offset some of the financial burden experienced by the displaced residents. Outreach workers, who typically work with people living on the streets, helped link residents with resources, and Metro Social Services also assisted in the transition process, including by distributing tenant-based Section 8 housing vouchers. On the final day of the move-out, Open Table Nashville held a press conference to bring attention to a situation that was unfortunately not isolated, while volunteers worked to pack and move the tenants who remained until the end.

As a result of the lack of affordable housing units in Nashville, the residents of James Robertson were pushed against time to find something that did not exist: a viable place to live. While most of the former James Robertson residents were relocated to other subsidized living facilities around Nashville, the process significantly disrupted their lives and communities, often moving them far from their work, families, churches, and social spheres. The crisis created an environment of anxiety for residents, testing their physical and mental health.

In 2016, James Robertson Apartments was sold again, this time for $18.2 million, roughly double the price Covenant Capitol had paid just a year earlier. The buyer, New Orleans–based real estate development company HRI properties, plans to convert the building into a 190-room luxury boutique hotel. Meanwhile, within the metro area there are more than eight thousand units of affordable housing with contracts set to expire in the coming years. Given the current rate of population growth in Nashville and increasing demand for housing, it is critical that Nashville preserve existing affordable housing and put in place policy measures that protect those who dwell at or below Nashville's poverty line.

ABOUT THE AUTHOR

Ingrid McIntyre is the executive director of Open Table Nashville and a clergy member of the United Methodist Church.

NEARBY SITES OF INTEREST

Frist Art Museum (919 Broadway): A renowned visual arts museum with major national and international exhibitions, the Frist is located in the city's historic US Post Office building and features interactive exhibits for youth as well as work by local, state, and regional artists.

Customs House (701 Broadway): An exceptional example of Victorian Gothic architecture, this federal building was built in 1877.

1.11 NASHVILLE PUBLIC LIBRARY CIVIL RIGHTS ROOM

615 Church St.,
Nashville, TN 37219
(615) 862-5800

Reaching this room on the second floor of the downtown Nashville Public Library, where scenes of injustice line the walls, requires physical and mental endurance. The space speaks of cruelty and fear, strategy and humanity, protest and progress. The Civil Rights Room features photographs, books, and videos that share Nashville's historic role in the 1960s movement for human rights; to get there from the main floor of the library, go up to the second floor, walk through the doorway marked Special Collections, and turn left. Two white pillars frame the room. A quote from Dr. Martin Luther King Jr., praising Nashville for its pivotal role in leading nonviolent protests, greets visitors from an opaque wall of glass. This is hallowed ground.

Figure 1.17. The Civil Rights Room in the Nashville Public Library. Photo courtesy of Joseph Gutierrez

For years, stifled by Jim Crow, African American residents of Nashville were allowed to shop in downtown stores but not sit and dine at lunch counters. The library, located at 615 Church Street, was built on the former location of the Watkins Institute Free Night School, a segregated restaurant called Candyland, and later a W. T. Grant department store. Across the street was the Castner Knott department store, where youth trained in nonviolent protest (most of whom were students in their late teens and early twenties) filled segregated lunch counters reserved for Whites only. For nearly three months, beginning on February 13, 1960, hundreds were abused and arrested for disturbing the peace while quietly tolerating violence.

The Civil Rights Room is a testament to the efforts of these and so many other members of the Nashville Movement. The space in the library is also the fulfillment of the dreams of Bill and Robin King, two local citizens with a strong interest in justice issues, who donated money for the creation of a room in the library dedicated to the story of the Nashville Movement. The Civil Rights Room—which also features a collection of oral history interviews with local and national activists—opened in 2003 to root Nashville's contribution in the international narrative of social justice. Visitors can read the "Ten Rules of Conduct" for nonviolent protest, etched in glass around a symbolic lunch counter, written by activists Bernard Lafayette and late Georgia congressman John Lewis. "Do show yourself friendly and courteous at all times," teaches one. Another warns: "Do not leave your seat until your leader has given you permission." Several of the black and white photographs surrounding the room display discipline, patience, solidarity, and transformation. One photo shows a protester gripping a lunch counter with his fingertips while angry segregationists yank him from his seat. Another shows a group of students, many of them from Fisk University, Meharry Medical College, Tennessee A & I State University (now Tennessee State University) and American Baptist College, sitting in a jail cell. Taken by photographers from the *Tennessean* and the openly segregationist *Banner* newspaper, few of the photos made it to print. Instead, those from the *Banner* were archived and later donated to the library, along with newspaper clippings and microfilm, after the newspaper closed in 1998. The images, once hidden from sight and significance, were first shared when the room opened.

Similarly, the room illuminates the stories of people who are often absent from history books. In this room, guests are invited to read about a range of activists, artists, and scholars ranging from Jim Zwerg and Afeni Shakur to Kadir Nelson and Irene Morgan. Here, book titles present a poetry of revolution. Biographies, memoirs, novels, children's literature, and dissertations announce themselves with prophecies such as *From Slavery to Freedom*, *Heeding the Call*, and *Long Time Coming*. Guests exit the room beneath a challenge inscribed in black: "If not us, who? If not now, when?" These questions are just as relevant today as they were when John Lewis first asked them in 1961.

The Civil Rights Room Collection includes an audio and visual collection, oral histories, periodicals, ephemera, photographs, records, and manuscripts. Visitors interested in local history, genealogy, and women's studies will find plenty in the Nashville Room to peruse, with its collections of local history and genealogy. The collections also include oral histories of military veterans, new Americans, survivors of the 2010 flood, and Latino artists. The Civil Rights Room is open seven days a week, 9 a.m. to 6 p.m. Monday through Friday, 9 a.m. to 5 p.m. Saturday, and 2 p.m. to 5 p.m. Sunday.

ABOUT THE AUTHOR

Tasneem Grace Tewogbola is a writer and a program coordinator with Special Collections at Nashville Public Library.

NEARBY SITES OF INTEREST

Downtown Presbyterian Church / The Contributor (154 5th Ave.): Downtown Presbyterian is the home of the *Contributor*, a nonprofit, social-enterprise, bi-weekly street newspaper. Look for the vendors wearing yellow nametags and support this newspaper written and sold by people experiencing homelessness in Nashville.

1.12 WALGREENS LUNCH COUNTER
226 5th Ave. N., Nashville, TN 37219

The downtown Walgreens is one of the last remaining site of the Nashville sit-ins, a protest that became one of the most celebrated examples of the sit-in movement in the South. In 1958—after receiving encouragement from Martin Luther King Jr. to move to the South—nonviolence advocate James Lawson relocated to Nashville. Upon his arrival in the city, he was pleased to find a well-organized group of Black ministers and students, including Kelly Miller Smith and C. T. Vivian, making plans for serious changes in the city. Their first goal was to integrate the downtown lunch counters of stores where African Americans could shop but not eat or use public restrooms. Lawson began a series of training courses in nonviolence to prepare students for their demonstrations.

While the Nashville students were planning the sit-ins of local lunch counters and had staged a sit-in of Oral Roberts Evangelistic Crusade, they learned

Figure 1.18. Walgreens Lunch Counter, 1960. Photo courtesy of Special Collections Division, Nashville Public Library

that four students at North Carolina A & T University had acted first, staging lunch counter sit-ins in Greensboro in early February 1960. The Nashville students told the adult leaders that they were ready to go, but Lawson and Smith urged them to wait and complete the training. The students prevailed, however, and the first Nashville sit-in took place on February 13, 1960. The Nashville students selected regional and national chains—including Woolworth, Kresge's, and McClellan's. Disciplined and adhering to their training, students showed up dressed for church, with homework to complete while they passed the time. As Congressman John Lewis recounts

in *Walking with the Wind: A Memoir of the Movement*, "We took our seats in a very orderly, peaceful fashion. . . . The managers ordered that the lunch counters be closed, that the restaurants be closed, and we'd just sit there, all day long."

Despite their peaceful demeanor, the students were frequently yelled at, spit on, burned with lit cigarettes, and assaulted with fists, knees, and boots from White patrons. When the police arrived, the students would be violently hauled off to jail, only to have another set of students take their place at the counter. As the lunch counter sit-ins continued during the first months of 1960, Nashville's Black community stood solidly

Before integration, one feature of downtown for Black people was that if you had to go to the bathroom, you peed in the alley. The main place for Black people to pee was on the east side of Fifth Avenue North, near Church Street and McKendree Methodist Church. Women peed at one end of the block behind boxes and men at the other end, also behind boxes, to give a little bit of privacy. When your grandparents have peed in an alley for fifty years, it was something you accepted. And when you questioned your parents about it, they said "That's the way it is. … God is going to change it, just pray about it." Except nineteen-year-olds don't pray about much, they make things happen. So when the Civil Rights Movement started, we said "When the lunch counters are done, we're going to pee in a real toilet."

Kwame Lillard

with the students. African American women who worked as maids in White homes surreptitiously relayed key pieces of information picked up while cleaning and serving food. Fisk student Matthew Walker recalled his mother driving students back and forth from their campuses to the downtown sit-in sites and preparing food so that no student would be hungry. Small amounts of money would be passed by working men and women to individual students, to be sure they had money for lunch.

When Dr. Vivian Henderson, a Fisk economics professor, suggested that an economic boycott of downtown merchants would send a powerful message to the business community about the importance of the Black community, the Nashville Christian Leadership Council (NCLC), led by Rev. Kelly Miller Smith and divinity student C. T. Vivian, immediately organized a boycott. As pressure on the business community intensified, Mayor Ben West offered to "compromise" by dividing the downtown lunch counters into separate Black and White sections. The NCLC and the students firmly rejected his proposal

and the sit-ins continued. In all, more than 150 students were arrested for refusing to leave lunch counters.

Things came to a head after the April nineteenth bombing of the home of Z. Alexander Looby, an esteemed African American city councilman and attorney representing student activists. Nearly three thousand protesters marched to city hall that day to confront Mayor Ben West, who finally agreed that lunch counters should be desegregated. Less than a month later, six downtown stores began serving Black customers.

ABOUT THE AUTHOR

Kwame Lillard was one of the organizers of the student movement, later serving as a Metro councilman and community leader. **Barbara Clinton** served as director of the Vanderbilt Center for Health Services and is a public health consultant.

ADDITIONAL READING

John Lewis and Michael D'Orso. *Walking with the Wind: A Memoir of the Movement.* New York: Simon and Schuster, 2015.

1.13 TENNESSEE STATE CAPITOL

600 Dr. Martin Luther King Jr. Blvd., Nashville, TN 37243
(615) 741-0830

The Tennessee General Assembly has been meeting in the State Capitol in Nashville since 1859, making it the oldest working capitol building in the country. Throughout its history, the building has been a source and site of political debate, as well as political protest. Many have protested the statue of Edward Ward Carmack—a former US representative, senator, and White supremacist—that overlooks Legislative Plaza, as well as the bust of Confederate War General and Grand Wizard of the Ku Klux Klan Nathan Bedford Forrest inside the capitol itself. Yet both confederate memorials still stand today.

Perhaps the most significant debate that took place inside the Tennessee General Assembly led to the 1920 ratification of the Nineteenth Amendment to the United States Constitution, which extended the right to vote to women. Passage is largely credited to Harry T. Burn (Rhea County). After the legislature was stymied by two tie-votes, Burn changed his no vote to a yes, later stating that his intention was to free millions of women

from political slavery. (See the Hermitage Hotel entry for a description of this event). Just five months later, Tennessee elected its first female state legislator—Anna Lee Keys Worley.

The Tennessee legislature has had a mixed record in the struggle for Black equality. Tennessee was the first state to ratify the Fourteenth Amendment, which recognized Blacks as full US citizens. Yet the state failed to pass the Fifteenth Amendment, guaranteeing people of all races the right to vote, until 1997, making Tennessee the last state to do so. Nevertheless, some African American men went to the polls as early as 1867. In 1873, Sampson Keeble (Davidson County) was elected to the General Assembly and served as Tennessee's first African American legislator. During the Jim Crow era, fourteen African American men served in the Tennessee State Legislature. Avon Williams, Tennessee's first African American senator, was elected in 1969 to represent North Nashville. Ironically, the State Capitol—a structure that was constructed using enslaved labor—was also the site where White Tennesseans passed Jim Crow Laws to create and maintain an unequal world for its Black residents. Legislation such as the Myers Law (1888), the Dortch Law (1889), the Lea Act (1893), and the imposition of a poll tax successfully undermined Black voting strength in the Volunteer State. The effects of these legislative acts would continue to negatively impact the ability of African Americans to vote until the passage of the Voting Rights Act of 1965.

Figure 1.19. TennCare sit-in, 2005. Photo © Al Levenson

Actions taken by the General Assembly continue to affect the quality of life for all Tennesseans. In recent years, legislation has expanded access to critical resources, such as higher education (the Tennessee Promise initiative guarantees two free years of community or technical college to all Tennessee high school graduates). Other bills have constrained access to opportunities, such as the 2016 "counseling discrimination bill," SB 1556, which allows a licensed counselor in a private practice to use personal or religious beliefs as an excuse to terminate care or refer away LGBTQ clients. Local engagement in political advocacy and protest remain essential to advancing social justice statewide.

The continued struggle for social justice across Tennessee has led the State Capitol to be a constant site of protest as well as policy-making. In January 2005, Tennessee governor Phil Bredesen proposed dropping 323,000 people from TennCare, the State's Medicaid Supplement program. This program provided medical insurance coverage for people with low incomes (but not low enough to qualify for standard Medicaid coverage), and for people denied coverage by private insurers because of pre-existing conditions. A broad coalition organized a protest in the governor's office at the State Capitol. Beginning June 20, 2005, the protest continued day and night into September and is believed to have been the longest protest sit-in at a government office in US history. Some concessions were won, but the governor prevailed in dropping thousands of people from coverage and curtailing benefits for thousands more.

The Tennessee General Assembly still meets in the Tennessee State Capitol on Dr. Martin Luther King Jr. Boulevard in downtown Nashville. The Capitol is open to visitors Monday through Friday from 8 a.m. to 4 p.m. The Tennessee State Museum provides free tours of the Capitol daily. More information can be found by calling (615) 741-0830 or visiting the Tennessee State Capitol's website, www.capitol.tn.gov.

ABOUT THE AUTHORS

Ashley Layhew is an educational specialist at the Tennessee State Museum. **Karl Meyer** is a life-long activist in Chicago and Nashville.

ADDITIONAL READING

A. Elizabeth Taylor. *The Woman Suffrage Movement in Tennessee*. New York: Bookman Associates, 1957.

NEARBY SITES OF INTEREST

Tennessee Judiciary Museum (401 7th Ave. N.): Next to the State Capitol in the Supreme Court Library, the Tennessee Judiciary Museum allows you to explore cases from Tennessee's history.

War Memorial Auditorium (301 6th Ave. N.): This classical structure has a storied history, including serving as the home to the Grand Ole Opry from 1939 to 1943, and still serves as a premiere event venue.

1.14 THE HERMITAGE HOTEL

231 6th Ave. N.,
Nashville, TN 37219

(615) 244-3121

The Hermitage Hotel has been a Nashville landmark since its opening in 1910. It quickly gained a reputation for its elegance, unique beaux-arts architecture, and Southern charm. Given its proximity to Tennessee's capitol, the Hermitage has also been a favorite of politicians and lobbyists throughout the years. It is a site that is symbolic of the city's Jim Crow past as its head waiter in

Figure 1.20. The Hermitage Hotel. Photo courtesy of Joseph Gutierrez

1917, W. C. Williams, was beloved by the hotel's patrons, but neither he nor any of the African American staff that found work at the stately hotel could find lodging in its rooms or eat in its restaurant. Paradoxically, in August of 1920, the Hermitage Hotel became the final battleground in the struggle for women to gain the right to vote.

Women in Tennessee began forming clubs to promote suffrage as early as the 1870s. The first large-scale league in Nashville arose in 1894. By 1897, there were ten women's suffrage leagues in Tennessee, and Lide A. Meriwether was named the president of the Tennessee Equal Rights Association. In 1915, Anne Dallas Dudley led the legislative committee that lobbied for suffrage. In April 1919, Tennessee became the only Southern state to allow women to vote in presidential elections. The following year, Tennessee became the deciding state to ratify the Nineteenth Amendment.

By July 1920, thirty-five states had voted to ratify the Nineteenth Amendment allowing women the right to vote, and

Figure 1.21. The Tennessee Woman Suffrage Monument by sculptor Alan LeQuire is located in Nashville's Centennial Park where suffragists Anne Dallas Dudley, J. Frankie Pierce, Sue Shelton White, Carrie Chapman Catt, and Abby Crawford Milton, among others, marched and gave speeches. Photo courtesy of Learotha Williams Jr.

only one more state was needed to secure the ratification. Tennessee Governor A. H. Roberts decided to call a special session of the state legislature in August to vote on the amendment. As a result, both pro- and anti-suffrage leaders flocked to Nashville. Most notably, Carrie Chapman Catt, president of the National American Woman Suffrage Association and the International Woman Suffrage Alliance, came to the city on July seventeenth and stayed at the Hermitage Hotel until ratification. Josephine Pearson, head of the Tennessee Association Opposed to Woman Suffrage, also booked a room at the hotel. Thus, with the ostensible leaders of both sides entrenched at the Hermitage, it became the de facto headquarters for much of the

political maneuvering around the passage of the amendment.

Catt fully recognized the extent to which opponents to women's suffrage would go to prevent ratification, writing that "at least two anti-suffrage men and one woman are here to pledge members against ratification. They will lie, misrepresent and appeal to all the sordid motives they may find." The suffragists' headquarters were in Catt's hotel room, and they worked to stop any vote changes by representatives supporting them. Opponents of woman suffrage, meanwhile, decorated the hotel mezzanine from floor to ceiling in anti-suffrage propaganda and red roses. The anti-suffragists distributed pamphlets

warning Nashvillians that ratification
of the Nineteenth Amendment would
reopen "the Negro suffrage question, the
loss of states' rights, and another period
of reconstruction horrors." As historian
Rebecca Price noted, "There was brib-
ery, illegal alcohol, public slandering, spy-
ing, wiretapping—and it all went down
at The Hermitage." After what seemed
a long and stressful day for both sides,
the amendment was ratified by a one-
vote margin. As word spread, the pro-suf-
fragists outside started celebrating. It
was said that Catt, who was sitting in
her hotel room waiting, heard the news
through her window at the Hermitage.

The Hermitage Hotel remains a
functioning hotel to this day. For hotel
information, contact 615–244–3121 or
visit www.thehermitagehotel.com. Those
interested in suffrage history might also
visit the new Tennessee Woman Suffrage
Monument in Centennial Park.

ABOUT THE AUTHORS

Hasina Mohyuddin is a board member of the
Nashville League of Women Voters. **Ashley
Layhew** is an educational specialist at the Ten-
nessee State Museum.

ADDITIONAL READING

Rebecca Price. "The True Story of Tennessee
    Suffragettes." *Nashville Lifestyles*, Decem-
    ber 26, 2015. http://www.nashvillelifestyles.
    com/bestof/the-true-story-of-tennessee-
    suffragettes.
The Tennessee State Museum, Tennessee4me,
    s.v., "Showdown in Nashville," accessed
    February 3, 2021, http://www.tn4me.org/
article.cfm/era_id/6/major_id/20/minor_
id/56/a_id/136.

NEARBY SITES OF INTEREST

Totem (Deaderick, near 5th Ave., in front
of Tennessee Performing Arts Center): This
sculpture was created by Tennessee folk artist
Homer Green, who died in 2002.

1.15 LEGISLATIVE PLAZA
301 6th Ave. N.,
Nashville, TN 37243

Legislative Plaza, easily the most accessible section of the capitol complex, was
constructed in the early 1970s just east
of the War Memorial Building. Located
at the bottom of the hill and next to the
State Capitol, Legislative Plaza became
an ideal gathering spot for public rallies,
social justice protest, and other noteworthy events.

In 2003, supporters of the Nashville
Peace Coalition organized a five-day vigil
and outdoor camp on Legislative Plaza
to highlight the deaths of hundreds of
thousands of Iraqi civilians as a result of
the embargo on food, medical supplies,
and other resources needed to restore
war-damaged infrastructure. Organizers
installed photograph displays facing Dr.
Martin Luther King Jr. Boulevard, and distributed literature featuring ordinary Iraqi
people suffering as a result of the stringent
economic sanctions in place against Iraq
between the 1991 Gulf War and the 2003
invasion. Full-time vigil participants sub-
sisted on a restricted portion of rice and

Figure 1.22. Legislative Plaza under construction. Photo courtesy of Special Collections Division, Nashville Public Library

as needed, is less expensive for public budgets than paying for nursing home residence. On March 20, ADAPT members and supporters known as TABS (temporarily able-bodied supporters) rolled or walked through drizzling rain to Legislative Plaza. They divided into six well-organized groups to block all intersections surrounding the legislative offices and parking garage entrances well into the evening, chanting, "Just like a nursing home, you can't get out" to frustrated legislators and staff trying to leave. By 8:00 p.m., police managed to clear the intersections by removing, arresting, or issuing citations to over one hundred protesters who refused warnings to disperse. Most were released because the city jail lacked facilities to detain so many people with disabilities. Actions continued for another day, and the ADAPT demands and actions were widely reported and discussed by all mass media outlets in Nashville. In the following year, Governor Phil Bredesen and the General Assembly adopted expanded options for home care in Tennessee.

Legislative Plaza was also the site of the 2011 Occupy Nashville movement, the local affiliate of the national Occupy Wall Street movement. Activists camped out

lentils, comparable to the ration provided to Iraqi civilians under the United Nations–supervised Oil for Food Program that allowed limited sale of Iraqi oil to ease the deadly effects of the trade embargo.

In March 2006, Legislative Plaza was also the site of Nashville's largest disability rights action. Members of ADAPT (American Disabled for Attendant Programs Today) held their annual convention in Nashville on the theme "Real People—Real Voices—No More Stolen Lives." ADAPT contended that public money earmarked for helping people with disabilities must allow people to continue living in their own homes with attendant services, instead of compelling people into nursing homes. During their convention, more than sixty people living with disabilities testified to the oppressive conditions in nursing homes, some vowing that they would rather die than be forced into nursing homes again to get care. They convincingly showed that paying for individualized care at home, only

I met Ahmed Al Uqualy in 2003, one month before the war in Iraq began. Ahmed showed up at a week-long Nashville Peace and Justice Center (NPJC) vigil called The Faces of Collateral Damage. The vigil was an interactive educational event detailing the damage a war would do—to Iraqi people, US soldiers, and the US economy. Ahmed had been in Nashville for several years, working sixty to one hundred hours a week behind the counter at Krispy Kreme. He lived on his own, having lost family members in Iraq, both from Saddam Hussain and from American bombs during the first Iraq war. After seeing the NPJC vigil on the news, Ahmed decided to come out publicly against the war. The night before joining us, he spray-painted "American Bombs Kill Iraqi Children" on his car. He arrived the next day with Krispy Kreme donuts and Iraqi food to share. He immediately made friends, shared his stories, and showed courage by his willingness to speak against US military action while still having only refugee status.

The last time I saw Ahmed was later that summer. In the wake of the Shock and Awe campaign—the bombing that demolished more buildings and killed more Iraqi civilians than ten Twin Towers combined in just the first two days—the NPJC began a support group for people of Iraqi, Muslim, and/or Arab heritage. Given rising Islamophobia in Nashville, this was one small safe space where people could be received with warmth, smiles, and a listening ear. After attending several sessions, Ahmed offered to host one in his home. A handful of peace activists of Muslim and non-Muslim heritage sat barefoot on Ahmed's floor, enjoying the feast he had prepared for us: rich beef dishes on yellow rice, pita bread, and a sweet juice.

A few weeks after that dinner, those of us working with NPJC found out that Ahmed had been detained by US Homeland Security and was now being held without bail in federal prison. Ahmed's name was listed as a successful domestic terrorist apprehension on the website of the newly appointed secretary of Homeland Security. We learned that undercover agents approached Ahmed, offered him weapons, and later arrested him as he attempted to buy grenades, AK-47s, and the like. We and his attorney believed Ahmed had been set up, and the NPJC developed a political prisoner support committee to raise awareness about his case.

After completing his five-year sentence in federal prison, Ahmed was deported. We don't know where he is now, but we hope Ahmed Al Uqualy is home with his family in southern Iraq, or someplace else in the world with people he loves and those who love him.

Matt Leber, community organizer

on Legislative Plaza for several months. When state troopers began arresting Occupy protesters, the American Civil Liberties Union filed a lawsuit asking for an injunction to stop the curfew and arrests. A federal judge agreed with the ACLU. In March 2012, the Tennessee General Assembly and Gov. Bill Haslam passed a bill outlawing camping on state property not designated for that purpose, ending the occupation of the plaza.

Legislative Plaza continues to be a site for protests and advocating for social justice reform. It is across the street from the State Capitol and is adjacent to the historic War Memorial Auditorium and Tennessee Performing Arts Center.

ABOUT THE AUTHORS

Karl Meyer is a life-long activist in Chicago and Nashville, a carpenter, and the founder of Nashville Greenlands. **Mary Skinner** is the community and media relations officer for the Tennessee State Museum.

NEARBY SITES OF INTEREST

Tennessee State Museum (1000 Rosa L. Parks Blvd.): Few sites in Nashville hold more evidence of the legacy of injustice and struggles for justice. Open Tuesday through Sunday; admission is free.

Tennessee Military Branch Museum (301 6th Ave. N.): This branch of the Tennessee State Museum is housed in the War Memorial Building across the street. It is open 10:00 a.m. to 5:00 p.m., Tuesdays through Saturdays.

1.16 MUSIC CITY CENTRAL BUS STATION BATHROOM

400 Charlotte Ave., Nashville, TN 37219

Just blocks from the Tennessee State Capitol lies the Music City Central bus station, which serves twenty thousand Nashville residents who ride the bus every day. Built in 2008, the building was constructed in order to provide a warm and inviting environment for riders, visitors, and employees. While the welcoming exterior of the building suggests the Nashville Metropolitan Transport Authority (MTA) met their goal, the state of the restrooms quickly

Figure 1.23. Meme created by Music City Riders United

proved otherwise. For years, the men's restroom at the station lacked dividing walls between the toilets and working sinks, and was incredibly dirty. For many, the lack of sanitation and the demeaning environment of the restroom reflected underlying tensions between development of the city for the visitor class and the basic rights of local residents.

In June 2016, a group of concerned riders formed Music City Riders United (MCRU) to demand improvements to Nashville's transit system. One of their first targets was the derelict Music City Central restroom. A meme designed to raise awareness of the unsanitary conditions and to demand dignity for everyday Nashvillians compared the bus station restroom to that of a state prison. It quickly went viral, successfully gaining the attention of city officials. MCRU members demanded that the MTA clean up and repair the bus station bathrooms. The MTA issued an apology, made initial repairs, and pledged to complete renovations in the future. Although this was an important win, it is unfortunately only one of many transit rights issues facing Nashville.

Music City Riders United continues to fight for rider dignity and justice. Additional projects have included getting the women's restroom fixed at the bus station and winning expanded hours of service on the Bordeaux bus route, which serves historically Black neighborhoods. MCRU aims to give voice to those residents who have been marginalized by the city's new multimillion-dollar projects in order to fight for the civil rights of public transit riders, such as a safe, clean place to use the restroom.

ABOUT THE AUTHORS

Michelle Estes and **Kutonia Smith** have served as dedicated members of Music City Riders United (MCRU). **Alexa Malishchak** was a Workers' Dignity organizer through 2018. **Tilden Davis** is a graduate of Vanderbilt University's Community Development and Action program.

NEARBY SITES OF INTEREST

Tennessee Falls (Deaderick St., near 6th Ave., in the lobby of Tennessee Performing Arts Center): In a nod to the state's abundance of waterfalls, this stone wall was built with three types of stone, with water gathering into a pool below.

Tennessee Performing Arts Center (505 Deaderick St.): Part of the James K. Polk Cultural Center, TPAC is home to the Nashville Ballet, the Nashville Opera, and the Nashville Repertory Theatre.

1.17 THE *NASHVILLE GLOBE*

441 4th Ave. N.,
Nashville, TN 37219

The *Nashville Globe* was the longest running Black owned and operated newspaper in Nashville. The paper was founded in 1906 by Richard Henry Boyd, a former slave from Texas. There, Boyd taught himself how to read and write and spent years organizing associations of freedmen. After moving to Nashville in 1896, Boyd and his son Henry founded the National Baptist Publishing Board (NBPB) and were involved in the creation of the One-Cent Savings Bank, among numerous other businesses.

The Boyds founded the *Nashville Globe* during the Nashville Streetcar Boycott of 1905. The two-year boycott was launched in response to the Nashville government extending Jim Crow to the public transportation system. Over the following years, the *Globe* reported extensively on the efforts of Black businessmen to create a self-serving streetcar business. While the business venture and boycott eventually failed, the newspaper continued to operate out of the National Baptist Publishing Board building for many years.

The Boyds believed Nashville's Black community was best served by self-advancement. The first issue of the *Globe* reflected the ethos of its founders, featuring quotes such as, "Good things come to those who wait, provided they are hustling while they wait," and "Get out of our sunshine." Editorials encouraged readers

Figure 1.24. The original office for the *Globe*, prior to constructing a new building in 1924. Photo courtesy of Special Collections Division, Nashville Public Library

to exclusively patronize Black businesses, stressed the importance of political participation, and rallied for equal educational opportunities for Black Tennesseans. In 1909, Boyd used the *Globe* to campaign for a state college for African Americans. The campaign was successful, and Tennessee State University remains to this day a testament to Boyd's leadership and tenacity.

Throughout its tenure, the *Nashville Globe*'s message of Black pride and self-reliance was read regularly by over twenty thousand people, or one-fifth of Nashville's total population at the time. After Richard Boyd's death in 1922, his son took over the newspaper's operations. In the 1930s, the *Nashville Globe* merged with another Black newspaper, the *Nashville Independent*, becoming the *Nashville Globe and Independent*. However, in the decades leading up to the Civil Rights Movement, the ethic of "separate but equal" and focus on economic advancement advocated by the paper became less popular. After the death of Henry Boyd in 1959, the *Globe and Independent* survived for only a few months, ceasing publication in 1960. Nonetheless, the *Nashville Globe* had a widespread influence on Black life in Nashville for over sixty years, and it is remembered for its devotion to improving the Nashville community.

ABOUT THE AUTHOR

Chelsea McQueen is a graduate of Vanderbilt University's Community Development and Action program.

ADDITIONAL READING

Bobby L. Lovett. *A Touch of Greatness: A History of Tennessee State University.* Macon, GA: Mercer University Press, 2012.

NEARBY SITES OF INTEREST

Sulphur Dell (19 Junior Gilliam Way): The *Globe* was located not far from the current location of the city's baseball stadium, First Horizon Park, which was built on top of an old salt processing site.

1.18 DUNCAN HOTEL

Southeast corner of 4th Ave. N. and Charlotte Ave., Nashville, TN 37219

Although the classic art deco building that once stood on this corner was razed in the 1970s, the Duncan Hotel—and the land beneath it—has been a site of racial and social justice struggles for more than a century. In Nashville's early days, slave brokers in the city once engaged in the selling of enslaved persons of African descent on this site. Later, Nashville financier William M. Duncan built the Duncan Hotel at the southeast corner of the intersection, where it operated from 1889 to 1916. The hotel played a significant role in Unites States labor history when in 1914 it became the birthplace of the Amalgamated Clothing Workers of America (ACWA), a union of garment workers who, during the early twentieth century, competed with the American Federation of Labor affiliate the United Garment Workers for power. In October

1914, delegates of the eighteenth convention of the United Garment Workers—a national union headquartered in New York and Chicago—convened in Nashville with the hopes of settling unrest that had developed among members. However, just the opposite occurred. Tensions rose when a considerable number of delegates were not given seats at the convention, an act which they took as an affront to the central union value of united brotherhood. Several delegates were vocally displeased with leadership and motioned for "lawful" delegates to abandon the convention. As a result, 130 unseated delegates and a majority of the Chicago members marched out of the hall, down the street, and into the Duncan Hotel, breaking away from the national organization and forming the ACWA. The new labor organization went on to become one of the most powerful industrial unions in American history. By 1964, the ACWA represented 97 percent of the workers in men's apparel.

The same year the ACWA was formed in the Duncan Hotel, African American leaders in Nashville began a fundraising drive to buy a permanent home for the city's Colored YMCA, an organization with roots in post–Civil War Nashville. The drive culminated in 1917 when Richard Henry, Henry Allen Boyd, Preston Taylor, and other Black Nashvillians purchased and remodeled the Duncan Hotel. At the time, the Colored YMCA was considered a "mission" of the White YMCA, which also held the facility's $70,000 mortgage. Disheartened by the display

Figure 1.25. Colored YMCA sign. Photo courtesy of Special Collections Division, Nashville Public Library

of White paternalism inherent in a Black space that was owned and controlled by Whites, preeminent leaders of the African American community sought an independent charter from the Y's national headquarters. The Boyds, Preston Taylor, James Napier, and William Beckam again stepped forward and collectively raised the $4,500 needed to secure the Duncan's mortgage. Once Black ownership of the building was guaranteed, Nashville's African Americans contributed greatly to its success by raising $18,000 for its support, serving 19,623 meals, and accommodating 20,166 boarders during World War I. By 1930, Nashville was one of sixty cities with a Colored YMCA and one of only thirty-six chapters with its own building. The Duncan Hotel and its location became a symbol of Black self-help and economic independence, organized labor in the United States, and a platform for the political organization of Black women in the community.

ABOUT THE AUTHORS

Linda Wynn is the Assistant Director for State Programs at the Tennessee Historical Commission and a professor of history at Fisk University. **Vonda McDaniel** serves as president of the Central Labor Council of Nashville/Middle TN (CLC). **Tilden Davis** is a graduate of Vanderbilt University.

ADDITIONAL READING

Bobby L. Lovett and Linda T. Wynn. *Profiles of African Americans in Tennessee.* Nashville: Local Conference on Afro-American Culture and History, 1996.

Bobby L. Lovett. *The African-American History of Nashville, Tennessee: 1780–1930, Elites and Delimits.* Fayetteville: University of Arkansas Press, 1999.

P. C. Cotham. *Toil, Turmoil, & Triumph: A Portrait of the Tennessee Labor Movement.* Franklin, TN: Hillsboro Press, 1995.

1.19 THE NASHVILLE FARMERS' MARKET

900 Rosa L. Parks Blvd.,
Nashville, TN 37208
(615) 880-2001

For over sixty years, the Nashville Farmers' Market has been an iconic institution in Middle Tennessee. Founded in 1954, the original market was one of the first city-operated farmers' markets in the country. It was constructed on Jefferson Street in the heart of the historically Black North Nashville community. At the time the market was established, most farmers sold their product directly

Figure 1.26. Historic image of the Nashville Farmer's Market. Photo courtesy of Nashville Metro Archives

to consumers through open-air markets. Yet as agriculture became more mechanized, relying on sales from farmer's markets alone became impractical for most growers. With more food choices in grocery stores, consumer preferences also changed. To adapt to growers' needs and meet consumer demand, the Nashville Farmers' Market evolved. Vendors supplemented their own produce offerings with crops from rural farms throughout the Southeast along with some imported produce from California and Florida. This allowed a balance of affordability and selection even when local and regional produce was not available. In addition, the facility also provided space for a flea market, where many North Nashville residents came to find basic goods, like socks and t-shirts.

In 1995, the city—in conjunction with its efforts to complete its Bicentennial Mall—constructed a new $6.2 million facility for the Nashville Farmers' Market and formalized its vendor standards. Stall rental fees were applied at graduated rates to incentivize Tennessee producers, while still allowing a wide array of vendors and products throughout the year. Yet over the course of the next decade, the Nashville Farmers' Market faced significant financial losses and was forced to request a greater financial subsidy from the Metro Council. After years of failing to break even, the market faced an ultimatum from the metro government to become financially self-sufficient.

In January 2015, the board and a newly

hired director rolled out a new vision for the Nashville Farmers' Market. Centered around refined culinary tastes, support for small-scale farmers, reconnection to agrarian roots, and the benefits of seasonal eating, this rebranding was accompanied by a "producer-only" rule stipulating that all vendors must "grow, bake or make" at least 90 percent of their products. This rule had an immediate effect on vendors—four of the market's long-time anchoring merchants, including produce resellers and flea market merchants— were asked to change their business model or leave. It also had an immediate effect on the area's largely Black residents who relied on the non-producer merchants for affordable and accessible food throughout the year. Further, the new policy created a hardship for many farmers who relied on resale to get their products to consumers.

Within weeks of the policy change announcement, produce merchants and concerned customers had collected over two thousand signatures from local residents who desired that produce merchants remain, to no avail. Many longtime customers who are experiencing displacement from their neighborhoods understood the shift to a producer-only model as intended to hasten the gentrification of North Nashville. Indeed, the Nashville Farmers' Market director has said the goal of the policy change was to turn the market into a "world class destination." A lingering question for some was who exactly the market was inviting to come as it had been a destination

for more than sixty years. Producer-only standards do not in and of themselves create a sustainable food system, ensure equitable access to quality produce, or support the growth of small-scale farm operations. Nevertheless, the Nashville Farmers' Market continues to provide an important outlet to some Nashville growers and also supports thirty-four local businesses and restaurants housed indoors—many of which are owned and operated by people of color. While we encourage people to support these local businesses, we also challenge the city to imagine alternatives to the current niche market model that caters to an affluent consumer base and consider a return to a more inclusive neighborhood market that benefits the local community as well as visitors. The Nashville Farmers' Market is open 362 days a year, 8 a.m. to 6 p.m., though individual merchant hours vary.

ABOUT THE AUTHOR

Austin Sauerbrei is a community organizer with the Edgehill Neighborhood Partnership. **Sam McCullough** is a life-long Nashvillian and grew up patronizing the Nashville Farmers' Market.

NEARBY SITES OF INTEREST

Tennessee State Museum (1000 Rosa L. Parks Blvd.): The Tennessee State Museum showcases objects of artistic, cultural, historical, and scientific importance to the Volunteer State.

Bicentennial Capital Mall State Park (600 James Robertson Pkwy.): This park spans from James Robertson Parkway to Jefferson Street.

Figure 1.27. Nashville Movement leaders, including John Lewis (right), being interviewed during a demonstration. Photo courtesy of Nashville Metro Archives

1.20 FIRST BAPTIST CHURCH, CAPITOL HILL

625 Rosa L. Parks Blvd.,
Nashville, TN 37203

(615) 255-8757

Situated near the state capitol building in the city center, First Baptist Church, Capitol Hill (FBCCH) is much more than a bastion of community, fellowship, and spiritual renewal for generations of Nashville's Black community; but it is certainly not less than that. For over 150 years, both its people and its space have been central purveyors of social justice and human dignity. FBCCH's origin is in the First Baptist Church of Nashville (located downtown) which, in 1834, welcomed Black residents, both enslaved and free, to hold monthly prayer meetings and later established the First Colored Baptist Mission in 1847. By 1853, founding pastor and slave Reverend Nelson G. Merry was ordained as the Mission's pastor. At the Civil War's end in 1865, the church gained full independence, renamed itself First Colored Baptist Church (FCBC) of Nashville, and, under Merry, swiftly grew to over 2,800 members. Other churches that grew out of FCBC, such as Spruce Street Baptist and Mount Olive Baptist Churches, also worked within the city to look after the spiritual and physical needs of African Americans, often laboring with public schools, Colored Women's Clubs, and civil rights organizations during the era of Jim Crow. Reverend Merry was later memorialized with a street in his name that borders the modern church campus.

Though rivalries and dissensions within the congregation characterized much of the late 1800s and early 1900s, many influential leaders held ties to FBCCH through this period. Author, abolitionist, and former slave Frederick Douglass spoke at FCBC in May 1892, and William N. Sanders, future organizer of the Nashville Colored YMCA, became a member in 1912. Renowned Women's Suffrage Movement (1919–1920) activists J. Frankie Pierce and Carrie Hull were longtime members as well. Reverend Russell C. Barbour, pastor from 1929 to 1944, boldly challenged Jim Crow bigotry and promoted civil rights from the pulpit. In 1951, the congregation elected Kelly Miller Smith Sr. as lead pastor, and he served faithfully for thirty-three years. This would come to be known as the Activist Church period for FBCCH.

Kelly Miller Smith Sr.'s bravery, leadership, and service in one of the most turbulent periods in history left an indelible mark on his church and the city of Nashville. The church building served as an organizing home and nonviolence training grounds to many student activists, like those in the Student Nonviolent Coordinating Committee (SNCC). As president of the Nashville NAACP branch, Reverend Smith Sr. helped found and led the Nashville Christian Leadership Council (NCLC), an affiliate of Dr. Martin Luther King's Southern Christian Leadership Conference. The NCLC often provided funding and mentorship to SNCC activists, such as future US congressman John Lewis. The Smith family and FBCCH also maintained close ties with Martin Luther King Jr. and Coretta Scott King, both of whom spoke at FBCCH on multiple occasions.

After a series of transient pastoral periods, in 2010 Reverend Kelly Miller Smith Jr. was elected to follow his father's footsteps and lead the church on its future course. Less than five years later, the church began a yearlong celebration of its 150-year anniversary (1865–2015). During this time, many notable civic leaders offered praise for the church's role in the nation's Civil Rights Movement

and beyond, including President Barack Obama, US senator Bob Corker, and Governor Bill Haslam. Despite its important place in national history, First Baptist Church, Capitol Hill remains at its core a home and a family with a cornerstone mission to be "spiritually empowered, culturally diverse, and socially relevant," all to "advance the Kingdom of Jesus Christ." Visitors are welcome to Wednesday and Sunday services. For more information, visit www.firstbaptist-capitolhill.org.

ABOUT THE AUTHORS

Vonda McDaniel is the president of the Central Labor Council of Nashville and Middle Tennessee (AFL-CIO) and longtime member of First Baptist Church, Capitol Hill. **Seth Gulsby** is a graduate of Vanderbilt University's Community Development and Action program.

ADDITIONAL READING

First Baptist Church, Capitol Hill: A Photographic Journal—The First 150 Years. Nashville, TN: First Baptist Church, Capitol Hill, 2016.

NEARBY SITES OF INTEREST

Historic Jefferson Street: For much of the twentieth century, Jefferson Street served as the business and entertainment center of Nashville's African American community.

Nashville Slave Market (Corner of 4th Ave. N. and Dr. MLK Jr. Blvd.): During the eighteenth century, Nashville served as Tennessee's second largest slave market.

2. NORTHWEST

2.1   Gateway to Heritage / I-40   77

2.2   American Baptist College   81

2.3   Clark Memorial Methodist Church   82

2.4   Fisk University   84

2.5   Jubilee Hall   86

2.6   Tennessee State University   88

2.7   Hadley Park   90

2.8   Meharry Medical College   93

2.9   Nashville Greenlands   94

2.10   Pearl High School   96

2.11   Planned Parenthood   98

2.12   The Tennessee State Penitentiary   100

2.13   William Edmondson Park   102

2.14   John Henry Hale Apartments   104

2.15   Z. Alexander Looby's home   105

2.16   Bordeaux Landfill   108

2.17   Southern Publishing Association   109

2.18   Beaman Park / Bells Bend   111

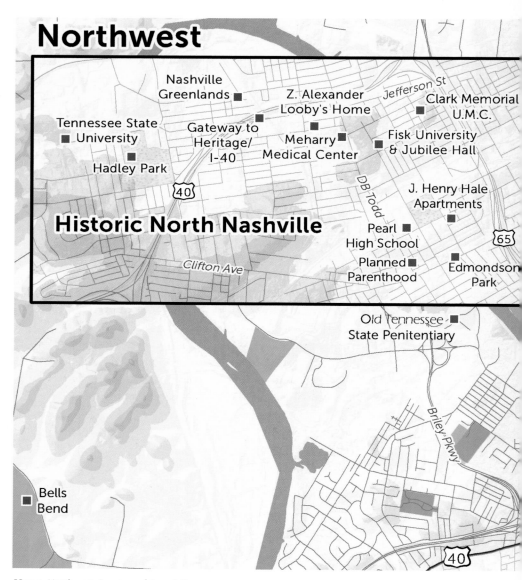

Map 4. Northwest. Courtesy of Joseph Speer

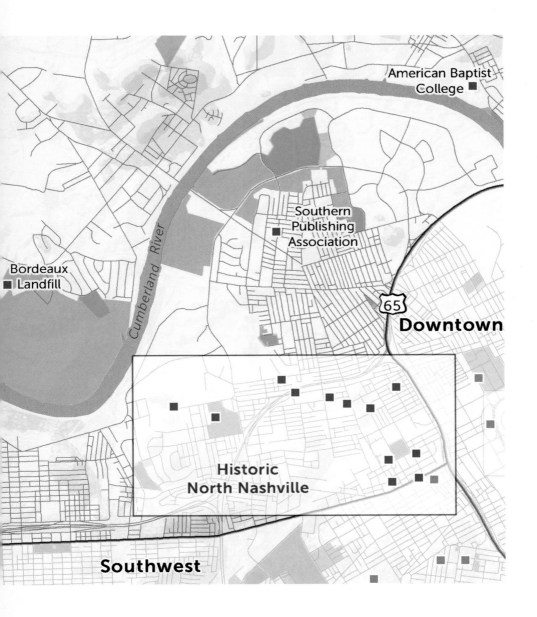

American Baptist
College

Southern
Publishing
Association

Bordeaux
Landfill

Cumberland River

65

Downtown

Historic
North Nashville

Southwest

AN INTRODUCTION TO NORTHWEST NASHVILLE

NORTHWEST DAVIDSON COUNTY IS a geographically diverse region, where the weaving Cumberland River and its tributaries serve as both a corridor and a barrier. Rich in natural resources, the region has also been subject to some of the most extreme environmental degradation in the city. This quadrant encompasses industrial, agricultural, and urban areas and a varied collection of neighborhoods, including Bordeaux, Germantown, Buena Vista, The Nations, Cockrill Bend, Whites Creek, Metro Center, and the iconic Jefferson Street, as well as the city of Goodlettsville. While North Nashville has long been "Black Nashville," the outer-ring areas of the Northwest region were largely White through the mid-twentieth century.

As is true throughout Davidson County, this land once served as seasonal hunting grounds and semi-permanent camps for a number of Indigenous groups. Later, some of Nashville's earliest settlements occurred in this area. In 1780, pioneers built Heaton's Station on a bluff overlooking the Cumberland, and other settlements formed further north, in the area of present-day Goodlettsville. The second oldest church in Davidson County, Walkers United Methodist Church, was founded near Goodlettsville in 1787. After the Revolutionary War, the Northwest region became known for fertile soil, mushrooms, limestone, and mineral quarries. Early settlers like James White, Benjamin Drake, and David McGavock staked claims in the area, and some of the sweeping plantations and antebellum homes, many of which were built by slave labor, remain today. Drawn by the rich resources, a farming community quickly established in this region, and within a few years, infrastructure developments connected these more rural settlements

Figure 2.1. The sculpture *Emergence* was completed by Buddy Jackson in 2013. It was commissioned by the Metro Nashville Arts Commission in response to the 2010 flooding of the Bordeaux neighborhood. Photo © 2017 Stacey Irvin

to the city's growing industrial core. By 1903, Tennessee Central Railroad laid tracks from Nashville to Ashland City, and three major corridors—Hyde's Ferry Turnpike, White's Creek Turnpike, and Buena Vista Turnpike, all of which still exist today—connected the region.

The violence of colonization and chattel slavery that marked the region's settlement continued into the nineteenth century. The Trail of Tears passed through this area, and multiple Civil War battles were fought in the region. Yet, following the war, the Northwest region also became a place where many Black Americans, displaced by slavery, sought to reunify their families and to create institutions for worship, education, and economic advancement.

North Nashville—particularly the area surrounding Jefferson and Buchanan Streets—developed into a vibrant and self-supporting Black community. In the latter twentieth century, some of North Nashville's most vital institutions were its universities, including Fisk, Tennessee State University, Meharry Medical College, and American Baptist College. As showcased in this chapter, many students from these institutions became leaders and activists in the Civil Rights Movement, and these institutions of higher learning remain points of pride on the Northside.

In 1927, as administrators at Meharry planned a move of their institution to North Nashville, Riverside Sanitarium and Hospital opened on the north bank

Figure 2.2. The Norf Collective's mural at the Elks Lodge. Photo courtesy of Learotha Williams Jr.

of the Cumberland River at 800 Youngs Lane, further increasing Black Nashvillians' access to quality healthcare. Yet, the Northwest region also became the dumping ground for the cities LULUs (locally unwanted land use). The 1897 construction of Centennial Boulevard ushered in an austere industrial footprint, and the area was soon home to plants, factories, and mills built to process and store lumber, chemicals, fertilizer, and phosphates. In 1898, the state relocated the Tennessee State Penitentiary from near downtown to Centennial Boulevard, and later the region became home to a landfill and a water treatment plant. This constellation of environmental hazards in the city's Black community is not an accident; the same pattern of siting LULUs in communities of color can be seen across the country. As you will read in this chapter, resident organizing has won some important victories, including the transformation of a landfill into a certified nature area and the preservation of open space for farming and recreation.

But not all of the region's fights have been won. One of the most devastating events in the area was the construction of Interstate 40. The vibrant commercial districts on Jefferson and Buchanan Streets suffered a rapid decline as many of their customers were displaced, and the area became difficult to navigate by car or foot. Several of the entries in this chapter speak to the damage caused in this era, as well as to local efforts to revitalize the area.

Today Northwest Nashville reflects the tension between equitable development—economic investments designed to improve quality of life for all residents—and gentrification—economic investments that attract high income residents and displace poor and working people. Within this region you will find the creative repurposing of underused historical spaces such as Germantown's Neuhoff Meat Packing Plant, which has been home to a range of commercial, cultural, and communal activities, including, at present, the Nashville Jazz Workshop. The cultural roots of Black Nashville are nourished through vivid mural arts projects by the Norf Collective, among others, and the annual Jefferson Street Jazz & Blues and African Street Festivals have become sources of local pride. The 28th/31st Avenue Connector has lessened the neighborhood's cultural and commercial isolation, and there is a swelling community of Black-owned businesses and others that

Norf Art Collective

If you speed down Jefferson Street too fast, without looking and without wondering, you have just missed a vital part of the city's, the South's, and the nation's cultural history. Chances are you have missed the larger-than-life rendering of the epic musical battle between Jimi Hendrix and Johnny Jones at Club Baron, now the Elks Lodge (2614 Jefferson St.). Chances are you have missed the powerful sprint of Wilma Rudolph, blazing along the side of the Jefferson Street Sportsbar (1022 Jefferson St.). And chances are you have missed the jubilant tribute to soul music icons pouring out of the side of Green Fleet Bike Shop (934 Jefferson St.) onto Jefferson Street. These and several more murals have been painted by the artists of Norf Art Collective (or simply Norf)—a multimedia creative team laboring day and night to immortalize the cultural history of North Nashville. They are feeding the varied aesthetic appetites of a multigenerational community, including young people from the area's four historically Black colleges. They are raising up issues of race, class, and gender that are often silenced in (and about) the surrounding neighborhoods. And they are making visible African American artists who have been hidden or ignored in the city more widely.

The Collective formed in 2015 after putting together Norf Wall Fest—a curated exhibit of large-scale murals addressing racial and capitalist struggles, with a day-long festival including spoken word poetry and live painting. The festival's epicenter, a space under the Jubilee Singer's Memorial Bridge, is the site of an old wheel and rubber factory turned junk lot that had for many years been a destination for both seasoned and new graffiti artists, including some Norf artists. Norf's success at beautifying and energizing a space for the North Nashville community has gained much attention, including from parties with competing visions for the space and desires based in profit. For now, the murals from the inaugural Norf Wall Fest remain intact, featuring the art of Woke3, Brandon Donahue, Abshalom, Arjae, Brad Wells, Ol'Skool, Elisheba Israel, Doughjoe, and Sam Dunson. Make note of these names—the spirit of the place was forever changed by the art they created there.

It's Norf. With an f. Because everybody from North Nashville says norf with an f. This is where the collective has put down its roots. It is from the history, knowledge, and experiences of the surrounding community that Norf draws its content and inspiration. Since the success of Norf Wall Fest, the artists have been sustaining each other's momentum and building up their capacity to take on new projects despite (and to face) the strains of fast-moving and displacement-threatening development. But Norf moves on its own terms. Norf navigates the changing terrain of the city on bikes, on ladders, in the sky, scaling walls, with the desire for their art, stories, and work to travel across the globe and back. For those who do stop: Don't just look. Read into what you see. Take some time. Ask questions. Learn the whole story.

Norf Art Collective with **Jyoti Gupta,** graduate student at Vanderbilt University

provide employment for local residents. At the same time, many neighborhoods in Northwest Nashville are rapidly developing, bringing new housing and commercial activity that cater to higher income residents. Parts of North Nashville—like Germantown—have all but fully gentrified, and many worry that redevelopment following the March 2020 tornado will accelerate gentrification of this area. While

Figure 2.3. The pocket park beneath I-40. Photo courtesy of Learotha Williams Jr.

some residents welcome improvements, others fear that long-time Black institutions and residents have been, and will continue to be, displaced as a result of the rising land values. Some worry that the cultural fabric of the community is at risk.

As you visit Northwest Nashville, we hope you experience the strength of its storied educational, faith, and community institutions; bear witness to the often-disastrous effects of urban development and infrastructure expansion; celebrate the power held in sites of Black Liberation Movements and community organizing victories; and imagine the possibilities for equitable development in the city.

ABOUT THE AUTHORS

Jackie Sims, long-time Nashville advocate and activist, Vanderbilt sociology professor

Joe Bandy, and Vanderbilt graduate students **Lauren Baer, Kayla DeCant, Chelsea Edwards, Nicole Escobedo, Seth Gulsby, Hannah Nell, Allie Mikels,** and **Chris Shefelton** contributed to this section.

2.1 GATEWAY TO HERITAGE / I-40

2412 Jefferson St.,
Nashville, TN 37208

If you were standing at the location of the Gateway to Heritage Plaza on Jefferson Street in the mid-twentieth century, you would be on Black Broadway, in the middle of a thriving African American community. Connecting downtown to Fisk University, Meharry Medical College, and Tennessee A&I (later renamed Tennessee State University), Jefferson

Figure 2.4. Staff preparing to welcome guests at Brown's Dinner Club. Courtesy of Fisk University, John Hope and Aurelia E. Franklin Library, Special Collections, Photographic Archives

Street was the pulse of Black Nashville. In the Golden Age of Jefferson Street (1935 to 1965), it was home to 80 percent of Nashville's Black-owned businesses, including cafes, barber and beauty shops, the Ritz Theater, and the Brown Hotel. Its live music clubs brought B.B. King, Nat King Cole, Duke Ellington, and Etta James to perform. Jimi Hendrix lived next door to the Del Morocco and played with the King Casuals in the early 1960s. Hendrix was a regular visitor to the legendary clubs. The area was also a hub for the student, citizen, and clergy activists of the Civil Rights Movement. W. E. B. Du Bois, one of the original founders of the NAACP, was a Fisk graduate, and later, other students from Fisk,

American Baptist College, Meharry, and TSU followed his example by staging the lunch counter sit-ins in 1960.

However, in 1967, after much debate about whether to locate the new Interstate 40 through the more affluent Belle Meade community, the federal government and local officials agreed to route it across the heart of Jefferson Street. Recognizing that this construction could destroy the cohesion of a thriving neighborhood, North Nashville residents vehemently opposed the plan. A forty-person steering committee of North Nashville residents took legal action, claiming that the plan was discriminatory and would disproportionately affect Black citizens by isolating businesses from

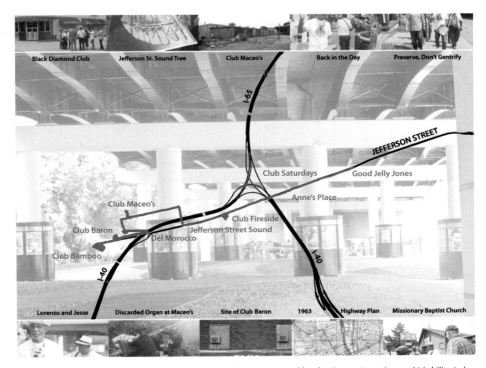

Figure 2.5. A Walk Down Jefferson Street Back in the Day. Created by the Space, Learning and Mobility Lab

the neighborhoods of their customers. A judge ruled in favor of the State, however, and construction commenced, forcing a 2.5-mile section of highway through the heart of Black Nashville. Many residents resisted construction to the end; long-time TSU communications professor Jamye Williams, along with several others, stood in front of the bulldozers during one attempt to halt the devastation.

Construction of I-40 had an immediate and lasting impact on the Jefferson Street community: 650 homes and 27 apartment buildings were torn down; an estimated 126 businesses closed ($4.5 million lost); and the loss of cultural identity was felt with the destruction of iconic businesses. The quality of housing dropped from 32 percent substandard to 67 percent, and the population fell by 13 percent within ten years. The interstate infrastructure now served as "a concrete barrier to commerce," and its noise and pollution posed health risks including asthma and pulmonary disease. When the 1968 Civil Rights Act enabled much of the Black middle class to leave the declining area, its downturn accelerated. In the words of *Nashville Banner* reporter David Henry, the construction of I-40 "wrecked the community."

In recent decades, there have been many efforts to breathe more life into Jefferson Street. Problems remain, however,

Back in the Day: A Walking Tour of Historic Jefferson Street

What was life like "back in the day" along Jefferson Street? Take a walk along this "digital spatial story line" (DSSL) with Lorenzo Washington and Jesse Boyce, both longtime community members and leaders of the only active recording studio along Jefferson Street today. Start by going to the Internet (https://tinyurl.com/yaqx7end) to access the map using a smart phone (iOS or Android). Using this digital spatial story line, you can follow Lorenzo and Jesse as they walk the neighborhood, hear parts of their conversation with visitors to Jefferson Street, and view digital media linked to places you pass by.

You will hear a number of themes along the way, as Lorenzo and Jesse discuss the Gateway to Heritage as an unfinished project and a desire to preserve and not gentrify the cultural heritage of North Nashville. They discuss notable music venues and businesses along Jefferson Street (then and now), sitting in with Jimi Hendrix at Club Baron, and how I-40 and urban renewal were experienced by Lorenzo and Jesse as young Black men making their way in the Music City. For those interested in learning more, check out some of the amazing artifacts on display at Jefferson Street Sound (2004 Jefferson St., Nashville, TN 37208), open Saturdays, 11 a.m. to 4 p.m.

And if you are inspired by this digital spatial story line, consider making your own! They are easy to make and share using DIY tools for creating, collecting, and sharing public history. Check out the functions in Google's My Maps, or open a public account in ESRI's ArcGIS StoryMaps.

This digital spatial story line was created by **Rogers Hall, Ben Shapiro,** *and* **the Space, Learning and Mobility Lab,** *with* **Lorenzo Washington** *of Jefferson Street Sound and* **Jesse Boyce** *of Sovereign Music Group, LLC.*

and the site of the Gateway to Heritage Plaza epitomizes them. Here, the Plaza, as well as the Freedom Riders mural across the street and to its west, are commemorations of both the historic contributions and resilience of North Nashville. Amidst the noise and shadows of I-40, the Plaza lacks the amenities (parking, crosswalks, lighting, and benches) necessary to allow visitors to fully access and engage with the community's history or its present. In this memorial space, we see tributes to the past and hopes for the future, but also lasting evidence of the ongoing social fractures and environmental damage suffered by this community.

ABOUT THE AUTHORS

Joe Bandy, Kwame Lillard, Noah Trump, Jack Lindenman, Jacob Graham, Katani Ostine-Franklin, and **Barbara Clinton** contributed to this entry.

ADDITIONAL READING

Edward. T. Kindall. *A Walk Down Historic Jefferson Street: From the 1940's to the early 1970's—Dark Clouds and Silver Linings during an Era of Segregation.* Nashville, TN: Self-published, Curtis' PrintAll, 2012.

Christine Kreyling. *The Plan of Nashville: Avenues to a Great City.* Nashville, TN: Vanderbilt University Press, 2005.

Figure 2.6. Entryway to American Baptist College. Photo courtesy of Learotha Williams Jr.

NEARBY SITES OF INTEREST

One Drop Ink Tattoo Parlor (1106 Ed Temple Blvd.): This Black-owned parlor is helping anchor a Nashville Black artists' renaissance on Jefferson Street.

Kidd Epps Art Shop (906 Buchanan St.): Head to nearby Buchanan Street to explore this shop featuring locally built, handcrafted furniture.

2.2 AMERICAN BAPTIST COLLEGE

1800 Baptist World Center Dr., Nashville, TN 37207

(615) 256-1463

Tucked on the banks of the Cumberland River, American Baptist College (formerly Baptist Theological Seminary) was arguably one of the greatest engines of the Civil Rights Movement, and it remains a powerful force educating college students for leadership, ministry, and social justice. American Baptist College opened on September 14, 1924. In his memoir, American Baptist College graduate John Lewis recalls one professor saying, "be ashamed to leave this world having done nothing to improve the human condition." Taking that message to heart, in 1960, Lewis and other American Baptist College students—including Julius Scruggs, Bernard Lafayette, James Bevel, C. T. Vivian, and William Barbee—were on the front lines of the Nashville sit-in movement for justice and change. On April 19, 1960, Lafayette helped lead the march to the historic confrontation with Nashville mayor Ben West. Influenced by the Rev. Kelly Miller Smith Sr., pastor of

Nashville's First Baptist Church, Capitol Hill, as well as the nonviolence teachings of James Lawson at Clark Memorial Methodist Church, these students often led their college into greater activism.

Though American Baptist College has served since its inception as a historically Black college, it was not until March 2013 that the US Congress officially recognized it as such. American Baptist College continues its tradition of academic excellence inspired by its motto, "Light a flame that lasts forever." The school aims to instill in all students a passion to advance justice, compassion, and reconciliation. American Baptist College stands as a powerful reminder of the critical role that the Black church and historically Black colleges and universities (HBCUs) played in fueling the Civil Rights Movement, and as importantly, the role of the young activists who pushed those institutions to put their principles into practice. Visitors to the campus are welcome. To schedule a tour, visit www.abcnash.edu/contact.

ABOUT THE AUTHORS

Ridley Wills II is a Nashville historian and author. **Dr. Forrest E. Harris Jr.** is president of American Baptist College.

ADDITIONAL READING

John Lewis and Michael D'Orso. *Walking with the Wind: A Memoir of the Movement.* New York: Simon and Schuster, 2015.

NEARBY SITES OF INTEREST

Riverside Sanitarium and Hospital Historical Marker (800 Youngs Ln.): This medical center served Nashville's Black residents from 1927 to 1983. The marker also commemorates Dorothy Lavinia Brown—the first Black surgeon in the South—who served as the Chief of Surgery at Riverside from 1957 to 1983. Visit the marker at the Riverside Chapel Seventh-Day Adventist Church.

Hartman Park (2801 Tucker Rd.): This neighborhood park features a striking concrete sculpture of an African American woman emerging from the earth. This piece was created after the 2010 flood, as a testament to the resilience of the Bordeaux community.

The National Baptist Convention, USA, Inc., (1700 Baptist World Center Dr.): The National Baptist Convention is one of the largest predominantly African American Christian denominations in the United States.

2.3 CLARK MEMORIAL METHODIST CHURCH

1014 14th Ave. N., Nashville, TN 37208

(615) 329-4464

A modest redbrick building in the heart of this working-class neighborhood, Clark United Methodist Church has been a force in the North Nashville community since 1865. Clark United played a mobilizing role in the Civil Rights Movement, hosting James Lawson's nonviolence seminars, which proved to be a training ground for the Nashville sit-ins.

James Lawson had studied nonviolence in India with disciples of Mahatma Gandhi and moved to Nashville in 1958. He enrolled in Vanderbilt's Divinity School and launched a series of Tuesday evening classes in nonviolence at Clark United

Figure 2.7. Clark Memorial United Methodist Church. Photo courtesy of Joseph Gutierrez

Methodist. Attended by students from American Baptist College, Fisk University, and Tennessee State University, Lawson made connections across the major religious traditions and introduced the group to philosophies of nonviolence. As one attendee of Dr. Lawson's seminars noted, "Clark was the birthplace of the Civil Rights Movement in Nashville. This is the cradle." When more and more students wanted to attend, Lawson started a second training series at First Baptist Church, Capitol Hill, and when Nashville activists decided to conduct lunch counter sit-ins to protest discrimination, Lawson prepared them. Meeting throughout the fall of 1959, the students—including Civil Rights Movement leaders Diane Nash and future congressman John Lewis—practiced the calm and peaceful responses they would use in the face of the insults and assaults they knew would come.

Today, 150 years strong, Clark United Methodist Church remains a pillar of the North Nashville community and continues to engage members in social justice activism in the city. The church is a member of Nashville Organizing for Action and Hope (NOAH), a multiracial and interdenominational coalition of congregations, community organizations, and labor unions that is organizing for affordable housing, economic equity, and criminal justice across Nashville.

ABOUT THE AUTHOR

Kwame Lillard was one of the organizers of the student movement in Nashville who later served as a Metro council member and community leader. **Barbara Clinton** served as director of the Vanderbilt Center for Health Services and is a public health consultant.

ADDITIONAL READING

Jim Carrier. *A Traveler's Guide to the Civil Rights Movement*. Boston: Houghton Mifflin Harcourt, 2004.

Michael Cass. "A Movement Emerges in Nashville: Area Students Led the Way." *Tennessean*, March 26, 2013, http://content-static. tennessean.com/civil-rights/index.html.

NEARBY SITES OF INTEREST

Mary's Old-Fashioned BarBQ Pit (1106 Jefferson St.): This iconic Nashville restaurant offers a simple dining experience with great food.

2.4 FISK UNIVERSITY

1000 17th Ave. N.,
Nashville, TN 37208

(615) 329-8500

Figure 2.8. Young man visiting Du Bois Statue on Fisk University campus. Photo courtesy of Learotha Williams Jr.

Fisk University was created in 1866 during the tumultuous period of Reconstruction to meet the desires of African Americans to obtain an education. First housed in barracks used by Union forces during the Civil War, the school became one of the nation's elite HBCUs. Over time, Fisk grew into one of the largest repositories of African American culture, a space where African American intellectuals developed and debated ideas about Black life and culture across the Diaspora, and one of the centers for social justice organizing in the Music City. Many of Fisk's faculty were considered the cornerstone of the Harlem Renaissance, among them Arna Bontemps, Aaron Douglas, Charles S. Johnson, and James Weldon Johnson. Since its inception, countless Fisk students

have become national and global leaders, including W. E. B. Du Bois, John Hope Franklin, Nikki Giovanni, and Diane Nash. Du Bois, arguably one of the greatest thinkers in American history, spent his formative years at Fisk, an experience that laid the groundwork for his future work in civil rights, sociology, Pan-Africanism, and other anti-racist movements.

As a crucible of social change, Fisk provided a space where faculty and students could study the impact of racism on American society. Through its historic summer Race Relations Institute, founded in 1942 by former Urban League research director and sociologist Charles Spurgeon Johnson (who was also the first African American president of the university), Fisk was at the forefront of researching the desegregation of public accommodations and major societal structures such as the

Figure 2.9. Fisk students getting organized. Photo courtesy of Nashville Metro Archives

armed forces. During the institutes, Johnson convened multiracial dialogues among activists throughout the United States, including Dr. Martin Luther King Jr. and future Supreme Court justice Thurgood Marshall. Those cutting-edge convocations served as the framework for racial discourse in contemporary diversity training activities. Fisk students and faculty continue to contribute to racial understanding through convenings with students, faculty, and staff of sister institutions such as Vanderbilt University, Ripon College, and Case Western Reserve University.

Perhaps Fisk's most celebrated activism occurred during the 1960s, when its students challenged Jim Crow in downtown Nashville stores, serving as leaders of the sit-in movement and later participating in the Freedom Rides throughout the South. Throughout this decade, students from Fisk worked with students from Nashville's other area HBCUs and local universities to change how America defined and practiced democracy. The strategies for challenging oppression implemented by these students, often at great risk to their lives, inform social justice efforts to this day.

Fisk continues to provide a rich intellectual and cultural environment in which students and the community at-large can embrace the journey of descendants of the African Diaspora. Students from across the globe are trained to become scholars and leaders, alongside students whose families and communities have supported Fisk throughout its existence and first-generation students. A leader in the sciences and arts, Fisk faculty are engaged in research on contemporary issues such as environmental justice, nanotechnology, and creating a pipeline of students and teachers in the STEM (science, technology, engineering, and math) disciplines. With the prestigious Alfred Stieglitz collection (which was gifted to Fisk by the photographer's wife, the celebrated painter Georgia O'Keefe) and the art of the Black Masters, Fisk provides a rich cultural learning environment for art enthusiasts. Young and old can become immersed in the fabric of American and Southern experiences dating back to the post-Civil War era. Visitors are welcome to explore Fisk's campus and learn more about the university's contributions to the educational, political, cultural, and spiritual life of the city.

ABOUT THE AUTHOR

Dr. Sheila Peters is a professor of psychology at Fisk University and past president of the Nashville NAACP. A version of this essay was published in The State of Blacks in Middle Tennessee (report of the Urban League of Middle Tennessee, 2010).

NEARBY SITES OF INTEREST

W. E. B. Du Bois Statue (near 1500 Jackson St.): This statue honors one of the University's most recognizable alumni.

Nashville Student Movement Headquarters (Corner of 21st Ave. N. and Jefferson St.):

A modest brick house on this corner once served as the Nashville headquarters for the Student Nonviolent Coordinating Committee. A historic marker for the site sits directly across the street in front of the redbrick building.

2.5   JUBILEE HALL
1000 17th Ave. N.,
Nashville, TN 37208

The roots of Nashville's "Music City" mantle are not traced to lower Broadway or Music Row, but to Fisk University's Jubilee Singers. Indeed, it is quite probable that the first documented use of that term resulted from a fundraising world tour embarked upon in 1871 by the Fisk Jubilee Singers. These young people lifted up songs of sorrow, hope, and jubilation from their enslaved ancestors in Tennessee's cotton and tobacco fields. According to the *Times Daily Mirror*, when their voices reached the ears of Queen Victoria, she was reported to have remarked, "These young people must surely come from a musical city."

The Jubilee Singers created global appreciation for music that articulated the psychological trauma endured by their ancestors, as well as admiration for the subversive hymns that the slave experience produced. Indeed, these were songs that their ancestors (who labored in the fields and the big houses owned by prominent Nashville families including the Acklens, Overtons, Hardings, and Donelsons) could sing at times only under their collective breaths. As the Jubilee Singers gained prominence, these

Figure 2.10. Fisk University's Jubilee Hall. Photo courtesy of Learotha Williams Jr.

songs, deeply rooted in their families' diasporic experiences and cultural expressions, made their way into White homes around the globe. The Fisk Jubilee Singers—many of whom were children of enslaved Africans—first sang classical pieces, but they began to receive national attention when they embraced what W. E. B. Du Bois described as the songs that "the slave sang to the world," songs they introduced to audiences in their own way and for their own benefit. The historic international tour raised enough money to begin construction of Jubilee Hall—a building that would become the first permanent structure on Fisk's new campus and the first permanent edifice built for the higher education of African Americans in the South.

Jubilee Hall became a visible representation of the perseverance and hope of African Americans in the city, yet not all sectors of Nashville welcomed its construction or the independence it symbolized. Indeed, when construction commenced, the very residents of North Nashville who labored on the magnificent structure during the day volunteered to guard the site at night, to protect it from destruction by the city's conservative White citizens. Their successful and largely forgotten efforts contributed to its completion, and today Jubilee Hall remains one of the most striking pieces of architecture in the city.

The building was designated a National Historic Landmark in 1976, on the centennial of its dedication in 1876. It remains a testament to the first Fisk

Jubilee Singers, who, less than a decade after emancipation, contributed to the further appreciation of the inherent artistry of African-derived melodies, rhythms, harmonies, and other nuances that have impacted the music of Nashville (and the world), sometimes in unintended, unacknowledged, and unrecognizable ways. Today's Fisk Jubilee Singers continue the tradition of singing Negro spirituals in local, national, and international venues, while visitors from around the world travel to Nashville to tour the campus grounds, and witness the "frozen music"—a physical manifestation the melodies of enslaved voices—symbolized by Jubilee Hall.

ABOUT THE AUTHORS

Fletcher Moon, a Nashville native and graduate of Fisk University, is an associate professor and head of the reference section of the Brown-Daniel Library at Tennessee State University. **Learotha Williams Jr.** is an associate professor of African American and Public History and coordinator of the North Nashville Heritage Project at Tennessee State University.

ADDITIONAL READING

Joe M. Richardson. *A History of Fisk University, 1865–1946.* Tuscaloosa: University of Alabama Press, 1980.

NEARBY SITES OF INTEREST

McKissack Park (Torbett St. and 28th Ave.): A small park with a playground named after the famous first Black architects.

Friends Quaker House (530 26th Ave. N.): Founded by Fisk's first president, the Nashville

Friends now operate out of this former AME church. The building also provides space to the Nashville Peace and Justice Center, yoga classes, various musical groups, and the Nashville Chinese Alliance.

2.6 TENNESSEE STATE UNIVERSITY

3500 John A. Merritt Blvd., Nashville, TN 37209

(615) 963-5000

Originally founded as Tennessee Agricultural and Industrial State Normal School for Negroes in 1912, Tennessee State University is one of Nashville's four remaining HBCUs. The main campus rests atop a hill at the intersection of Twenty-Eighth Avenue and Jefferson Street in the heart of North Nashville, a historically Black neighborhood. TSU's first president, William Jasper Hale (1912–1943), worked diligently to navigate two seemingly disparate constituencies—a Black community that welcomed the school, and many reluctant White citizens, including legislators, who distrusted any hint of Black ambition. Despite limited funding from the state, within ten years, the school grew into a four-year college and awarded its first degrees in 1924.

TSU's student body took the motto "Enter to learn; go forth to serve" seriously. Their participation in civil rights demonstrations as a means of serving their communities often placed TSU's second president, Walter S. Davis, at odds

Figure 2.11. The Olympic Statue, honoring famous TSU alumna Wilma Rudolph and TSU's Olympic excellence under the leadership of Coach Ed Temple (1927–2016). Photo courtesy of Learotha Williams Jr.

with White legislators and legal officials. President Davis's tenure (1943–1968) roughly coincides with the emergence of a more assertive turn in the Black Freedom Struggle that was fueled by Black veterans returning home from military service. This revolutionary fervor in Black communities did not bypass TSU's campus. Its proximity to Fisk University and Meharry Medical College placed the three educational institutions in a unique position to garner a critical mass of support for the growing Civil Rights Movement of the 1950s and '60s.

With an increase in the numbers of young people placing their bodies on the line for nonviolent demonstrations, TSU could not escape the revolutionary spirit of the time. President Davis had to walk a racial tightrope between addressing students' calls for social justice and appeasing White Nashvillians who remained hostile to the growing modern Civil Rights Movement. This tension sometimes placed him at odds with the student body. Most notably, President Davis expelled fourteen TSU students as a result of their participation in the sit-in movement. Despite these tensions, the school received full land-grant university status in 1958 and continued to expand. The school officially changed its name to Tennessee State University after President Davis's retirement in 1968.

While some TSU students advocated for social justice at home, others competed for international acclaim abroad. Wilma Rudolph (1940–1994), arguably TSU's most internationally known alumna, became a legend for outrunning polio and any woman who set foot on a racetrack in her presence. Her 1956 Olympic debut and three record-breaking gold medal sprints in 1960 solidified her place in sports history. Back home in the United States, her triumph was another example of Black success on a global stage in the face of legalized discrimination. Her victory filled students with pride and emboldened them to continue the struggle for progress in Tennessee and their home states. Rudolph remains a symbol of TSU's illustrious past and the promise of its future students.

With its eighth president, Dr. Glenda Baskin Glover, at the helm, Tennessee State University has responded to the challenges facing HBCUs in the twenty-first century. Its diverse student body represents a number of countries while remaining true to its mission to provide access to higher education for members of historically underserved groups. Visitors are welcome to explore the five-hundred-acre main campus, set in a North Nashville residential neighborhood, as well as the Avon Williams campus,

located downtown near the center of Nashville's business and government district. For more information or to schedule a tour, visit www.tnstate.edu.

ABOUT THE AUTHOR

K. T. Ewing is an assistant professor of history at Tennessee State University and a third generation HBCU graduate.

NEARBY SITES OF INTEREST

Tennessee State University Olympic Plaza Statue (near Ed Temple Blvd.): This statue at Tennessee State University honors Wilma Rudolph, class of 1963, one of the most internationally recognized Black female athletes of the 1960s.

Swett's (2725 Clifton Ave.): For over sixty years, Swett's has offered cafeteria-style Southern food to college students, the surrounding neighborhood, and local celebrities.

2.7 HADLEY PARK
1039 28th Ave. N.,
Nashville, TN 37208

The city of Nashville dedicated Hadley Park for the exclusive use of its Black residents on July 4, 1912. The first of its kind in the nation, these thirty-four acres of attractive grasslands, abundant shade, and natural beauty seemed to validate the efficacy of the 1896 Supreme Court Case *Plessy v. Ferguson*. At the time, many thought the park, which resulted from a collaborative effort between public officials and leaders in the African American community, stood as powerful

Figure 2.12. Hadley Park in the fall. Photo courtesy of Learotha Williams Jr.

evidence that a separate but harmonious relationship between the Nashville's Black and White populations could be achieved if all parties worked together to achieve their desired goals.

Benjamin Carr, North Nashville's renowned farmer-citizen, was the driving force behind the park's creation. An ex-slave who emerged as a prominent activist in the city—Carr was part of the committee that convinced the state to create Tennessee Agricultural and Industrial State Normal School for Negroes (now Tennessee State University) in Nashville—his tireless advocacy convinced the city leaders to purchase part of the farm once owned by John L. Hadley, a slaveowner, to be used as a park for African Americans. As the crowd stood in the sunshine that July listening to addresses from the porch of Hadley's old plantation house, many observers wondered why the park was not named after Benjamin Carr, their fearless populist leader who was instrumental in its creation.

Hadley Park's opening represented an attempt by the city to move beyond its slaveholding past into a future that would be characterized by "goodwill and brotherly interest." For most of the attendees, that day became a perfect metaphor for Nashville's race relations. When the city's residents awoke that morning, dark skies and inclement weather threatened to delay the ceremony or limit its participation to only its most enthusiastic supporters. Nevertheless, the breaking of the clouds and the resultant sunshine seemed to usher in a spirit of jubilation with residents celebrating the transformation of the former plantation into a recreational space. A place once characterized by compulsory labor and emotional trauma was to become a refuge where African Americans could relax and find peace.

The sun shone brightly that day, but Nashville's enthusiasm for the park as well as that of those who used it quickly declined, and the space that once represented the viability of Jim Crow became one of the city's most visible indictments of the system. Six years after its grand opening, the *Nashville Globe* described Hadley Park as a "monumental joke" possessing no "redeeming features." In contrast to public areas reserved exclusively for Whites, including Centennial, Watkins, and Shelby Park, Hadley Park was ill-maintained, lacked amenities, and had become a "grotesque failure," demonstrating the lack of real power possessed by Nashville's African American leaders.

Much has changed since then, and the park now boasts a large modern community and fitness center, an indoor swimming pool, indoor and outdoor walking/running tracks, sports fields, and a computer lab. Today, many long-time North Nashville residents' most vivid memories of Hadley Park are not the stories of Benjamin Carr and other African Americans who made the park a reality, but the mixed accounts of prominent events in Nashville's history. Some remember the staging of tanks among its trees and benches in anticipation of race riots during the late 1960s. For others, memories of the park's legendary Sunday car shows—events

that often drew visitors from as far away as Alabama and Mississippi—remain among the most enjoyable recollections. Today, Hadley Park draws visitors from around the globe for the annual African Street Festival, a three-day event organized during the late twentieth century to celebrate African culture. Though there is still an ongoing dispute among locals over whether the park was named after the former planter, John L. Hadley, who owned the land where the park now sits, or the prominent local African American physician W. A. Hadley, the park has been a fixture in the community for more than a century.

ABOUT THE AUTHOR

Learotha Williams Jr. is an associate professor of African American and Public History and coordinator of the North Nashville Heritage Project at Tennessee State University.

NEARBY SITES OF INTEREST

PearlCohn Entertainment Magnet High School (904 26th Ave. N.): To take a tour with youth ambassadors of this nationally renowned music magnet school, contact the main office at (615) 329-8150.

Figure 2.13. Mayor West at Meharry. Photo courtesy of Nashville Metro Archives

2.8 MEHARRY MEDICAL COLLEGE

1005 Dr. D. B. Todd Jr. Blvd., Nashville, TN 37208

(615) 327-6000

Today, Meharry Medical College is one of the nation's oldest and largest historically Black academic health science centers, and its legendary beginnings sprang from a single act of kindness. As folklore has it, during the 1820s, a young White man named Samuel Meharry was hauling salt in a loaded wagon through Kentucky when he lost control and his wagon tumbled into a ditch. Nightfall quickly approaching, Meharry went searching for shelter and assistance. He came upon a cabin, home to a newly emancipated Black family, who risked their very freedom by letting an unknown White man into their home. At the time, slave hunters were notorious for rounding up free African American men and women throughout Kentucky and other border states and kidnapping them for eventual sale into slavery. The next morning, the family helped Meharry pull the cart out of the ditch, and the young salt seller was on his way. He left with a promise, "I have no money now, but when I am able, I shall do something for your race." True to his word, in 1876 he provided a grant of land and $30,000 deeded to the Central Tennessee College's Medical Center, which evolved into Meharry Medical College. It is this act of kindness that inspires the mission of Meharry Medical College to this day: educating African Americans to serve the underserved.

Meharry is distinguished by its student population and social justice mission. In the first half of the twentieth century, Meharry had educated half of the nation's Black doctors. In 1931, the college moved from its original location in the Chestnut Hill neighborhood downtown to North Nashville, one of the centers of the city's

African American community. Meharry remains the nation's largest historically Black medical college and has the highest percentage of African Americans graduating with PhDs in the biomedical sciences in the country. Eliminating health disparities is central to Meharry's education, research, and patient care.

Persistent racial disparities in health are a key concern in Nashville. Uneven access to health-promoting resources—such as parks, grocery stores, and accessible and affordable health care—in addition to concentrations of environmental risks—such as hazardous waste, poor housing quality, and pollutants—have produced stark racial health disparities across the city. Nashville's Black and Latino residents are twice as likely to live below the poverty level as their White counterparts, are less likely to have health insurance, and suffer from higher rates of heart disease, stroke, respiratory disease, diabetes, and infant mortality.

Although comprehensive policy changes are needed to close the gap in health outcomes, Meharry has long served as a leader in reducing health disparities in Nashville, operating a number of community outreach programs to improve health of vulnerable Nashvillians. Every day, Meharry students and faculty help realize the vision of Samuel Meharry and pay homage to the memory of the family that risked their well-being to help a stranger. Visitors are welcome to walk the campus grounds, including the school's beautiful amphitheater, which faces Twenty-First Avenue North between Alameda and Albion Streets.

ABOUT THE AUTHOR

Chris Shefelton is a graduate of Vanderbilt University's Community Development and Action program.

NEARBY SITES OF INTEREST

Woodcuts Gallery and Framing (1613 Jefferson St.): Visit this locally owned frame shop and gallery space, featuring Black artists.

2.9 NASHVILLE GREENLANDS

2407 Heiman St.,
Nashville, TN 37208
(615) 322-9523

You can find the homes and residents of Nashville Greenlands surrounded by apple and fig trees, chicken coops, and grapevines. This residential "intentional community" began in January 1997 with the purchase and restoration of a vacant, vandalized house at 2407 Heiman St. for $18,000. Since then, the community has grown to include a network of six restored houses in the neighborhood. These homes provide low cost housing for twenty-four resident members at any given time, and over a hundred Nashville activists have been part of the Greenlands Community.

The community's purpose is twofold. First, Nashville Greenlands restores vacant properties in an economically distressed area of the urban core, creating affordable housing for young activists devoted to social justice organizing. Second, Nashville Greenlands serves as a model for using yards and unoccupied lots for intensive

Figure 2.14. Residents of Greenlands. From the personal collection of Karl Meyer

organic cultivation and production of food crops—vegetables, berries, fruit trees, nuts—and fostering other plant and animal diversity—wildflowers, small meadows, decorative shrubs—using sustainable organic methods.

Living cooperatively, growing food, and reusing salvaged lumber and other building materials reduces the residents' living expenses. Low-cost living in turn allows residents time for peace and social justice activism. Greenlands resident members have had key roles as founding members and lead organizers for Open Table Nashville, Workers' Dignity, and Occupy Nashville. Over the years, residents have served as staff organizers, interns, and volunteers with Nashville Peace and Justice Center, Nashville Food Project, Tennessee Health Care Campaign, Homeless Power Project, Cayce United, Tennessee Coalition Against State Killing, Room in the Inn, Hands on Nashville, Tennessee

Immigrant and Refugee Rights Coalition, Tennessee Alliance for Progress, North Nashville Organization for Community Improvement, Black Lives Matter, and other organizations and movements. Greenlands resident members have been arrested and jailed many times for nonviolent protest actions in support of the rights of homeless people, disability access and rights, and healthcare for all, and in opposition to death penalty executions, US wars in Iraq and Afghanistan, the US Army School of the Americas, and the manufacture of nuclear weapons at Oak Ridge, Tennessee.

Public authorities have not always appreciated the contributions and public advocacy of Greenlands members. In the early years, the Metropolitan Public Health Department cited Greenlands garden projects four years in a row as "a danger to the health, safety and welfare of the people of Metro/Davidson County." Greenlands prevailed in court and at the Metropolitan Council, ultimately leading to changes in the Metro Code to allow gardens and natural vegetation growth. Greenlands members also had active roles in "No Spray" initiatives to limit aerial insecticide spraying to control mosquitos, and UCAN legislation to allow backyard chickens. Although the Health

Department vigorously opposed these initiatives, both campaigns ultimately succeeded. For those interested in seeing an alternate model of living in which people consume less, destroy less, and share the wealth of the Earth around us, the Greenlands welcomes visitors.

ABOUT THE AUTHOR

Karl Meyer is a life-long activist in Chicago and Nashville, a carpenter, and the founder of Nashville Greenlands.

NEARBY SITES OF INTEREST

Southern V (1200 Buchanan St.): Looking for vegan Southern cuisine? Stop by this North Nashville–owned and –operated soul food restaurant!

2.10 PEARL HIGH SCHOOL

Corner of 17th Ave. N. and
Jo Johnston Ave.,
Nashville, TN 37203

Pearl High opened its doors one year after the 1896 US Supreme Court decision *Plessy v. Ferguson*, which legally sanctioned Jim Crow. As author Andrew Maraniss concluded, "Jim Crow and a segregated school system didn't crush a community, but instead inspired a purposeful resistance, and greatness in both academics and athletics." From its beginning through the 1980s, Pearl Senior High School was the bedrock of secondary education for Nashville's African American community. Despite unequal

treatment from the world outside, Pearl High created a family atmosphere that is still celebrated by its alumni. Closely connected to civil-rights activities at neighboring Fisk University and Tennessee A&I State College, Pearl High students and teachers were part of the force that challenged Nashville's segregated society.

Pearl School, the precursor of the senior high school that bore its name, began in 1883 as a grammar school for African Americans on what is now Fifth Avenue South. It remained in the area known as Black Bottom until 1917. Three years after Pearl opened, Meigs School became Nashville's first Black high school, though within a year, the high-school classes at Meigs were transferred to Pearl. On June 2, 1898, Pearl graduated its first high school class. Due to overcrowded conditions, the mayor and the city authorized the building of a new facility for Pearl High School at Sixteenth Avenue North and Grant Street. By 1936, the academy again outgrew its facilities, and a new building was erected on Seventeenth Avenue North and Jo Johnston Avenue. Designed by the African American architectural firm of McKissack and McKissack, in the fall of 1937 students moved into what "eminent authorities considered one of the most modern, best constructed, and well-equipped buildings for Negroes in the South."

One of the most historic events in the school's history took place on January 4, 1965, when the Pearl High School basketball team played Father Ryan High School at Nashville's Municipal Auditorium.

Figure 2.15. Pearl High School teachers, 1910. Photo courtesy of Nashville Metro Archives

The first game in the South between a predominantly White school and an African American school drew approximately 8,300 attendees, the largest crowd ever for a regular season event. The game lived up to expectations. The teams traded the lead throughout the game. Eventually, Pearl took a 51–50 lead. However, the game came down to a final shot for Father Ryan. Willie Brown, an African American and Ryan's star, took a shot from the corner that bounced off the rim and into the hands of his teammate Lynn Dempsey, who hit the last shot as the horn sounded, giving Ryan a 52–51 victory. The following year, Pearl won the TSSAA State Championship, becoming the first African American team in Tennessee to win that title. Each of the Pearl Tigers went on to play collegiate level basketball, and Pearl's forward Perry Wallace became the first African American varsity athlete to play basketball under an athletic scholarship in the Southeastern Conference at Vanderbilt University.

Nonetheless, the integration of Nashville's public school system progressed slowly, and more than a decade after *Brown*, two schools on Nashville's south side, Rose Park and Cameron Junior Highs, did not have a single White student enrolled. In 1983, the city's federal desegregation plan combined Pearl High School and West Nashville's predominantly White Cohn High School into the new Pearl-Cohn Comprehensive High School. With the departure of many of Pearl's teachers and administrators to other Metro Nashville Public Schools, the intimate relationship the school had with its students and the North Nashville community declined, leaving a void that no school or school cluster has successfully filled. In more recent history, the city converted the old Pearl High School facility into the Martin Luther King Jr. Academic Magnet for Health Sciences and Engineering at Pearl High School. Like its predecessor, this school is now nationally recognized for academic achievement.

ABOUT THE AUTHOR

Linda T. Wynn is the assistant director for state programs at the Tennessee Historical Commission. She is on faculty at Fisk University in the Department of History and Political Science, and a graduate of Pearl High School.

ADDITIONAL READING

Andrew Maraniss. "The Legacy of Pearl High School and Its Success during Segregation." *The Undefeated*, July 19, 2016. https://theundefeated.com/features/the-legacy-of-pearl-high-school-and-its-success-during-segregation.

NEARBY SITES OF INTEREST

Nashville Christian Institute (2420 Batavia St.): The site of one of the earliest Christian schools for Black residents, today all that remains of the Nashville Christian Institute is the gymnasium, which hosts a café and Islamic Community Center.

2.11 PLANNED PARENTHOOD

412 Dr. D. B. Todd Jr. Blvd., Nashville, TN 37203

(866) 711-1717

It may be difficult to imagine this unassuming health center as a site of social struggle, but for more than fifty years it has been just that. When Planned Parenthood opened, faith-based opposition to the use of birth control methods ran deep, and women had little access to information and services related to their reproductive health. In the early 1960s,

Figure 2.16. Anti-choice protesters in the 1970s. Photo courtesy of Special Collections Division, Nashville Public Library

student activists, health professionals, and civic groups grew increasingly concerned about the need for access to family planning education and the lack of information and agency related to women's sexual and reproductive health. The Nashville Planned Parenthood center opened in 1965 to provide sexual and reproductive health resources to families in Nashville and the surrounding rural counties. After *Roe v. Wade* legalized abortion in 1973, the health center added pregnancy tests, a full range of contraception options, and abortion to its services.

The addition of abortion services was as controversial locally as it was nationally. Annual protests, such as the Pastor's Protest against Abortion, attracted as many as 850 people, making it difficult for patients to access any of the clinic's resources. In 1989, two anti-choice protesters were arrested for assaulting a Planned Parenthood staff member in Nashville, and since the nineties there has been a constant legislative battle to protect the rights guaranteed by *Roe v. Wade*. Despite the ongoing struggle for reproductive rights, thousands of Nashvillians of all ages rely on Planned Parenthood for reproductive, sexual, and complementary healthcare and comprehensive sexuality education each year.

In recent decades, Tennessee has imposed a number of restrictions that impact access to sexual and reproductive health, including a mandatory forty-eight-hour waiting period for abortion services, a twenty-week abortion ban, the closure of rural hospitals and medical centers, and votes against Medicaid expansion for the state. As of this writing, a legislative attempt to block Tennessee patients from accessing care at Planned Parenthood is also pending. This legislative context makes the work of Tennessee's four Planned Parenthood health centers—located in Nashville, Memphis, and Knoxville—a critical component of sexual and reproductive health care in the state.

However, the struggle for reproductive rights and reproductive justice in Tennessee has always been larger than a single organization. In 2019, Tennessee garnered national attention when lawmakers hosted a "summer study" examining the effects of six-week abortion bans. The hearings reached their pinnacle when Senate Judiciary Chairman Mike Bell cut the microphone of SisterReach founder and executive director Cherisse Scott after she accused the committee of perpetuating White supremacy. She was the only Black woman to present and the only person blocked from finishing their testimony.

Scott's testimony reflected broader calls from Black, Brown, Indigenous, and people of color who for decades argued that the reproductive rights movement did not recognize that the conversation about reproductive oppression was much larger than access to abortion and birth control. In order to move toward reproductive freedom, the movement must also acknowledge the history of White supremacy and eugenics within the United States, including but not limited to the forced sterilization of Black, Brown, disabled, poor, queer, and incarcerated people; gynecological experimentation on Black and Brown bodies; and genocide of Indigenous/Native people. In 1994, twelve Black organizers from SisterSong developed and shared the Reproductive Justice framework. Reproductive Justice is led by women of color and expanded the movement to incorporate a human rights framework connected to bodily autonomy, including pleasure; the right to parent; the right to not parent; and the right to raise families in safe and healthy communities.

Planned Parenthood's provision of sexual and reproductive health services, education, and advocacy is one part of a larger movement for reproductive rights and reproductive freedom. In addition to Planned Parenthood, Tennesseans benefit from the strong leadership in Reproductive Justice organizing provided by Sister-Reach, a Memphis-based educational and advocacy organization, and many other organizations advocating for reproductive rights and freedom across the state, such as Healthy and Free Tennessee, Knoxville and Memphis abortion doula collectives, countless birth workers and sex educators, and several independent abortion centers including Knoxville Center for Reproductive Health, Bristol Women's Center, and Memphis CHOICES.

ABOUT THE AUTHORS

Lizzy Thomas is a Nashville-based community organizer for Planned Parenthood of Tennessee and North Mississippi. **Elise Krews** and **Amie Thurber** are graduates of Vanderbilt University.

NEARBY SITS OF INTEREST

OutCentral (1709 Church St.): Nashville's LGBT community center, featuring drop-in groups, yoga classes, film nights, and more. Visit outcentral.org for a calendar.

2.12 THE TENNESSEE STATE PENITENTIARY

100 Bomar Blvd.,
Nashville, TN 37209

One of the most architecturally striking buildings in Nashville is also the site of one of the most inhumane prisons in American history. Located on 1,200 acres on the Cockrill Bend of the Cumberland River, the prison was primarily built by incarcerated men from nearby penitentiaries. Despite having an initial capacity of 800, when the fortress-like prison opened in February 1898, 1,403 inmates were admitted on the first day. Immediately, the prison suffered from massive overcrowding and quickly devolved into atrocious living conditions plagued by medical, sanitation, and safety hazards. The surpassed capacity was not matched with increased staffing, and the supervision and protection of the inmates suffered.

In 1902, a band of prisoners blew up the right wing of Cell Block D, killing one inmate and allowing two others to escape. Another incident involved an eighteen-hour siege of the segregated White wing. A mass escape occurred in 1938, and later a fire destroyed the dining hall. Major riots broke out in 1975 and 1985. As threats, attacks, riots, and escapes became a daily norm, the prison acquired a reputation for negligence and corruption. Inmate health was further compromised by forced labor, initially on the large farm surrounding the then-rural prison, and later, making durable goods. It was not uncommon for inmates to work sixteen-hour days, laboring in high heat with no water, safety gear, or breaks, and to be paid in pennies. In 1990, the death toll at the Tennessee State Penitentiary (excluding those whose lives were ended by execution) was the highest of any prison in the country.

In 1983, Scotty Grubbs and four other inmates filed a lawsuit contesting the inhumane living conditions. They claimed that "the conditions were so bad as to guarantee inevitable serious physical and psychological deterioration." Ultimately, the United States District Court agreed, ruling the Tennessee State Penitentiary unfit for human habitation. The prison closed, never to hold prisoners

Figure 2.17. Tennessee State Penitentiary, 1960. Photo courtesy of Special Collections Division, Nashville Public Library

again. For many, the memories of pain and suffering live on, and the future of the infamous building—which sustained heavy damage in the March 2020 tornado—remains uncertain. While some would like to see those memories buried and the building demolished, others have mobilized a robust grassroots movement to preserve the building and the prison history. In an era of increased concern over the privatization of prisons, the building stands as a stark reminder of the inhumanity so often associated with incarceration, whether publicly or privately operated.

The building is closed to the public, though visitors can still view the Gothic-style facility from the road, and glimpses of the building's dilapidated interior can be seen in movies such as *The Green Mile* (1999), *The Last Castle* (2001), *Ernest Goes to Jail* (1990), and *Marie* (1995).

ABOUT THE AUTHORS

Samantha Forcum is a graduate of Vanderbilt University's Community Development and Action program, and **Frank Lee** is a historian and professor at Middle Tennessee State University. The authors were assisted by a former inmate, who wishes to remain anonymous.

NEARBY SITES OF INTEREST

West Park (6105 Morrow Rd.): This community park features *Anchor in the Storm*, a sculpture exploring the lifesaving role of the nearby quarry during the May 2010 flood.

Thistle Stop Café (5128 Charlotte Ave.): Serving up coffee, home-cooked food, natural bath and body products, handcrafted global items, and more, Thistle Farms has become a nationally recognized social enterprise model that employs survivors of prostitution, trafficking, and addiction and embodies the motto, "Love is the most powerful force for change in the world."

2.13 WILLIAM EDMONDSON PARK

1624 Charlotte Ave.,
Nashville, TN 37203

The city's first art park stands as a testament to one of Nashville's most important artists, William Edmondson. Born in 1874, William Edmondson was a child of freed slaves. He grew up in and around Nashville, spending most of his life working as a janitor. As Edmondson approached age sixty, he felt a religious calling to begin carving stone. Working from limestone that he collected from demolished buildings, Edmondson developed his craft. He progressed from carving tombstones to sculptures and quickly gained renown. In 1937, Edmondson was the first African American to have a solo show at the Museum of Modern Art in New York City. Although he enjoyed some acclaim during his lifetime, many in the art world were swift to marginalize his work as that of a folk

Figure 2.18. Dedication to William Edmonson. Photo courtesy of Special Collections Division, Nashville Public Library

artist, and his art never garnered large sums. Though Edmundson created about three hundred pieces in his short career, he died in 1951 with limited financial resources to his name. He is buried in an unmarked grave in Mt. Ararat, Nashville's oldest African American cemetery.

In 1979, Metro dedicated a park near John Henry Hale Homes (a public housing community) in Edmondson's memory. However, many felt that the barren stretch of grass—lacking a playground, benches, or fence to buffer Charlotte Avenue traffic—was an affront to the artist's legacy. This changed when a group of thirteen neighborhood youth participated in the local Design Your Neighborhood program. Though some believed Edmondson Park was underutilized, the group saw the park's potential. Working in conjunction with the Nashville Civic Design Center, the Oasis Center, and Watkins College of Art, the students produced a park revitalization plan that included public art, sustainability features, and play areas for neighboring children.

The new William Edmondson Park opened in the summer of 2014 as

Figure 2.19. Sherri Warner Hunter, The Gathering, 2001, Metro Nashville Arts Commission. Photo © 2017 Stacey Irvin

Nashville's first art park. It features three permanent installations, including Thornton Dial's piece *Road to the Mountaintop*, Lonnie Holley's work *Supported by the Ancestors*, and Sherri Warner Hunter's sculpture *The Gathering*. Through the vision of neighborhood youth and a collaboration between government, nonprofits, artists, and community members, the park is now a worthy honor to the late great sculptor. Participating in the Design Your Neighborhood project also served as a stepping-stone for many of the student's career goals, encouraging one to study architecture at the University of Tennessee, and another to study Community Development at Vanderbilt University.

William Edmondson Park is located on Charlotte Avenue and can be visited by the public daily during daylight hours. Additionally, some works of William Edmondson can be viewed at the Cheekwood Estate and Gardens in Southwestern Nashville.

ABOUT THE AUTHORS

Allison Plattsmier and **Shanese Brown** were student participants in the Design Your Neighborhood program. **Betsy Mason** was a design fellow at Nashville Civic Design Center during the program.

NEARBY SITES OF INTEREST

Youth Opportunity Center (1704 Charlotte Ave.): This striking building functions as a one-stop shop for youth seeking a wide range of services and support.

2.14 JOHN HENRY HALE APARTMENTS

1433 Jo Johnston Ave.,
Nashville, TN 37203

Figure 2.20. John Henry Hale housing in 1954.
Photo courtesy of Nashville Metro Archives

As the city entered into the third month of 1953, the city of Nashville and many African American families eagerly anticipated the opening of the John Henry Hale Homes in North Nashville. Named after the renowned physician, professor of surgery at Meharry Medical College, and president of the National Medical Association, the new 498-unit complex generated much excitement for the city and Nashville's African American residents that met the requirements for occupancy. As was the case with many of the housing projects built and renovated in North Nashville during the Great Depression and post–World War II period, such as Cheatham Place and the Andrew Jackson Homes, construction of the new units provided the city with the tools to remove urban blight while simultaneously providing new affordable housing for long-term residents of the area.

At first glance, the John Henry Hale homes seemed to epitomize African Americans' dreams of homeownership in the city, ones that they had clung to fervently since emancipation. The service industry, businesses that included funeral homes, barber and beauty shops, and restaurants, thrived in the shadows of the newly constructed homes. Similarly, residents packed the pews of nearby Baptist churches each Sunday, filling the streets surrounding the community with the songs of joy and praise rooted in the experiences of African Americans in the Volunteer State.

Still, the John Henry Hale Homes existed in a city that was firmly committed to White supremacy, and its residents faced restrictions on how they lived and interacted in the new complex. Indeed, its residents endured similar injustices and humiliations to the ones they had experienced when they dwelled in the slums the city cleared to make way for the new dwellings.

The construction of Interstate 40 during the 1960s demolished substandard housing along the Twelfth and Thirteenth Avenues corridor and destroyed or displaced a number of businesses. As late as 1968, many of the remaining homes were not equipped with running water or adequate lighting. It must also be noted that crime increased substantially after the interstate project.

Though Nashville created the John Henry Hale Homes to remove almost a century's worth of dilapidated shanties and blight, throughout its existence the housing project became one of the spaces in the Music City that served to warehouse some of its poorest residents. The families that called the area home developed deep lifelong bonds and created a rich culture that enabled them to survive and negotiate the boundaries Jim Crow segregation placed upon their lives. The residents managed to survive and make lives for themselves in a city that appeared to be firmly committed to their marginalization. This spirit of perseverance persists today despite the fact that many of its long-term residents have moved away as a result of gentrification in the area.

Figure 2.21. Z. Alexander Looby (center), flanked by Thurgood Marshall and A. Z. Kelley. Photo courtesy of Nashville Metro Archives

ABOUT THE AUTHOR

Learotha Williams Jr. is an associate professor of African American and public history and coordinator of the North Nashville Heritage Project at Tennessee State University.

NEARBY SITES OF INTEREST

Marathon Music Works (1402 Clinton St.): This event venue is located in what used to be the Marathon Motor Cars factory.

2.15   Z. ALEXANDER LOOBY'S HOME

2012 Meharry Blvd., Nashville, TN 37208

The home of Nashville City Councilor and prominent NAACP attorney Z. Alexander Looby sat across the street from what is currently the Meharry-Vanderbilt Alliance, on Meharry Boulevard. At 5:30 a.m. on April 19, 1960, an unidentified assailant detonated a bomb at the corner of the attorney's home. The blast was so powerful that it not only destroyed Looby's home, but reportedly also blew out over one hundred windows at Meharry Medical College across the street. Amazingly, neither Looby nor his wife Grafta sustained major injuries. After the bombing, Looby demolished and rebuilt the home's front wall to protect his family from future violence, eliminating the large front windows and adding a bomb shelter in the basement. Today, the front wall of the home is fully bricked, except for slim windows at either end.

Born in the British West Indies in 1899, Looby arrived in the United States in 1914. A brilliant student, he attended Harvard and then Columbia Law School.

Figure 2.22. (above) Looby's Home, 1960. Photo courtesy of Special Collections Division, Nashville Public Library

Figure 2.23. (left) Ms. Grafta Looby, following the bombing. Photo courtesy of Nashville Metro Archives

At the time of the bombing, Looby was the only member of the Nashville Bar to have two law degrees, one a PhD. In 1926, he moved to Nashville to work at Fisk University. Over time he also served as a city council member and a leader in the NAACP, was an active member in the city's historic Holy Trinity Episcopal church and other religious organizations with his wife Grafta, and maintained numerous legal positions, including owning his own legal practice. Having established himself as a legal advocate for civil rights activists, Looby filed the first desegregation lawsuit against Nashville public schools shortly after the 1954 *Brown v. Board of Education* decision.

When the student-led sit-ins of prominent segregated stores in downtown Nashville began, Looby was the first to represent the arrested students. Soon, he and his colleagues were the legal backbone of the Civil Rights Movement in Nashville, defending student activists in court, making sure that bail was set, monitoring jail conditions, and getting students released. His visible efforts in support of the movement made his family a target for terrorism.

In the hours following the bombing, more than 1,500 people gathered at TSU before marching downtown in protest of the racial animus at the root of segregation and the violence toward the Looby family. By the time the crowd neared City Hall, where Mayor West met the marchers, its numbers had doubled. While the mayor and the crowd waited silently for the full group to assemble in front of the courthouse, Guy Carawan, a young musician from the Highlander Center, sang "We Shall Overcome," a song that later became an anthem of the movement.

When the crowd finally gathered in front of the courthouse, C. T. Vivian spoke, condemning segregation and terrorist violence. Tension was high as student leader Diane Nash approached the mayor. She asked him if he felt, "as a man, as a person, that segregation is right?" He looked out at the crowd of thousands and saw his political future. He said it was "wrong for citizens of Nashville to be discriminated against at the lunch counters solely on the basis of the color of their skin." To cheers from the protesters, the mayor appealed to all citizens "to end discrimination, to have no bigotry, no bias, no discrimination." The momentum created by this confrontation at the public square contributed to Nashville becoming the first major Southern city to integrate its public facilities.

Despite the significance of the Looby home bombing to Nashville's Civil Rights Movement, it was not until November 2014 that a historic marker was placed at the home. And the home's current owner personally paid to have the State of Tennessee mount the marker on the lawn.

ABOUT THE AUTHOR

Kwame Lillard was one of the organizers of the student movement, later serving as a Metro councilman and community leader. **Barbara Clinton** is a public health consultant.

NEARBY SITES OF INTEREST

Z. Alexander Looby Theater and Community Center (2301 Rosa L. Parks Blvd.): Named after the Nashville civil rights leader, this community center has a library, recreational center, and theater that hosts a variety of events.

2.16 BORDEAUX LANDFILL

1400 County Hospital Rd., Nashville, TN 37218

Figure 2.24. Bordeaux residents Annie Jarett and Melvin Jarett hold up protest signs outside the Bordeaux landfill before dawn. Photo courtesy of Special Collections Division, Nashville Public Library

A nature preserve is now growing where the city's garbage was dumped for more than twenty years. This transition from a despised landfill to a desired amenity is a testament to the power of resident-led organizing to confront environmental racism. The Bordeaux community is a historically Black neighborhood tucked along the Cumberland River in North Nashville, and one of the first areas where upwardly mobile African American families were allowed to buy land. When the landfill opened in 1973, Bordeaux quickly became Nashville's dumping ground. For nearly every day of the next twenty years, neighboring residents—some many blocks away from the landfill—complained of garbage blowing throughout their neighborhood. At first, garbage trucks heading for the landfill were uncovered, and garbage flew freely through the air. In response to resident concerns, the city eventually required the loads to be covered with tarps. Still, fumes from garbage and toxic waste continued to blow from the trucks and the landfill

itself, marring this otherwise peaceful neighborhood.

Bordeaux residents, including Wilma Springs, John Hall, and current state senator Thelma Harper, fought for years to achieve safety and well-being in their community. They publicized the potential health risks of the landfill at neighborhood meetings and advocated for public officials to restore the neighborhood's tranquility. In 1982, Ms. Springs requested that Vanderbilt University researchers test the runoff from the landfill to determine whether it was dangerous to residents' health. When the testing showed evidence of contaminants in the landfill's water and soil, the community redoubled its efforts. Ms. Springs and Tony Britten, a Vanderbilt student intern, organized a team of community members and students who systematically walked the landfill, mapping the site and measuring the amount of daily garbage intake. With the landfill's dangers becoming more apparent to others in the city, a coalition of neighborhood groups called Nashville Communities Organized for Progress (NCOP) dedicated its 1983–84 annual report to documenting the landfill's threat to the neighborhood's health. Citywide media attention grew, and with continuing community advocacy, the landfill finally closed in 1996.

In the years that followed, the neighborhood's activism led to significant improvements in the area. In 2004, the Metro Public Works department began transforming three hundred acres of the former landfill into a natural habitat. Over sixteen native plants and thirty-six native species have been introduced, and in 2013, the area received the Wildlife Habitat Council's "Wildlife at Work" certification.

Over the course of more than twenty years of citizen determination and resilience, Bordeaux residents mobilized their community, leveraged scientific research, built coalitions, and garnered hard won investments from the city in order to close and transform this former environmental hazard. As a result of these efforts, the land is once again a space where both nature and people can co-exist.

ABOUT THE OTHERS

Barbara Clinton is the former director of the Vanderbilt Center for Health Services, and a public health consultant. **Janelle Wommer** is a graduate of Vanderbilt University's Community Development and Action program.

NEARBY SITES OF INTEREST

Ted Rhodes Golf Course (1901 Ed Temple Blvd.): This eighteen-hole course is named after Theodore "Ted" Rhodes, a Nashville native who was the first African American to participate in a PGA tour.

McGruder Family Resource Center (2013 25th Ave. N.): This former school now functions as a family resource center and arts hub for the neighborhood.

2.17 SOUTHERN PUBLISHING ASSOCIATION

2119 24th Ave. N.,
Nashville, TN 37208

An empty lot on the corner of Twenty-Fourth Avenue and Pecan Street was once the heart of the Buena Vista Heights community. From 1901 to 1983, the site was home to the Southern Publishing Association, the main publishing house of the Seventh Day Adventist Church. The legacy of the publishing house lives on in the millions of religious texts printed here that still circulate the world, and in the model of collective economics and racial integration the company long demonstrated. The Southern Publishing Association, in addition to publishing houses owned by the African Methodist Episcopal Church and the National Baptist Convention (located in downtown Nashville in the Morris Building), helped to solidify the city's reputation as one of the centers of Christian publishing in the United States.

The Southern Publishing Association was founded by James Edson White, a White man who was deeply influenced by his mother's advocacy for abolition and racial equity. In 1891, Ms. Ellen White wrote a passionate appeal, titled *Our Duty*

Figure 2.25. Southern Publishing Association, 1951. Photo courtesy of Special Collections Division, Nashville Public Library

free of charge. True to Ms. White's vision of racial equity, the publishing house employed people of all races and ethnicities, and many employees settled in the neighborhood immediately surrounding the building. As a result, Buena Vista Height became one of the first racially integrated neighborhoods within Nashville. The 1930s to the 1950s were times of prosperity for the publishing house, and by extension, for the community.

to the Colored People, in which she chastised White Christians' mistreatment of Black people, writing "those who have spoken harshly to them or have despised them have despised the purchase of the blood of Christ. . . . The color of the skin does not determine character in the heavenly courts." After Ms. White had a vision for a Southern outpost for the church, her son built the publishing house from an old chicken barn in a historically Black Nashville neighborhood.

As the publishing house became more successful, White expanded the company's footprint and invested in the community, creating something of a company town. In 1917, Southern Publishing opened an employee-only store with lower costs than were available elsewhere in the city, and designated an area for employees to grow their own produce

After the Southern Publishing Association left Nashville in 1983, the former factory sat vacant and the neighborhood as a whole suffered. Within a decade of its closure, the property's value dropped by almost a half. In July 2010, a massive fire engulfed the buildings, with flames visible from all over Nashville. After a protracted legal battle between Metro and an absentee owner and developer, Metro Codes obtained the property in 2012 and demolished the remaining buildings. Today, the site looks like any other abandoned lot, with some remnants of the original structures visible under the overgrown brush.

The Buena Vista Neighborhood Association hopes to see this once significant site restored to its former glory.

Drawing on its legacy, the neighborhood envisions a new space of vitality where community members can work, garden, socialize, and more.

ABOUT THE AUTHORS

Dr. Arthur Lee is a lifetime resident of Buena Vista Heights and president of the neighborhood association. **Kate Goodman** is a former resident of the area and a graduate of Vanderbilt University's Community Development and Action program.

NEARBY SITES OF INTEREST

Temple Jewish Cemetery (2001 15th Ave. N.): Established in 1871, this cemetery offers insight into the history of Nashville's Jewish community. Learn more with a tour through the Temple (www.templenashville.org).

John Early Museum Magnet Middle School (1000 Cass St.): Visit the first museum school in the country and take a tour with the Junior Curators. Call (615) 291-6369 for more information.

2.18 BEAMAN PARK / BELLS BEND

5911 Old Hickory Blvd., Nashville, TN 37015

"Keep It Country!" You might encounter this on signs in northwest Nashville-Davidson County between Beaman Park and Bells Bend Park. The slogan reflects residents' efforts to preserve the rural character of the thirteen-thousand-acre corridor on either side of the Scottsboro community where Old Hickory Boulevard crosses TN-12. After fighting off a host of incompatible development schemes, the neighbors have laid the groundwork for permanent protection.

The Beaman Park–to–Bells Bend corridor is rich in archeological and historic sites, wildlife habitat, creeks, deep abundant forests, and open fields. It has remained so due to its isolation and the lay of its land. Bells Bend is one of the nine giant Cumberland River bends in Davidson County, and it is almost a stone's throw from some of Nashville's most intensive residential, commercial, and industrial development. For many years, visitors could gain access to the area via a ferry. The only way in and out of the bend is via a twisting dead end stretch of Old Hickory Boulevard. North of the gently rolling bend, the steep and geologically unstable escarpment of the Western Highland Rim is not suitable for extensive development.

Since the 1970s, citizens of the area have successfully resisted plans for a chemical plant, a landfill, a two-thousand-unit residential development, and most recently, the $4 billion May Town Center extravaganza, which proposed three river bridges, eight thousand condos, and six hundred thousand square feet of retail and office space designed to accommodate forty thousand workers. That plan failed in 2009.

Area residents recognized that simply trying to beat off the next proposal was not a satisfactory long-term solution. So, under the creative leadership of Minda Lazarov, they came up with the "Third Vision"—a plan for their community that

Figure 2.26. Railroad bridge heading into Bells Bend, where residents hung "Keep It Country" signs to protest the May Town Center development. Photo courtesy of Jennifer Mokos

Figure 2.27. Bells Bend in winter. Photo courtesy of Jennifer Mokos

involves something more than merely rejecting all change or allowing the bend area to become like everyplace else. The neighbors organized the Beaman Park–to–Bells Bend Conservation Community.

The group supports activities compatible with the rural character, including outdoor recreation at the two parks that bookend the corridor: 1,688-acre Beaman and 808-acre Bells Bend. Both parks have nature centers that host a variety of naturalist-led programs. Long-range plans include a trail along the forested ridges between the two areas. The community has launched a number of successful farming operations, including Bells Bend Farms (products are available on site and at the Nashville Farmers Market) and the Old School Farm, which produces quality farm-to-table food while employing workers with intellectual disabilities. A group of women started Humble Flowers, a flower farm, and some of the hops used by craft brewery Yazoo come from Bells Bend.

In Bells Bend, Nashville's once-prevailing attitude of promoting growth at all costs has evolved into a keen awareness that the city will continue to thrive only by protecting and promoting the characteristics unique to Nashville. This massive swath of rural land, a mere six miles from the State Capitol as the crow flies, is unique. Citizens of the Bells Bend area continue to demonstrate how focused citizen activism can conserve neighborhood character and sustain viable economic activity. Beaman and Bells Bend Parks are located, respectively, north and south of TN-12 on Old Hickory Boulevard.

ABOUT THE AUTHOR

Robert Brandt is a Tennessee native, active conservationist and nature writer, and a retired judge and attorney.

NEARBY SITES OF INTEREST

Bells Bend Outdoor Center (4187 Old Hickory Blvd.): An 808-acre facility, the Bells Bend Outdoor Center is a natural and cultural education center.

Sally Beaman Park (5911 Old Hickory Blvd.): Stop by the park's nature center and try one of its three trails.

3. NORTHEAST

3.1 John Seigenthaler Pedestrian Bridge   122

3.2 Greenwood Cemetery   124

3.3 Edgefield House   125

3.4 Sunday Night Soul at the 5 Spot   127

3.5 QDP   129

3.6 Hattie Cotton Elementary   130

3.7 First Baptist Church of East Nashville   132

3.8 Winfrey's Barber Shop   134

3.9 Stratford High School   135

3.10 Cornelia Fort Park   137

3.11 Nashville National Cemetery /
            US Colored Troops National Monument   139

3.12 Mansker Station   141

3.13 Gass's Store / Cinco de Mayo Mexican Restaurant   143

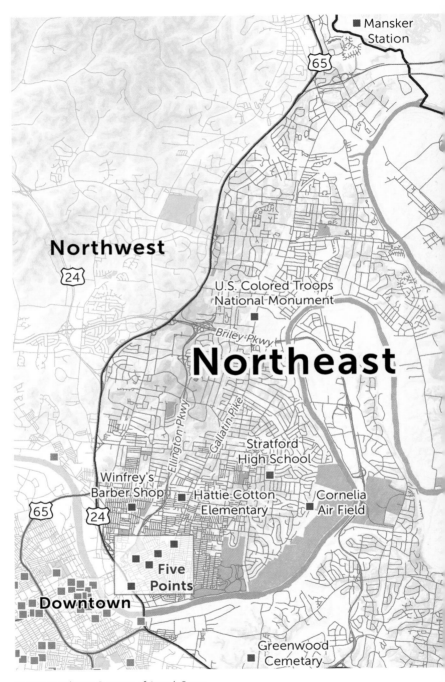

Map 5. Northeast. Courtesy of Joseph Speer

AN INTRODUCTION TO NORTHEAST NASHVILLE

THE NORTHEAST REGION OF Davidson County is bounded by the Interstates to the west and south, Briley Parkway to the north, and the Cumberland River to the east. Most guidebooks limit their attention east of the Cumberland to the urban neighborhoods collectively known as East Nashville that surround the Five Points commercial and cultural district. These include a number of historic urban neighborhoods, including Cleveland Park, Edgefield, and Lockeland Springs, as well as some older suburban neighborhoods, such as Inglewood, Rosebank, and South Inglewood. Given its proximity to downtown, its reputation as having a "hip" urban aesthetic, and the expansive Shelby Bottoms greenway and recreational area, East Nashville is now one of the most sought-after areas to live in the city. But the Northeast quadrant of Davidson County expands well beyond East Nashville and includes parts of the incorporated city of Goodlettsville, a rural area home to numerous working farms, and the suburban communities of Donelson, Hermitage, Old Hickory, and Madison.

Some of the most well-recorded struggles between settlers and Indigenous people fighting to protect their land occurred in this quadrant of Davidson County. An entry in this chapter describes Cherokee efforts to halt the settlement of Mansker's Station, built in 1780 in present-day Goodlettsville. East Nashville proper—the land just across the Cumberland from downtown—was settled in the late 1700s by soldiers who received 640-acre land grants from the State of North Carolina following their service in the Revolutionary War. Some of the early homes remain today, including the Riverwood Mansion in Inglewood

Figure 3.1. Revelers at the fourteenth anniversary of the Tomato Art Festival. Photo courtesy of Solar Cabin Studios/Tomato Art Festival

and the Two Rivers Mansion on the east side of the Cumberland River. As is the case throughout Nashville, these historic buildings were largely constructed by enslaved Africans, and the structures' enduring presence on the landscape is a testament to both the skill of the laborers and the city's legacy of slavery.

Northeast Nashville was also home to a contraband camp during the Civil War. Once the Union Army claimed Nashville, thousands of enslaved Blacks fled the country for the city. There, the Union army provided lodging in exchange for labor to fortify Nashville. The Edgefield contraband camp was located where the Clarion Hotel stands today, on North First Street between the Cumberland River and I-24. A number of Black families in East Nashville trace their ancestry to this camp. Following the Civil War, several Black communities formed in East Nashville. Rock City, for example, was founded in the late 1800s, and originally consisted of forty families who settled around a quarry where the South Inglewood Community Center stands today.

In 2018, a historical marker was placed at 1515 Ann Street, honoring the legacy of this tight-knit community characterized by mutual support and collective economics.

For much of East Nashville's history, Black and White residents lived in relatively close proximity to one another but attended separate schools, frequented different businesses, and were buried in separate cemeteries. This legacy of segregation—and the strength of the area's Black cultural institutions—can be found throughout this chapter's entries, which include burial places, a historic church, a barbershop, and an elementary school bombed the night after the first Black child enrolled. This history is critical to understanding current struggles involving gentrification and the displacement of people, businesses, and other sites of cultural significance.

As is true throughout Nashville, the history of the Northeast region has also been heavily shaped by natural disasters. Straddling a large bend in the Cumberland River, both East Nashville and Donelson have been particularly vulnerable to flooding, which, on numerous occasions, has left thousands of people homeless. In addition, major tornadoes in 1933, 1988, and 2020 destroyed thousands of homes and businesses. Although these disasters brought some communities together, they also triggered urban development plans that have accelerated gentrification in the region. Following the 1988 tornado, the city launched a revitalization plan for East Nashville. Within

Figure 3.2. East Nashville flooding. Photo courtesy of Special Collections Division, Nashville Public Library

includes a major suburban shopping center, numerous established suburban neighborhoods, the historic downtown Madison shopping corridor, and the national cemetery, home to the Colored Troops monument. Numerous supermercados and Mexican restaurants dot Madison's major corridor, reflecting the area's growing Latino community. To the east of Madison are three historic communities: Donelson, Hermitage, and Old Hickory. A traditional post–World War II suburban community, Donelson features an older commercial corridor along Lebanon and Donelson Pikes. Hermitage includes mostly newer suburban neighborhoods, but it is also home to the Hermitage, the former residence of President Andrew Jackson, a slave owner and architect of the Trail of Tears. Given the degree of published material on the Hermitage Plantation, it is not included in this guide. It should be noted, however, that in recent years, the visitor center has added archival materials documenting the lives of the slaves who lived, worked, and died at the historic site. Old Hickory also has an interesting history; it was founded as a company town for DuPont's gunpowder plant during World War I. As the housing

a few years, new coffee shops, bars, and restaurants catering to a younger, wealthier crowd replaced the small businesses that had previously served the working-class White and African American residents. The mix of brightly painted historic homes and modern commercial construction has made the area attractive to millennials. A number of entries explore alternative venues for the arts and music that have drawn residents who often do not feel as welcome in other parts of the city, including LGBTQ Nashvillians. At the same time, land values and rents have risen dramatically, displacing many long-time residents, particularly in the African American community.

While most of the entries in this chapter focus on East Nashville, other areas of the Northeast are worth exploring. Davidson County annexed the Madison community to the north in 1963. Madison

values closer to Nashville's urban core continue to rise, both the Madison and Donelson-Hermitage-Old Hickory areas are seeing rapid population growth and increasing ethnic diversity.

As you travel through Northeast Nashville, we encourage you to look for the legacy of segregation visible in the landscape and within the sites you visit. If you enjoy the Shelby Bottoms Greenway, take note of the natural beauty as well as the vulnerability of the surrounding area to the effects of flooding. We hope you enjoy the unique artistic and cultural spaces East Nashville has to offer, while also considering the costs of continued development to long-time low-income and working-class residents in the community.

ABOUT THE AUTHORS

Vanderbilt graduate students **Ryan Anderson, Marisa Flores, Lisa Freeman, Katie Goodman, Lauren Marlar, Anna Warren, and Hollie Williams** contributed to this section.

3.1 JOHN SEIGENTHALER PEDESTRIAN BRIDGE

Between S. 1st St., near Victory Ave., and 3rd Ave. S., Nashville, TN 37213

Named after the esteemed Nashville journalist, writer, and outspoken proponent of First Amendment rights, the John Seigenthaler Pedestrian Bridge is one of Nashville's most popular attractions. Spanning the Cumberland River, the bridge connects East Nashville to the city center and is heavily used by residents who commute to school and work, as well as by those seeking easy access to amenities on both sides of the river. Given its visibility from dozens of Nashville buildings and passing cars, the bridge is also a frequently used route for protests.

On April 5, 2014, the bridge carried nearly five hundred immigrant families, activists, and allies across the Cumberland River for the "Two Million Too Many" march. Organized by the Tennessee Immigrant and Refugee Rights Coalition (TIRRC) and led by undocumented youth activists, the march was part of a national day of action. Organizers sought to pressure President Obama's administration to stop deportations, to end the disastrous Secure Communities program (which facilitated cooperation between local jails and federal immigration enforcement agents to carry out deportations), and to expand the Deferred Action for Childhood Arrivals (DACA) program to protect all eleven million undocumented immigrants, not just Dreamers. The march was also held to draw attention to the shameful milestone the federal administration had just reached: deporting two million people, more than all previous presidents combined.

The march started near Nissan Stadium. The atmosphere was joyful and defiant as musicians played protest songs and activists led chants through megaphones. Immigrant families held giant

Figure 3.3. The pedestrian bridge from the eastern bank of the Cumberland. Photo courtesy of Learotha Williams Jr.

banners that read "OBAMA DEPORTS PARENTS" and "OBAMA: DEPORTER IN CHIEF." Children held colorful hearts that read, "Don't deport my mom," and "Keep families together." Undocumented youth carrying a banner that read "Two Million Too Many" led the march, and hundreds of protestors followed them across Seigenthaler Bridge toward the city center.

As the marchers entered downtown, some observers initially stared, perplexed. But then Latinos working on the rooftop of Joe's Crab Shack began to wave, shout, and cheer for the marchers, and street performers joined in, singing and dancing with children. The march culminated in a press conference at Public Square Park. Organizers spoke of the harmful effects that deportations had on their families and community, made demands of the Obama administration,

and pledged to keep fighting. In a Tennessean article published the day of the protest, one youth activist explained, "[President Obama] gave deferred action to me. . . . He has the power to give deferred action to my parents, too."

The voices of the hundreds of protesters in Nashville joined thousands more across the country, and within a few months of the Nashville march, President Obama signaled that he would use his executive authority to take action on immigration. Finally, in November of 2014, the president revealed his much-anticipated executive order. While the ultimate order fell short of activist's demands, it was a major victory for the immigrant rights movement. Unfortunately, the State of Tennessee joined twenty-five other states and sued the administration to block the program from going into effect. The order stalled in court, ultimately leading to a deadlock in the Supreme Court, before President Donald Trump formally rescinded the order in June 2017.

The "Two Million Too Many" march was part of an important shift in the immigrant rights movement across the country. In the face of punishing policies and mass deportations under the Trump administration, an increasing number of people are outraged, and the fight to stop deportations in Nashville has continued to grow.

ABOUT THE AUTHORS

Stephanie Teatro, co-director of TIRRC, **Jazmin Ramirez**, an organizer with TIRRC, and **Jewlz Davis**, a graduate of Vanderbilt's Community Development and Action program, contributed to this entry.

NEARBY SITES OF INTEREST

Cumberland Park (592 S. 1st St.): A park on the riverfront with attractions for kids and a variety of public art, including *Ghost Ballet for the East Bank Machineworks,* a one-hundred-foot-tall installment by Alice Aycock that represents the river's transition from industry to entertainment.

3.2 GREENWOOD CEMETERY

1428 Elm Hill Pike,
Nashville, TN 37210

Created to house the tombs and remains of those who often carried the weights of prejudice, oppression, and segregation, Greenwood Cemetery joined Mount Ararat Cemetery as one of the earliest cemeteries in Middle Tennessee to exclusively offer a place for African Americans to be buried with pride and dignity. In the aftermath of slavery, Whites no longer wanted African American bodies to be buried in private cemeteries, and given African Americans' disproportionate rates of death due to disease and illness, burial space was desperately needed. When Thomas Winston, Nashville's only African American undertaker, died in 1888, African American minister and community leader Preston Taylor stepped up to fill the void. Taylor served initially as an undertaker, and ultimately a cemetery owner, providing an African American burial ground. With his purchase of thirty-seven acres of land, Taylor officially opened Greenwood Cemetery in 1888, intending to provide a high-quality, low-cost burial space for Nashville's growing African American community. He was the sole provider of this service for several years. In 1908, the *Nashville Globe* highlighted the care Taylor put into the cemetery, noting "the Negroes of Nashville have the most beautifully arranged cemetery in the vicinity. One does not feel that he is among the dead when in Greenwood."

Upon his death in 1931, Taylor deeded the cemetery to the National Christian Missionary Convention, and it remains a nonprofit establishment committed to honoring the legacy of Nashville's African American community. In 1982, the Greenwood Cemetery Board of Directors agreed to assume management of Nashville's first

Figure 3.4. Greenwood Cemetery entrance. Photo courtesy of Joseph Gutierrez

ABOUT THE AUTHOR

Janet Walsh is the founder and chief tea officer of Tea Tea and Company and former professor of library sciences at Tennessee State University.

ADDITIONAL READING

Bobby L. Lovett. *The African-American History of Nashville, TN: 1780–1930.* Fayetteville: University of Arkansas Press, 1999.

African American cemetery, Mount Ararat, which had experienced years of neglect and disrepair. Many of the names of those interred have been lost; while 1,400 people per year were buried at Mt. Ararat, only 410 gravestones have been recovered. Mt Ararat is now known as Greenwood West. Together, these two cemeteries hold the remains of thousands of Nashville's African American residents.

NEARBY SITES OF INTEREST

Ararat Cemetery (Orr Ave., off Elm Hill Pike): You can pay your respects at Nashville's first Black cemetery, now known as Greenwood East.

3.3 EDGEFIELD HOUSE
714 Russell St.,
Nashville, TN 37206

Today, many notable figures in African American history rest at Greenwood Cemetery, including Harlem Renaissance poet Arna Bontemps, suffragist Mattie Coleman, the first Black president of Fisk University Charles S. Johnson, country music and blues star DeFord Bailey, College Football Hall of Fame coach John Merritt, and Preston Taylor, the cemetery's founder. Greenwood Cemetery stands as a monument to strong voices now quieted. When we view Greenwood Cemetery as a history book, we chronicle the voices of those who carried centuries of oppression. To this day, the cemetery offers a living history of Nashville and the injustices it has overcome.

Edgefield House, the only residence on the 700 block of Russell Street, stands tall and proud overlooking East Park, not unlike the woman who fought to preserve it. The large seventeen-room house, built in 1878, harkens back to the post–Civil War expansion of residential East Nashville. Despite its stature, the house and many others in the historic neighborhoods became vulnerable during the 1950s. During this time, a Federal urban renewal program provided funding for cities to "rehabilitate" neighborhoods by demolishing areas deemed to be slums and building new housing stock in their place. While many areas faced overcrowding and poor health conditions, the slum clearance

Figure 3.5. Historic Edgefield house. Photo courtesy of Amie Thurber

disproportionately targeted Black neighborhoods.

When the East Nashville urban renewal program began in 1958, the Nashville Codes Department determined that most of the historic homes in the predominantly Black area of Edgefield were unlivable and must be torn down. In total, the Nashville Housing Authority razed more than two thousand homes. As a result, many working class and African American residents were forced out. The lost wealth from these homes has had generational effects on the families who once lived here, and the city lost many historic buildings as well.

One woman fought back. Sarah Hamilton and her husband purchased the home at 714 Russell Street in 1952. When the urban renewal code inspectors came, Hamilton refused to leave and would not allow the home to be destroyed. In an interview published in the *Tennessean* in January 1972, Mrs. Hamilton recounts that for over a decade her neighborhood was filled with bulldozers. During this time, Hamilton invested heavily in the 714 Russell Street Victorian she dubbed Edgefield House. As she explained, "one's home—what's inside the walls—determines what your children will be." But Hamilton also wanted to show her neighbors that anyone, including people with limited means, could improve their condition and fight to remain in the community.

Her son, Kendrick Hamilton, remembers his mother's efforts to help their neighbors. Many residents were elderly and afraid of the inspectors, but Hamilton's crusade kept inspectors at bay. Although Hamilton inspired many to follow suit and refurbish their homes, others could not afford to do so. On average, it cost residents more than $4,000 to bring their homes up to code. Nonetheless, neighbors and city officials credit Hamilton with possessing a vision for what Edgefield could become, long before anyone else in the city did. The Hamiltons sold the house in the 1980s to future Nashville mayor Bill Boner.

The Edgefield House has remained a crown jewel in the neighborhood for many decades. During the Hamiltons' residency, Edgefield transitioned from one of the most dilapidated areas of the city to one that now attracts upper-income families seeking to live in renovated historic homes. As a proponent of revitalization, Hamilton would be happy to see Edgefield House and other Victorian homes standing strong today. But her vision was one of preserving families *in* their homes, and on that front, East Nashville has fallen short.

ABOUT THE AUTHOR

Kate Goodman is a graduate of Vanderbilt University's Community Development and Action program.

ADDITIONAL READING

Bill Carey. "A City Swept Clean." *Nashville Scene*, September 6, 2001. https://www.nashvillescene.com/news/article/13006140/a-city-swept-clean.

NEARBY SITES OF INTEREST

Metropolitan Development and Housing Agency (701 S. 6th St.): This publicly funded agency is the largest provider of low-income housing in the city—managing public housing and Section 8 programs—and also one of the largest commercial and residential developers in the city. It is headquartered in James Cayce Homes, the largest remaining public housing project in Nashville.

3.4 SUNDAY NIGHT SOUL AT THE 5 SPOT

1006 Forrest Ave.,
Nashville, TN 37206

(615) 650-9333

From the 1930s to the 1960s, Nashville had a robust soul, blues, R&B, and gospel scene. As a stop on the Chitlin' Circuit, Nashville offered a number of venues where Black musicians could perform under Jim Crow. On a nightly basis, crowds danced to the likes of Etta James, Ray Charles, B.B. King, Aretha Franklin, and Otis Redding. Nashville supported these soul artists by providing quality venues, strong Black radio stations, independent record labels, and a loyal and growing audience. Yet, the vibrant soul scene took a blow after urban renewal programs in the 1950s and 1960s gutted the Black music districts downtown and on Jefferson Street, and the "Music City" moniker was rebranded to be synonymous with country music. Today, one of

Figure 3.6. Jason Eskridge and his band at Sunday Night Soul. Photo courtesy of Ciann Photography

musicians from all walks of life would come to get, like, a refill musically. . . . We all just hug and love on each other and laugh and have a good time."

Off the typical tourist path, at Sunday Night Soul you will find one of the most diverse audiences in Nashville: people of all ages, ethnicities, and walks of life. Featuring a rotating line-up of musicians, visitors will also find some of the most talented and passionate rising soul artists the South has to offer. Sometimes the night is about folks blowing off a little steam because they know Monday is right around the corner, other times it's about passing the tip jar to help someone in need. But it's always about the love of soul music, and how music brings us together in ways that few other things can.

Though Nashville has yet to rebuild the soul scene of the past, a new generation of artists is making sure the folks in Middle Tennessee can get a healthy dose of soul music. Homegrown Nashville musician and Grammy award-winning producer Shannon Sanders is the music director for radio station 102.1, the Ville, featuring local soul music. And, if you are looking for live soul music, you can find it: check out "Soul at the Factory" at the Little Brick Theater at the Factory

the few places to reliably hear live soul music is inside an East Nashville bar, two nights a month.

Sunday Night Soul launched in April of 2014 to meet two needs: Nashville's soul artists were longing for a platform to share their craft, and Nashville music fans were hungry for a consistent venue to hear quality soul music. The 5 Spot offered a fitting venue for this musician-driven project; the owners understand that Nashville offers more than just country music, realize that the city has broad musical tastes, and attracts and employs good people—from the management to the door man.

Over the last few years, Sunday Night Soul has blossomed into an eclectic community of fans and artists with genuine appreciation for one another. As Emoni Wilkins, one of Nashville's most renowned soul artists, reflects, "Sunday Night Soul is probably one of the places where I've found so much peace, because it felt like that's where all the working

Figure 3.7. QDP attendees, from author's personal collection. Photo by Steve Cross Photography

in Franklin, Tennessee; or catch Emoni Wilkins at Bourbon Street Blues and Boogie Bar in Nashville's Printer's Alley, or Dynamo at ACME Feed and Seed on Broadway. And of course, Sunday Night Soul takes place every second and fourth Sunday from 6 p.m. to 9 p.m. at the 5 Spot.

ABOUT THE AUTHOR

Jason Eskridge is a Tennessee native, the founder of Sunday Night Soul, and a full-time musician. In addition to being an independent singer-songwriter and session singer, Jason sings backup for musicians including Keb' Mo' and Zac Brown Band.

ADDITIONAL READING

Jewly Hight. "Just off Music Row, Nashville's R&B Scene Thrives." *The Record: Music News from NPR*, March 24, 2017. https://www.npr.org/sections/therecord/2017/03/24/521276599/just-off-music-row-nashvilles-r-b-scene-thrives.

NEARBY SITES OF INTEREST

Five Points (11th and Woodland St.): Walk down any street of this intersection to explore restaurants, shops, and more.

3.5 QDP

917 Woodland St., Nashville, TN 37206 (The Basement East)
(615) 254-6268

LGBTQ spaces have been few and far between throughout the history of this Southern, overwhelmingly conservative, and Christian city. Where they do exist, they have almost always been in bars. In the early twentieth century, bars such as Juanita's downtown provided a sanctuary for some—though these spaces primarily existed for Nashville's White gay men. Today's gay district on Church Street is markedly more inclusive and still functions as a sanctuary for many LGBTQ people. For those looking for an alternative to the bar scene, Queer Dance Party—known as QDP—may be for you.

Launched in 2012, QDP is a monthly celebration and party for Nashville's LGBTQ community. Although you'll still find plenty of elaborate drink specials and sweaty people dancing into the late hours to Robyn and Lady Gaga, the organizers started QDP as a monthly gathering that is more casual than some club environments and more explicitly inclusive for people of all sexualities and gender identities. To that end, QDP offers a "QDProtocol" for creating a safe space, which includes providing gender neutral restrooms and encouraging the correct pronoun usage. The event is known for the mainstay photo booth, where revelers holding the red, yellow, and blue QDP letters work the camera at their very best, reflecting the spirit of joyful community created within QDP.

In addition to the monthly dance party, organizers offer additional events throughout the year. QDProm, hosted annually in February, is particularly popular as it provides many LGBTQ Nashvillians their first chance to have a prom experience in a space where they can bring whoever they want, wear whatever they want, and freely be themselves. Although most QDP events take place at the Basement East, organizers occasionally host the party at other traditionally straight institutions around town, "queering" these locales for a night as part of their vision to create a vibrant queer community in all corners of Nashville. In addition, QDP frequently raises money to support LGBTQ causes in Nashville and beyond. Recently, the event raised funds for Just Us (a program for queer youth at Oasis Center in Nashville), the Orlando chapter of a drag-based service organization, and for a local trans woman and military veteran who was the victim of a hate crime.

In an era of political backlash against LGBTQ people, spaces of convening and celebration remain as important as ever. On the third Friday of every month, QDP provides a space unlike any other in Nashville. Those who are twenty-one and older can find the next QDP events by following the Facebook group (www.facebook.com/QDPnashville) or @QDPnashville on Twitter.

ABOUT THE AUTHOR

Hannah Nell is a queer woman, Vanderbilt graduate student, and Queen Latifah's biggest fan.

NEARBY SITES OF INTEREST

Penny Campbell Historical Marker (1615 McEwen Ave.): Pay tribute to one of the state's leading organizers for LGBT rights and visit the first historical marker in TN related to the struggle for LGBT equality.

Lipstick Lounge (1400 Woodland St.): Visit Nashville's only lesbian bar, known for its laid-back neighborhood feel, game nights, and karaoke.

3.6 HATTIE COTTON ELEMENTARY

1033 W. Greenwood Ave., Nashville, TN 37206

Today, this modern-looking brick elementary school tucked in a residential neighborhood serves as a model of innovation in urban education. On a daily basis, partners from Vanderbilt's esteemed Peabody College of Education work with educators to develop best practices in teaching and learning. But leading the pack is not new for Hattie Cotton, which, in 1957, was one of the first Nashville elementary schools to desegregate.

Within hours of the 1954 *Brown v. Board of Education* US Supreme Court decision, Nashville attorneys Z. Alexander Looby and Avon N. Williams Sr., representing the local chapter of the NAACP, officially requested that Nashville's Board of Education immediately end racial segregation in its schools. The stair-step desegregation plan finally adopted by Nashville's Board of Education planned to integrate the schools one grade per year, beginning with the first grade in 1957 and extending to all twelve

Figure 3.8. Investigators surveying the wreckage of the Hattie Cotton Elementary School bombing. Photo courtesy of Special Collections Division, Nashville Public Library

grades by 1968. Nashville's grade-a-year was a model approach to desegregation until May 1963, when grade-a-year integration plans were ruled unconstitutional by the Supreme Court.

On Monday, September 9, 1957, nineteen apprehensive African American six-year-olds walked with their adult chaperones past angry hordes of White adults to register for admission at eight previously all-White Nashville elementary schools. Six of these schools—Buena Vista, Jones, and Fehr on the north side, and Bailey, Caldwell, and Glenn on the east—received much public attention, due in part to extensive advance coverage by the city's newspapers. Two additional elementary schools also desegregated that morning—Clemons, south of downtown, and Hattie Cotton, to the northeast. Having not been listed in the papers, these two schools drew no sign-waving protesters. On that Monday, Patricia Diane Watson became Hattie Cotton's first and only African American student, and her first day passed without

disruption. However, in the wee hours of the following morning, Hattie Cotton School was bombed. The blast, from a reported thirteen sticks of dynamite placed at the east end of a main hallway—could be heard miles away; it was one of the most severe attacks in Nashville's modern Civil Rights Movement. Hattie Cotton reopened eight days later, but Watson's family chose to send her to her former elementary school.

Today, Hattie Cotton STEM Magnet Elementary is the only science, technology, engineering, and math elementary magnet school in Nashville, and it has a diverse student body. Recognized as a Reward School by the Tennessee Department of Education in 2012, the school was also recognized by the National Magnet Schools of Merit. A calendar of student events can be found on the school's website, schools.mnps.org/hattie-cotton-stem-magnet-elementary-school.

ABOUT THE AUTHOR

Linda T. Wynn is the assistant director for state programs at the Tennessee Historical Commission and on faculty at Fisk University in the Department of History and Political Science.

NEARBY SITES OF INTEREST

Rock City Historical Marker (1515 Ann St.): Pay tribute to the African American community established in this neighborhood in 1881, named after the centrality of a quarry to the community's self-sufficiency.

3.7 FIRST BAPTIST CHURCH OF EAST NASHVILLE

601 Main St.,
Nashville, TN 37206

(615) 254-6268

The front steps of First Baptist Church of East Nashville used to cascade directly to Main Street, lending even more grandeur to the sanctuary's striking Greek-temple-inspired façade. Built between 1929 and 1931, the historic church remains unchanged but for altering the front steps to allow for the widening of Main Street in the mid-1960s. Founded in 1866 by Rev. Randall B. Vandavall, the First Baptist Church of East Nashville serves as testament to the Reconstruction Era roots of East Nashville's African American community. The small congregation was part of a burgeoning African American population that was home to many early Black leaders, a thriving business district, and the Meigs School—Nashville's first high school for Black children.

Throughout its 150-year history, the church's mission of evangelism and community service made it a site for political, social, and religious activism. In the 1930s and 1940s, Rev. W. S. Ellington became nationally known for his annual soul-stirring "Prodigal Son" sermon, which was eventually held at the Ryman Auditorium and broadcast on Nashville's WSM AM radio station. In the post–World War II years, Rev. Charles Dinkins and Rev. Jonathan Rucker expanded the church's education and outreach programs, highlighted the role of women in the church, and welcomed the brave organizers of the Civil Rights Movement. In 1955, prominent church member A. Z. Kelley served as the lead plaintiff in a class action lawsuit filed by Nashville attorneys Z. Alexander Looby and Avon N. Williams to desegregate Nashville schools. The success of *Kelley vs. Board of Education* forced Nashville schools into action, though the Board of Education continued to resist integration efforts for many years. At a Women's Day event sponsored by the church in 1958, Daisy Bates, known for her effort to desegregate Little Rock's Central High School, affirmed the critical role of women in the Nashville Movement. And in 1960, church leaders encouraged members to support the downtown sit-in campaign and boycott racist businesses.

While the First Baptist Church of East Nashville served an indispensable role during the Civil Rights Movement, its history did not end there. In the 1970s and 1980s, while the African American community in East Nashville grew, school desegregation and the construction of Interstate 24 and Ellington Parkway caused social upheaval and economic decline in the neighborhood. Under the leadership of Rev. James Campbell, the church expanded to meet growing neighborhood needs, adding Boy Scouts and Girl Scouts programs, a day care center, aid for the homeless, and outreach to the elderly and incarcerated. In 2000,

Figure 3.9. (above) First Baptist Church of East Nashville. Photo courtesy of Amie Thurber

Figure 3.10. (right) Reverend Ellington. Photo courtesy of Nashville Metro Archives

the church took action on a global scale when Rev. Floyd Lacy led an effort to resettle Sudanese refugees. And in 2005, the National Register of Historic Places named the First Baptist Church of East Nashville a site of valuable architectural and cultural heritage.

Today, Rev. Morris E. Tipton Jr. continues the First Baptist Church of East Nashville's legacy of responding to the spiritual and physical needs of East Nashville's African American community through fellowship, positivity, and activism. Yet, as is the case with many Black churches in East Nashville, gentrification of the surrounding neighborhoods has decreased its congregation size. Indeed, a number of East Nashville Black churches have sold their property in recent years. Developers are transforming these properties into high end residential, commercial, and event spaces. For now, First Baptist Church of East Nashville remains,

holding its place overlooking Main Street and preserving a critical piece of East Nashville's history. Visitors are welcome to attend worship service Sundays from 10 to 11:30 a.m.

ABOUT THE AUTHOR

Sam McCullough is a life-long resident of East Nashville and a member of First Baptist Church of East Nashville. **Denise Gallagher Fisher** is a public historian.

NEARBY SITES OF INTEREST

Frederick Douglass Park (210 N. 7th St.): Named Fred Douglas Park in 1935, the park was officially renamed Frederick Douglass Park in March 2017, to properly honor the famous Black abolitionist and statesman for whom the park is named.

Figure 3.11. Neighbors with Vernon Winfrey (center) in front of the barber-shop. Photo from Sam McCullough's personal collection

3.8 WINFREY'S BARBER SHOP

1001 Lischey Ave.,
Nashville, TN 37207

(615) 262-9993

Winfrey's Barber Shop is a cherished institution with a fifty-year history of deep family ties, civic engagement, and economic development. A cornerstone of the Cleveland Park neighborhood, proprietor Vernon Winfrey has made it his mission to improve the lives of those around him. Winfrey's daughter, television and film star Oprah Winfrey, credits his strict parental guidance and steady support for setting her on a path to success. It is this same fatherly wisdom and generosity that has made Winfrey a well-respected community leader and a life-long friend to many.

The shop's history begins in 1965, when Winfrey saw potential in a vacant barbershop located in an old concrete block grocery store on the corner of Lischey Avenue and Bayard Street. At the time, East Nashville was being radically re-made by a massive federal urban renewal project that included carving out land for Ellington Parkway and the creation of Cleveland Park Community Center and surrounding green space. The sizable neighborhood located north of Cleveland Street became known as Cleveland Park and was largely home to African American families.

Long-time residents recall the neighborhood as a peaceful place to live, populated by working people and homeowners. Within a few years, Winfrey purchased the entire building and hired employees to operate the grocery store. Like many other Black-owned barbershops, Winfrey's became an informal gathering place where news from around the neighborhood and beyond could be freely discussed. Contrary to popular notions, the shop was not just for men. Winfrey got to know entire families as young boys often came in accompanied by their sisters, aunts, mothers, and grandmothers.

Concerned about the need for economic development in a district that was becoming one of the poorest in the city, in 1975, Winfrey successfully ran for Metro City Council, representing the Fifth District. Winfrey's barbershop became a field office where constituents could easily find an ear for their concerns. Meanwhile, the newly completed Interstate 24 siphoned traffic away from Dickerson Road, eventually creating a haven for drug-related crime and prostitution that spread into the surrounding neighborhoods. Winfrey's Barber Shop remained open, despite the corner becoming one of the city's most dangerous.

Winfrey was re-elected four times, serving until 1991. In recognition of his outstanding service, Bayard Street was re-named Vernon Winfrey Avenue. Though retired from public service, Winfrey has remained active in community life. In 2003, the newly formed Cleveland Park Neighborhood Association received a federal block grant that sparked a community-led effort to reduce crime and increase opportunities in the neighborhood. The grassroots effort to revive Cleveland Park spurred Winfrey to envision a new chapter for his legendary barbershop: as the anchor of a mixed-use development called Winberry Place. Although the recession delayed and scaled back the project, in 2010, the historic concrete building was torn down to make way for Winfrey's new barbershop. The new face of the building matches the now rapidly gentrifying neighborhood, but inside, Winfrey's remains exactly the same. During an interview with his neighbors as part of the Cleveland Park Story Project, Winfrey reflected on the changes happening in the neighborhood: "The folk who

has moved out, years from now, they're going to be coming back . . . and I'm going to have something here when they come back." If you stop by, most days you can still find Winfrey cutting hair.

ABOUT THE AUTHOR

Sam McCullough is a life-long resident of East Nashville, and **Denise Gallagher Fisher** is a public historian.

NEARBY SITES OF INTEREST

Cleveland Park (N. 7th St. and Vernon Winfrey Ave.): This park and community center has long served as a place for recreation and fellowship within the Cleveland Park neighborhood.

3.9 STRATFORD HIGH SCHOOL
1800 Stratford Ave., Nashville, TN 37216

For the last fifteen years, students in one of Nashville's most stigmatized high schools have been fighting to improve their school and community. In the early 2000s, Stratford High School had a reputation for crime, violence, and poor academics. Many students in the school were indeed struggling—only 10 percent went on to college—and the public narrative largely placed blame for these struggles on Stratford students and their families. But the stigmatization of Stratford veiled the larger context in which Stratford families lived. On Gallatin Road, predatory lending institutions outnumbered banking institutions, charging consumers as much as 400 percent interest. Many

Figure 3.12. (above) Members of the Stratford Story Project, who created a documentary of the school. Photo courtesy of the Stratford Story Project

Figure 3.13. (left) Stratford High School. Photo courtesy of Joseph Gutierrez

East Nashville families were constrained by the lack of educational and economic opportunities in their neighborhood.

In the summer of 2003, a youth-led initiative engaged young people as change agents in their community. Community Impact! Nashville (CI!) employed about twelve students from Stratford and nearby Maplewood high schools as youth mobilizers. The students identified lack of college access and financial literacy as root causes of the many issues faced by their community. In response, they researched, networked, developed, and implemented community change strategies to increase college access for their peers and to limit the adverse effect of predatory lending in their neighborhood.

Stratford High School served as an office space and a safe space for these young people to conduct their activism.

On the economic front, the youth mobilizers educated their community regarding predatory lending practices and supported legislation intended to curb such practices. In their efforts to increase the number of their peers who attended college, the students tirelessly fought to change the college-going culture in East Nashville high schools. They advocated for increased funding so that each high school in the district could have a college counselor on staff to help students navigate the college application process. The students also published a report, "College Access: From the Inside Out," examining college access in low-income communities and offering concrete solutions to increase the college enrollment rate for East Nashville students.

By bringing attention to the issue of college access, the report helped spur the creation of the Oasis College Collection—Nashville's only college access center dedicated to making college a reality for first generation college students. In addition, new leadership at Stratford increased investments in the school's infrastructure, academics, and student support. Today, Stratford has a robust STEM program, increasing numbers of students are earning academic recognition, and nearly 75 percent of all graduates attend college.

Although more Stratford students are succeeding academically, the school still struggles to shake the negative reputation. Recently, the Stratford Story Project engaged students, alumni, parents, and neighbors to research and document the history of the school. The project culminated in a feature-length documentary film that traces the historical forces that have shaped the school's reputation over time—from desegregation to disinvestment to gentrification—and serves as a call to action to change the Stratford Story. Despite being cast as "the problem" in their neighborhoods, Stratford students have long demonstrated their potential and power to improve their community. Student Ambassadors provide tours of Stratford STEM Magnet High School throughout the academic year. Call (615) 242–6730 to schedule a tour, and search for the Stratford Story Project on YouTube to find the documentary film about the school.

ABOUT THE AUTHORS

Tayo Atanda is a 2003 graduate of Stratford High School and an attorney at Bone McAllester Norton in Nashville, Tennessee; **Amie Thurber** facilitated the Stratford Story Project.

NEARBY SITES OF INTEREST

Riverwood Mansion (1833 Welcome Ln.): The area surrounding Stratford High School was once part of a 580-acre farm. The mansion and surrounding grounds—which today serves as an event space—was built and maintained by and home to a number of enslaved African Americans.

3.10 CORNELIA FORT PARK
1199 Shadow Ln., Nashville, TN 37206

One of East Nashville's open space gems also pays tribute to the first woman in uniform to die in active military duty. Cornelia Fort was born in 1919 and raised on the family farm, near where Cornelia Fort Park stands today. After attending Sarah Lawrence College in New York, Fort pursued her dream of becoming a pilot. At twenty-one she made her first solo flight in Nashville and soon after moved to Honolulu to become a flight instructor. It was there, on December 7, 1941, that she witnessed the attack on Pearl Harbor from the air, and narrowly escaped an air strike. Stirred to patriotism by her experience, when the US military launched the first Women's Auxiliary Ferrying Squadron (WAFS) to ferry military planes during WWII, Fort

Figure 3.14. (above) Cornelia Fort Park in spring. Photo courtesy Amie Thurber

was one of the first to volunteer. Tragically, just six months into service, while on a ferrying mission from San Diego to Texas, Fort died in a plane crash. She was twenty-four years old.

Fort's letters home are a testament to her passion for flying and her commitment to her craft. She wrote to her mother, "as to your question of whether I felt I had to do this—It's something so deep inside of me—a need so vital to my happiness as sunshine and sleep—I want more than I ever wanted anything in my life to be . . . a scientific pilot and command respect from all corners of aviation but even more important—for my own satisfaction. And so my dear, I guess that's it." At a time when many women of her class aspired to marry well and be provided for, Fort wrote of the deep joy

that results from "earning a living for myself with my hands and the skill that they can produce."

Fort and the other WAFS pilots were initially treated as something of a spectacle and viewed with skepticism by civilians and soldiers alike. However, they quickly earned respect for their competence. Yet it was not until 1977 that the US Congress declared the WAFS active members of the military, making Cornelia the first women to die in active military service.

Fort's family home, Fortland, was destroyed in a fire while she was enlisted. In a letter home just months before her death, she mourned, "Wherever I have been, whatever lands my eyes have beheld, the white columns of Fortland were always in my heart, a place of refuge

Figure 3.15. Cornelia Fort. Photo courtesy of Special Collections Division, Nashville Public Library

Shadow Lane and Airpark Drive in East Nashville.

ABOUT THE AUTHOR

Chloe Fort is the niece of Cornelia Fort. **Amie Thurber** has found much solace in Cornelia Fort Park.

ADDITIONAL READING

Rob Simbeck. *Daughter of the Air: The Brief and Soaring Life of Cornelia Fort*. New York: Atlantic Monthly Press, 1999.

NEARBY SITES OF INTEREST:

Shelby Park and Shelby Bottoms Greenway (1900 Davidson St.): This 906-acre natural area has a nature center and a community center, as well as trails for walking, hiking, and biking.

and return." The year after her death, Norman Thomas built an airport for his aviation company on the land adjacent to the Fort family farm, naming the airport in honor of the fallen pilot. Cornelia Fort Airport was an active commercial airport from 1945 to 2010, when it closed after sustaining significant flood damage. With the help of the Land Trust for Tennessee and financial support from the Fort family, the city of Nashville purchased the land in 2011. Cornelia Fort Park is now part of the Shelby Bottoms Greenway system. Offering a rare sense of space in the densely foliaged Cumberland River valley, the park provides a place of refuge for neighbors and visitors alike. You can access Cornelia Fort Park from the north end of the Shelby Bottoms Greenway, or at the intersection of

3.11 NASHVILLE NATIONAL CEMETERY / US COLORED TROOPS NATIONAL MONUMENT

1420 Gallatin Pike S., Madison, TN 37115

(615) 860-0086

One of the nation's few memorials to US Colored Troops stands in the Nashville National Cemetery. Beneath the nine-foot bronze statue of a solitary soldier reads the inscription: "In Memory of the 20,133 who served as United States Colored Troops in the Union Army." Indeed, the Thirteenth Regiment of the US Colored Troops was the third largest contingent

Figure 3.16. The Memorial in fall. Photo courtesy of Learotha Williams Jr.

of Black Union soldiers in the nation. Recruitment for the Thirteenth began in Murfreesboro, Tennessee, and was completed in Nashville. The Colored Ladies of Murfreesboro made and presented the unit its regimental flag. Unlike Northern Black regiments, the Thirteenth was primarily composed of ex-slaves.

The Thirteenth was initially stationed at the Nashville and Northwestern Railroads as laborers and guards to other laborers, protecting them from Confederate raiders. The services of the Thirteenth on the railroad and their military participation in engagements at Johnsonville and Nashville had a critical impact on the defeat of Confederate forces during the Civil War.

In 1862, Nashville became the headquarters for the Union armies in the Western Theater, and the main hub for troops and supply movements throughout the South. Yet efforts to re-supply Nashville via the Cumberland River were hampered by the river's low waters. Union authorities determined that a railroad was needed to provide the Union forces with a dependable year-round port to receive shipments of supplies by boat up the Tennessee River. During construction and after completion, Confederate forces attacked this vital supply line but were repelled by members of the Thirteenth.

In December of 1864, in anticipation of a Confederate attack on Fort Negley and the massive supply depot, a portion of the Thirteenth was ordered back to Nashville. Upon arriving in Nashville, members of the Thirteenth were consolidated into the Second Colored Brigade and placed under the command of Colonel Charles Robinson Thompson. On December 16, 1864, the Thirteenth anchored the middle of a decisive Union assault on Peach Orchard Hill. In what would later be called "a charge into hell itself," the Thirteenth attacked head-on and without support. As federal forces trapped on the slopes watched in amazement, the Confederate forces concentrated their fire on the lone regiment, and the Thirteenth made straight for the line of blazing breastworks. While sustaining heavy casualties, they kept charging Peach Orchard Hill. During the assault, five different color bearers were killed. One soldier after the other seized

Figure 3.17. Reenactors at Mansker Station in 1985. Photo courtesy of Nashville Metro Archives

the fallen flag with "the colored ladies of Murfreesboro" embroidered in the cloth. One color-bearer jumped on top of the parapet and furiously shook his flag in the face of the Confederate fire. A Confederate commander was so impressed by the valor of the Thirteenth that he formally cited their bravery in his battle report, an almost unheard-of circumstance involving a Southern general.

The Thirteenth played a critical role in the subsequent defeat of Confederate forces. They were mustered out of service on July 7, 1865, yet there was no memorial to their service. In 2003, a grassroots group led by civil rights activist Kwame Lilliard raised $80,000 to establish this permanent monument to the fallen soldiers. You can visit the memorial Monday thru Friday 8:00 a.m. to 4:30 p.m. If you come on Memorial Day, you may catch a glimpse of the re-enactors of the Thirteenth USCT Living History Association.

ABOUT THE AUTHOR

George Smith, MD, was a practicing physician and a Thirteenth United States Colored Troops reenactor. He died in 2018.

NEARBY SITES OF INTEREST

Amqui Station (303 Madison St., Madison): This train station was originally built in 1910 and now serves as a welcome center and museum.

3.12 MANSKER STATION

705 Caldwell Dr., Goodlettsville, TN 37072

One of the earliest colonial settlements in Davidson County, Masker Station also serves as a reminder of Indigenous resistance to the colonization of their ancestral lands. Born in 1750 on an immigrant ship bound for the new world, Kasper Mansker traveled from the Virginia area to hunt in Tennessee and Kentucky at age nineteen. At the time, the region was inhabited by Cherokees and other Indigenous groups, though colonial hunters and French fur traders also frequented the area, and settlements such as Fort Nashborough were being established. In 1780, impressed with the abundant hunting and natural resources of the Cumberland Valley, Masker built a log fort along a creek outside of what is today the city of Goodlettsville. Conflict between the area's Indigenous inhabitants and colonists were frequent, and the small fort, known as Mansker Station, was intended to lay claim to the land and protect other colonists who were settling or passing through.

The Chicamagua Cherokee did not look kindly on this encroachment, especially given the settlers' seemingly insatiable appetite for game. That fall, a single hunting party reportedly killed 105 bear, 75 buffalo, and 87 deer in a five-day excursion. While not all Cherokee were militant toward the settlers, Chief Dragging Canoe attracted a strong band of warriors when he promised to rid their ancestral lands of the colonists. Knowing settlements threatened their survival, the Cherokee attacked Mansker Station, ultimately burning it to the ground. Some of the colonists living in the area retreated to Fort Nashborough, and others left the region altogether.

As a result of their attack, the Cherokee effectively stalled the settlement of the Goodlettsville area for two years. In 1783, Mansker returned and built a larger fort not far from the original location. Able to accommodate more people, the expanded fort was easier to defend against attack. Mansker Station served as a boarding house for colonists traveling through the area, including future president Andrew Jackson, the author of the devastating policy that later resulted in the forced removal of Indigenous people from the area. At the northern edge of what is now Davidson County, Mansker Station expanded the colonial reach of the Nashville settlement. Indeed, the first road out of Fort Nashborough—the

precursor to the city of Nashville—went to Mansker Station in 1783. For White colonists, Mansker Station represented a place of refuge and safety. For the Indigenous inhabitants of the area, it represented the deepening threat to their sovereignty and continued existence on the land they had called home for generations.

Today the site features a reproduction of the original fort, and interpretive exhibits celebrate the "pioneer spirit and dedication" of one of Nashville's founders. Indeed, Kasper Mansker helped form the first government in Nashville, and served as the first Captain in Davidson County. But this site is also a place to consider the costs of that pioneering spirit, and to remember the bravery of those who fought to preserve their homes, land, and way of life. Other sites of resistance include Renfro's Station, near present day Clarksville, and the Battle of the Bluffs in downtown Nashville, where the Chickamauga Cherokee fought the Donelson party.

ABOUT THE AUTHOR

Amie Thurber is a former resident of East Nashville.

NEARBY SITES OF INTEREST

Moss-Wright Park (745 Caldwell Dr., Goodlettsville): This park, adjoining Mansker Station, has 147 acres of recreational space, including trails, picnic areas, and a large playground.

Figure 3.18. Reverend Will Campbell outside his Mount Juliet home in 1992. Photo courtesy of Special Collections Division, Nashville Public Library

3.13 GASS'S STORE / CINCO DE MAYO MEXICAN RESTAURANT

580 Nonoville Rd.,
Mt. Juliet, TN 37122

On the outskirts of the Northeastern region sits the small city of Mount Juliet, home to a popular Mexican restaurant that was formerly the favorite juke joint of one of Nashville's most iconic and outrageous civil rights leaders. A White Southern preacher who preferred singing country songs to talking to the press, "Brother Will" Campbell was born July 18, 1924, on a Mississippi cotton farm. At age seventeen, Campbell was ordained as a minister, and in 1956 he and his wife Brenda moved to Nashville, settling on a small farm near Mount Juliet. It was there he lived out his ministry, in his words, "as a bootleg preacher with neither parish nor pulpit."

An outspoken proponent of racial integration, Campbell was active throughout the Civil Rights Movement. He was the only White person to participate in the founding of the Southern Christian Leadership Conference led by Dr. Martin Luther King Jr., and in 1957, was one of four escorts of the Little Rock Nine in their first attempt to integrate Central High School. While his ministry took him throughout the South, Will's efforts were particularly significant in Nashville. He was a trusted advisor to the student activists organizing the Nashville sit-ins and worked behind the scenes with business owners to help negotiate policy change. But what most distinguished Will was not only his staunch support of the Civil Rights Movement but his commitment to also ministering to White racists.

Campbell frequently declared, "If you love one, you gotta love 'em all." He had little faith in politics or mainstream religion to bring racial reconciliation. But he did believe in love. Campbell built relationships with members of the Ku Klux Klan, and he famously visited James Earl Ray, the man who assassinated Dr. Martin Luther King Jr., in prison. As Campbell reflected in his book *Brother to a Dragonfly*, "I have seen and known the resentment of the racist, his hostility, his

Will Campbell was a man of legend, and many knew him better than I. But the window of my world opened fifty years ago because of Will. I saw Will's ability to love and minister to everyone—on both sides of any conflict. I have tried to live into his theology, which he summed up in *Brother to a Dragonfly* when he concluded, "We are all bastards, and God loves us anyway." As is true for so many others, Will's example affected the lives of everyone in my family. A fierce opponent of the death penalty, at one time Will had visited nearly every person on death row in the United States. Inspired by his actions, my daughter and son-in-law faithfully visited a man on death row in Nashville for seventeen years, until his execution. Over the course of their at-least-monthly visits, they came to see each other as family.

After Will's stroke, I visited him weekly for the remaining two years of his life, often reading him excerpts from his books. His wife, Brenda, is now in the same assisted living facility her husband once was. There would not have been a Will without Brenda, who is a force in her own right, having raised the children and handled the finances while Will was frequently on the road. Now I visit Brenda weekly as well, bringing her a rose and conducting what I call the ministry of cigarettes—taking her to a park where she can enjoy a smoke. I will be forever grateful to Will and Brenda for their friendship and fellowship, and especially to Will, for opening my world so many years ago.

Floyd Craig

frustration, his need for someone upon whom to lay blame and to punish. With the same love that we are commanded to shower upon the innocent victim, the church must love the racist."

For much of his life, Will and Brenda could be found Saturday nights at Gass's Market, their local juke joint. Though he reportedly had a poor sense of tempo, Will loved to sing, and many of his Mount Juliet neighbors loved to listen. Some nights he'd end up at the microphone, but every night he'd be there ministering—lending an ear to neighbors in need. As his wife reflects, Gass's came as close to being his church as any place. Campbell retired from singing and ministering after a 2011 stroke, and died two years later, on June 3, 2013.

Campbell's obituary in the *Tennessean* aptly describes his ability to build his version of a beloved community: "Will's 'church without a steeple' attracted a wonderful menagerie of humanity—defrocked ministers, country music 'outlaws', alienated academics, hard-bitten journalists, Ku Klux Klan members, student protesters, Black Panthers, Vietnam War resisters, runaway children, death-row inmates and sundry other untouchables shunned by polite society." Though Will Campbell eschewed praise and avoided press, his work did not go unnoticed. President Clinton awarded him the 2000 National Endowment for the Humanities medal, and PBS profiled him in its documentary *God's Will*. You can learn more about Brother Will from the seventeen books he authored, the most renowned of which is *Brother to a Dragonfly*. Though Gass's Market closed in the mid-1990s, the Mexican restaurant at this address occupies the same building.

ABOUT THE AUTHOR

Floyd Craig is a retired pastor and resident of Franklin, Tennessee. He was a longtime friend of Will Campbell.

ADDITIONAL READING

Campbell, Will D. *Brother to a Dragonfly*. New York : Seabury Press, 1977. Reprinted with forewords by Jimmy Carter and John Lewis. Jackson: University Press of Mississippi, 2018.

NEARBY SITES OF INTEREST

Shutes Branch Recreation Area (Saundersville Rd. and Needmore Rd., Mt. Juliet): While you are in the area, check out this popular recreation area for boating, mountain biking, and more.

Williamson County CME Church Complex / Needmore Community (1576 Needmore Rd.): The Needmore Community is the oldest rural African American community in Wilson County, with roots tracing back to 1850. For much of the twentieth century, the church and attached school were the center of the community.

4. SOUTHEAST

4.1   Nashville International Airport /
      Nashville Metro Taxi Drivers Alliance   154

4.2   The Camps of Saint Cloud Hill   156

4.3   Wilson Park   158

4.4   Nashville Fairgrounds   160

4.5   Casa Azafrán   163

4.6   Clairmont Apartments   165

4.7   The Buddhist Temple   167

4.8   La Hacienda Taqueria y SuperMercado   168

4.9   Workers' Dignity   171

4.10   Global Mall at the Crossings   172

4.11   Hands On Nashville Urban Farm   174

4.12   Salahadeen Center   175

4.13   Nashville Zoo at Grassmere   177

Map 6. Southeast. Courtesy of Joseph Speer

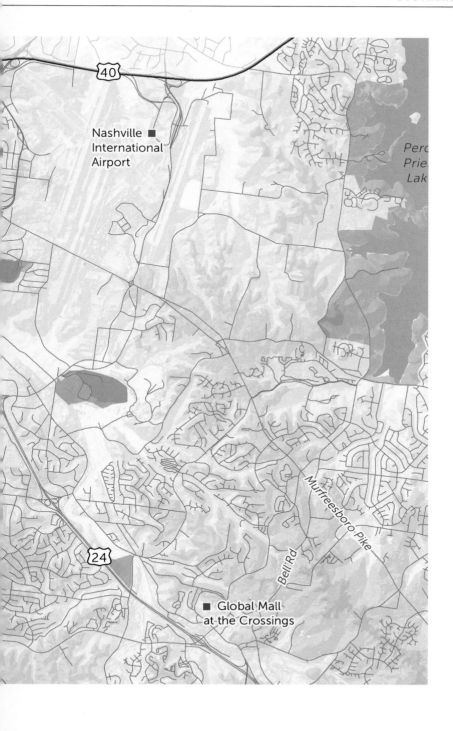

40

Nashville ■
International
Airport

Perc
Prie.
Lak

Murfreesboro Pike

Bell Rd

24

■ Global Mall
at the Crossings

AN INTRODUCTION TO SOUTHEAST NASHVILLE

SOUTHEAST NASHVILLE IS ONE of the most demographically and geographically diverse regions of the county. It includes
a wide range of neighborhood types: the older, rapidly gentrifying
urban neighborhoods of Chestnut Hill, Wedgewood-Houston, and
Woodbine; the mid-twentieth-century suburbs of Glencliff, Caldwell
Hall, and Crieve Hall; and a mix of mid-century and newer suburbs
and working agricultural land. Further to the southeast, the region
includes one of Nashville's largest recreation areas, Percy Priest Lake,
which offers ample hiking, biking, camping, and water activities.

Although all of Nashville was once populated by Indigenous people,
the Southeast region is distinct in that it is today home to a number
of Indigenous advocacy, service, and organizing groups. These include
the federal Indian Health Services Nashville Area Office, which serves
twenty-nine tribes or nations whose members are dispersed across
twenty-four states, as well as United South and Eastern Tribes, Inc.,
an inter-tribal organization providing policy advocacy, health support,
and environmental resource management to twenty-six nations with
ties to the multi-state southeastern region. Nashville's annual pow-
wow is also held in this area, drawing hundreds each October to Long
Hunter State Park on Percy Priest Lake.

Some of the region's earliest European settlers settled in what is
now the southeast quadrant of the county and played pivotal roles
in the founding of Nashville. Legacies of colonial violence and slavery are entangled in the histories of these settlers. For example,
John Overton built his historic home, Travellers Rest, on a 1,050-
acre plantation eight miles south of downtown Nashville. A wealthy

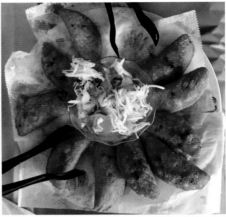

Figure 4.1. (above) Pupusas from Delicias de El Salvador on Murfreesboro Pike. Photo courtesy of Amie Thurber

Figure 4.2. Cultural celebration in the Woodbine neighborhood. Photo © Al Levenson

landowner, Tennessee supreme court judge, and advisor to President Jackson, Overton owned approximately eighty slaves who farmed the main Travellers Rest cotton and tobacco crops. Overton had his home built upon a Mississippian burial ground, and he originally named the house Hill of Skulls. He later renamed the home Travellers Rest to reflect the respite provided from his work as a circuit judge, which required frequent long travel by horseback. The irony in the name—given his desecration of those who had been laid to rest beneath his feet—may have been lost to him. Indeed, Indigenous activism to protect the burial site on this land from further disruption continued through the 1990s.

The Southeast region grew as an agricultural and industrial hub in the 1800s, and many of its residents worked in these fields. The Nashville & Chattanooga Railroad began operation in 1851, supplying access to more distant regions and markets. Much of the railroad work was done by enslaved Blacks and recent immigrants from Ireland. In addition to transporting goods and services to and from Nashville, the railroad provided an essential shipping link for the Union Army during the Civil War. During this period, freed and runaway slaves flocked to Nashville. As described in this chapter, many of these former slaves were conscripted, along with free Blacks, and forced to assist Union forces with the construction of Fort Negley.

With the arrival of the post–Civil War Reconstruction, many Black families began to settle in what is now the southeast part of Nashville. Important Black communities developed in several parts of the region, such as Trimble Bottom—now the Chestnut Hill neighborhood—located near downtown along what are now Second and Third Avenues South. Trimble Bottom was the original home of a number of important Black institutions, including Central Tennessee College, which was opened by Freedmen's Aid Society shortly after the war and chartered by the Methodist Episcopal Church in 1867. It was located where Cameron Middle School sits today. Central Tennessee College was among the first colleges in the city for African Americans, and the medical department, founded in 1876, went on to become Meharry Medical College. The Hubbard House, listed on the National Registry of Historic Places, is the last remaining structure from the original Meharry campus (the school is now located in North Nashville). Several sites discussed in this chapter speak to the early African American influences in the region.

During the 1930s and 1940s, Southeast Nashville was nearly evenly split between Black and White residents, albeit living in segregated neighborhoods. The 1950s ushered in suburban development in the outer-ring of the region and the beginning of White flight. Indeed, the Southeast region saw an influx of White residents to these suburbs, which peaked in the 1970s, when White residents made up 86 percent of the area's population. Since then, the demographic trends have changed,

with decreasing numbers of White residents and increasing populations of Latinos and other ethnic groups.

Commonly referred to as the International District, the neighborhoods bordering Nolensville Pike have the largest population of immigrants in Nashville, with robust communities hailing from Mexico, Honduras, Iraq, Burma, Nepal, Syria, and Somalia, among other countries. Much of the economic and civic development in Southeast Nashville has been driven by immigrants and refugees. Indeed, Nolensville Road and Murfreesboro Pike brim with international markets, food trucks, and restaurants, as well as diverse religious institutions, social service organizations, and community organizing centers. On Nolensville Road alone there are eighteen places of worship catering to different faiths and ethnic backgrounds, and in the Southeast region as a whole, there are more than two hundred churches and three mosques. While a number of entries in this chapter explore contributions to the city by Nashville's immigrant communities, they barely scratch the surface.

The built environment of Southeast Nashville has been shaped by a patchwork of zoning regulations that geographically separate single-family housing, multi-family homes, and commercial and institutional areas. As a result, the region is starkly segregated—often by ethnicity as well as economics; the zoning has also contributed to transit difficulties. The region's primary arteries are often clogged with traffic, and much of the area lacks sidewalks and bike lanes. Residents who depend on public transit to access employment and education can be stuck for hours a day on buses sitting in bumper-to-bumper traffic.

Despite these challenges, the Southeast is also characterized by a high level of resident engagement in civic life. In 2009, the immigrant community played an important role in helping defeat a proposal that would have required that all official city business be conducted in English. An estimated ten thousand immigrants went to the polls to vote— many for the first time—and the bill was defeated. In 2015, residents formed Southeast Nashville United (SENU) in response to the city's plan to relocate the main jail from downtown to the Southeast. With support from allied council members, the group won the fight, and the jail was not relocated. SENU continues to provide a platform for residents to organize for power in shaping the future of their community.

The diverse communities in Southeast Nashville take pride in their vast natural reserves, cultural hubs, and community power. Despite the civic engagement and entrepreneurial spirit evident in the region, income levels in this area are far below the Davidson County average. While exploring this area, we encourage you to visit and support the many immigrant-run businesses and organizations. While not the most walkable region of Nashville, you will find people who welcome the chance to connect. Save time

for compelling conversations as you learn more about this dynamic part of Nashville.

ABOUT THE AUTHORS

Vanderbilt graduate students **Julian Humphrey-Davis, SamiJo Forcum, Sarah Imran, Diamond Joy Luster, Dan Moranville, Kelly Smith, Sarah Stephanoff,** and **Bailey Via** contributed to this introduction.

4.1 NASHVILLE INTERNATIONAL AIRPORT / NASHVILLE METRO TAXI DRIVERS ALLIANCE

1 Terminal Dr.,
Nashville, TN 37214

Branded as the "gateway to the city," the Nashville International Airport features rotating and permanent art exhibits, four stages of live music, and an open container law allowing guests to carry alcoholic beverages throughout the terminal. Designed to exemplify Southern hospitality toward Nashville's guests and travelers, the airport has also been a site of struggle to extend that same hospitality to workers. In the past, labor groups have criticized the airport for the limited number of contracts awarded to minority- and women-owned businesses, a gap that is now improving. The airport has also been a critical site of struggle among the city's taxi drivers, many of whom are East African and Kurdish refugees.

Figure 4.3. Protesting taxi drivers being interviewed by the news. Photo © Al Levenson

In 2008, Middle Tennessee Jobs with Justice partnered with Middle Tennessee State University to research taxi drivers' out-of-pocket daily costs. Survey data from nearly three hundred drivers demonstrated that Nashville's taxi drivers were among the lowest paid workers in the United States, with their average gross income lower than the federal and state minimum wage. At the time, many drivers worked fourteen- to fifteen-hour days and seven-day workweeks, supporting on average a family of five on those wages alone. In 2008, the average gross income for taxi drivers was $106 per day, with the cab companies requiring the drivers spend up to $83 a day out of pocket for gas, permits, insurance, and airport fees. This amounted to an average take-home pay of less than $30 a day, an average of $2.40 an hour. At this rate, a driver who worked every day of a thirty-day month would take home less than $1,000 per month—half the federal poverty guideline for a family of five. The research also identified additional health risks suffered by Nashville taxi drivers. Despite the fact that drivers work in hazardous conditions, drive in dangerous neighborhoods, and are targets of discriminatory attacks, the taxi industry had a poor workers' compensation policy. Further, almost 75 percent of the drivers did not have employer-based, government, or private health insurance, and only 32 percent said their children and spouses had health insurance.

On June 6, 2008, the Nashville Metro Taxi Drivers Alliance (NMTDA) organized a rally to highlight the working conditions of immigrant taxi drivers. The rally received support from the Urban

EpiCenter, Jobs with Justice, the Homeless Power Project, and the Tennessee Immigrant and Refugee Rights Coalition. Over three hundred marchers rallied in solidarity with the taxicab drivers, including many African Americans who believed in the importance of alliances with the largely East African taxicab work force. NMTDA insisted that Metro's taxicab code be amended to cap weekly fees and to ensure the drivers' right to unionize within Nashville's unregulated taxi industry.

Despite the NMTDA's efforts, the regulating government agency did not change the industry's rules and procedures. It did, however approve two driver-owned taxicab companies, allowing NMTDA members to free themselves from the taxicab corporations (principally Allied Cab and Nashville Cab) who had proprietary influence at the airport. Volunteer Taxi, formed by Ethiopian drivers in 2012, is the first taxi company owned exclusively by the drivers. Two years later, the commission approved permits for TennCab, a Somali-based, driver-owned company.

If you have the opportunity to travel by taxi whether on your way to or from the airport, or during your time in the city, take the time to visit with your driver, learn more about his or her experiences, and don't forget to tip!

ABOUT THE AUTHOR

Sekou Franklin is an associate professor in the Department of Political Science at Middle Tennessee State University (MTSU) and was the lead researcher for the taxi-driver study.

A version of this essay was published in *The State of Blacks in Middle Tennessee* (2010).

NEARBY SITES OF INTEREST

Buchanan Log House (2910 Elm Hill Pike): Built in the early 1800s, it is one of the oldest historical sites in Middle Tennessee.

Clover Bottom Mansion (2941 Lebanon Pike): Now home of the Tennessee Historical Commission, Clover Bottom Mansion has nineteenth-century former slave quarters that can be toured during business hours.

Percy Priest Lake (3361 Bell Rd.): Need a place to cool off? Visit the reservoir to swim, boat, kayak, or picnic.

4.2 THE CAMPS OF SAINT CLOUD HILL

1100 Fort Negley Blvd., Nashville, TN 37203

The land surrounding Fort Negley on Saint Cloud Hill has been contested since the 1800s, when it became a contraband camp for slaves seeking freedom. In 1862, Confederate forces surrendered Nashville without a fight, enabling the Union to establish the city as a key military stronghold. Under pressure to quickly fortify the city, Fort Negley was the first of five forts built in Nashville. More than 2,700 Black laborers were conscripted for its construction. Working in harsh conditions with little rest, scraps for food, and in many cases, only the night sky over their heads for shelter, an estimated eight hundred Blacks died before the fort was complete.

Figure 4.4. Fort Negley. Photo courtesy of Learotha Williams Jr.

As the news of the Union takeover of Nashville spread, the city became a destination for people seeking to escape the bonds of slavery. To manage the rapid influx of refugees, the Union army established three "contraband camps" around the city, including one on Saint Cloud Hill. While the camps provided protection from Confederate forces and their former owners, the Union army saw runaway slaves as another easily exploitable labor source, and they were put to work constructing military infrastructure. Though enduring brutal work and living conditions, the buildings and railroads that were constructed by these men and women ultimately played a crucial role in the defeat of the Confederacy.

Following the end of the war, the original Fort Negley contraband camp evolved into the Edgehill neighborhood. After World War II, the area surrounding Fort Negley became a park, baseball field, and the site for the Adventure Science Center. During the twentieth century however, people struggling to find affordable housing began squatting in the woods surrounding Fort Negley. In 2008 and subsequent years, police removed squatters from the area, but without enough housing and shelter options, people continued to come back. In recent years, some squatting residents built elaborate campsites with pallet decks and hospitality wings, and welcomed others who could not access shelter or housing. In 2014, city officials threatened to close the camp again, by then home to over forty residents. Homeless advocates joined with residents and held off the camp's closure, but in 2015, Mayor Megan Barry announced that the camp would close on April 15, 2016.

Homeless advocates and residents involved the media and held demonstrations, marches, and a sleep-out at Fort Negley to call attention to the lack of affordable housing and safe places to rest. The advocates' action delayed the camp's closure, giving dozens of Fort Negley residents time to access permanent housing. The city gave many of the homeless residents vouchers so they could peacefully vacate the land, and others moved to other unsanctioned encampments. The camp was forcibly closed on May 11, 2016, when bulldozers razed the area, a move that took many supporters of the Fort and the nearby community by surprise. At the time, camper Chris Scott said, "They don't hear the birds sing in the early morning. They don't hear the whippoorwills cry after sunset. They don't see the bats fly against the night sky. They don't

Figure 4.5. Fort Negley residents took pride in their campsites. Photo courtesy of Lindsey Krinks

know what they're destroying." Later that year, the forest itself was completely razed, with every last tree removed. Now the forest, birds, whippoorwills, and bats are also gone.

You can walk the grounds of Saint Cloud Hill daily. The Park is open year-round from dawn to dusk for self-guided walking tours. Site maps are available in the mailbox posted behind the stone gates at Fort Negley. While aspects of the park's contested history are visible in the Fort Negley interpretive center, many of its former residents remain invisible, displaced, and in search of affordable housing and safe places to rest.

ABOUT THE AUTHORS

Austin Sauerbrei and **Lindsey Krinks** are community organizers working for housing justice.

ADDITIONAL READING

Lindsey Krinks. *Praying with our Feet: Pursuing Justice and Healing on the Streets.* Grand Rapids, MI: Brazos Press, 2021.

NEARBY SITES OF INTEREST

Fort Negley (1100 Fort Negley Blvd.): The Fort Negley Visitor's Center is free and open to the public Tuesday through Saturday, and features films, exhibits, artifact displays, and a gift shop, as well as an outdoor fossil collection site and a milkweed garden.

Adventure Science Center (800 Fort Negley Blvd.): An educational science center with hands-on activities for kids of all ages.

4.3 WILSON PARK
2nd Ave. S. and Chestnut St., Nashville, TN 37203

Tom Wilson Park and baseball stadium once stood at the intersection of Chestnut Street and Second Avenue South, right in the heart of the Chestnut Hill neighborhood. Nashville has a rich baseball history: in 1885, it became one of the charter cities for the Southern Baseball League (minor league baseball). However, it was not until the early 1900s, with the formation of the Capital City League, that African Americans were allowed to play.

In 1918, Thomas T. Wilson, an African American businessman, purchased the Nashville Standard Giants and in 1921 he renamed the team the Elite Giants. Encouraged by the team's increasing popularity across the South, in 1929, Wilson built the team its own stadium. Tom Wilson Park opened in Trimble Bottom neighborhood, now known as Chestnut Hill. The eight-thousand-seat stadium was one of only three venues in the nation explicitly built for a Negro

Figure 4.6. Nashville's Elite Giants 1935 roster. Photo courtesy of Nashville Metro Archives

Baseball League team, and one of two owned by an African American. Wilson, deliberate in his business decisions, opened the park to community events for both White and Black communities, in addition to baseball. The location of the stadium was also intentional, as the neighborhood was, and continues to be, Nashville's oldest surviving African American neighborhood.

Trimble Bottom, formed in the early nineteenth century during Reconstruction, was one of five distinct African American neighborhoods. Originally an encampment after the Civil War, living conditions in the neighborhood were poor as it sat on low-lying land and was prone to flooding. Yet the neighborhood soon became an educational center for African Americans. In 1867, Central Tennessee College was founded in Trimble Bottom, and in 1875 Meharry Medical Department opened, becoming Meharry Medical College in 1927. Meharry was the first medical school for African Americans in the South,

and also where Tom Wilson's parents had studied. The medical school helped Trimble Bottom attract and develop a middle class of African Americans, making it an ideal spot for Wilson's stadium. Today the George W. Hubbard House, constructed for Dr. Hubble in 1921 when he retired as president of Meharry Medical college, remains the last building from what was the original Meharry campus.

In 1930, the Nashville Elite Giants were invited to join the Negro National League (NNL), bringing the team to a new level. Although the NNL disbanded the following year, the Elite Giants joined the Southern Negro League for the 1932 season. After the NNL was reborn, the Elite Giants rejoined and played for two more seasons. Throughout this time, the stadium was also used for spring training and by minor league teams including the Nashville Vols, who played at the Sulphur Dell baseball park located on Jefferson Street.

With the nation in the grips of the Great Depression, and Wilson eager to capitalize on a larger market, he moved the Elite Giants to Columbus, Ohio. Perhaps coincidentally, Meharry Medical College had recently relocated to a campus near Fisk University, taking much of the Black middle class with it to the new North Nashville location. These losses sparked an economic downturn in Trimble Bottom. With the departure of the Elite Giants, African Americans in Nashville were again barred from professional baseball until 1947, when Jackie Robinson broke the color barrier. That same year, slum clearance programs and the construction of Interstate-40 cut Trimble Bottom off from downtown, further damaging the economic vitality of the neighborhood. Wilson retired from baseball, and the stadium was torn down to make way for Wilson's new nightclub, the Paradise Ballroom. Stars such as Cab Calloway and Lena Horne performed there before it too closed. Although the area continued to experience economic troubles, as of today community groups and housing nonprofits are actively working to preserve the historic neighborhood and ensure affordable housing for residents.

ABOUT THE AUTHOR

Kate Goodman is a graduate of Vanderbilt University's Community Development and Action program.

NEARBY SITES OF INTEREST

Nashville City Cemetery (1001 4th Ave. S.): Pay your respects at the oldest continuously operated public cemetery in Nashville.

4.4 NASHVILLE FAIRGROUNDS

625 Smith Ave.,
Nashville, TN 37203
(615) 862-8980

One of Nashville's biggest fights for equitable development in recent history centered around the future of the Tennessee Fairgrounds, a 117-acre swath of land in the heart of Southeast Nashville. Though often regarded as a central public space for Nashvillians to gather, the Fairgrounds has also long been a contested space, raising questions about what sorts of "recreation" are valued and valuable, and for whom. The land's recreational use dates back to 1891, when the privately owned horseracing track Cumberland Park opened. The sport was saturated with gender, race, and class divisions that shaped who could own, train, jockey, groom, watch, and profit on horses, and, over time, it was also sullied by concerns of cruelty to the animals at the center of it all. In 1906, Cumberland Park hosted the Tennessee State Fair, and soon after the Davidson County government purchased the land as a "public" recreational space for the annual state fair, as well as regular horse and automobile racing. In 1952, Fair Park opened on the site. Over the course of its thirty-five-year history, this regionally renowned theme park featured an enormous wooden roller coaster, impressive swimming pool, and eighteen-hole mini golf course.

I would say that 2017 and 2018 were very challenging years for Nashville; we were in the boom of being the "It City," dealing with a revolving door within our Mayor's office, and losing the battle of gentrification, while dealing with the second death of an unarmed Black male at the hands of the police. The feeling of hopelessness and frustration was quickly becoming part of our identity, and we decided to do our best to change that narrative.

In 2017, the ironworkers' strike on the Westin Hotel and the Just Hospitality campaign were happening at the same time the city was giving tax breaks to Westin and other projects that were stealing employee wages. After months of digging, it was apparent that rampant city development with no community input or accountability was having the largest impact on these looming issues. It was a particularly deadly year for construction workers; the release of the Build a Better South report underscored this reality and attracted the attention of several Metro council members. The Mayor's Office released an Affordable Housing Report showing that, by 2025, Nashville would need thirty-one thousand affordable housing units.

So there we were, in a time where the majority of minorities—especially African Americans—were not making living wages, out-of-state workers were being brought into Nashville to work instead of making local hiring a priority, affordable housing was being ravaged by the short-term rental market (such as Airbnb rentals), and local residents were being pushed out of the city, and even though the city was trying to address some of these problems, the state was undermining our efforts.

The MLS stadium and ten-acre development was a slap in the face for many in Nashville who were feeling the stress of Nashville's growth, and we at Stand Up Nashville were committed to not just talking about this issue, we wanted to change that stress to hope. Which meant we need different strategies . . . the community benefits agreement (CBA) was the tool we used to make that happen.

Building this healthy coalition was hard! For one thing, five years ago I didn't know what organizing was. I had to learn what advocacy was while learning to advocate for others. We had to build trust with people, build our capacity to do this well, strategically navigate through different priorities posed by the community, and put in an absurd number of hours daily, often giving up weekends too. Keeping clear lines of communication internally and externally were the keys to our success. This campaign became something more than an issue raised by Stand Up Nashville, it became the moral voice and reflection of our city. To have thousands of people say "this CBA represents me and my values, and I'm proud to have fought for it" is the real victory.

We built power with the people, not for them, and that was the difference needed to restore hope and pride.

Odessa Kelly

While a beloved recreation and entertainment site to many Nashville families, Fair Park was open almost exclusively to Whites into the 1960s, and investment in maintaining the park declined following desegregation. In 1987, as the Nashville Convention Center was being opened, Fair Park was being closed. Though the space continued to host a variety of fairs, flea markets, and races for more than thirty

Figure 4.7. Around 350 Stand Up Nashville supporters showed up at the courthouse to demand the CBA be signed. Photo courtesy of Stand Up Nashville

years, more days than not, the sprawling fairgrounds was largely vacant. One of the most consistent draws to the fairgrounds has been auto-racing, yet many residents of the surrounding neighborhood have long argued that the noise from the track is intolerable and advocated for an alternative use of the space to once again serve the area's families and children. As Debbie Young, a long-time resident of the area and community activist, lamented, "Metro government has taken everything away from the youth of Nashville," and this has felt particularly true in this historically low- and moderate-income, racially mixed neighborhood.

After years of petitioning by residents, in August 2016 the Mayor's Office released plans for a massive overhaul of the fairgrounds, proposing its transformation to a mixed-use residential, retail, office, and civic space. Soon after, Nashville was selected as Major League Soccer's (MLS) twenty-fourth franchise, and talk quickly turned to building an MLS stadium and surrounding mixed-use development at the Tennessee Fairgrounds. With a price tag soaring past $325 million, the *Tennessean* reported that this would be the largest stadium built for soccer in North America. But Stand Up Nashville, a coalition of community organizations and labor unions, raised concerns over who will benefit from the giveaway of land and investment of tax dollars. As leaders of Stand Up Nashville put it in a press release, "Using tens of millions of public dollars and land to create more dead-end jobs, displacement of vulnerable residents, and debt that jeopardizes vital public services like schools just won't do!" Stand Up Nashville negotiated a Community Benefits Agreement—a binding contract between the stadium developer and the community coalition—to create pathways out of poverty for residents currently being excluded from Nashville's growth and prosperity. Among the commitments outlined in the CBA are that all employees directly employed by Nashville Soccer Holdings will receive wages of at least $15.50 per hour, that developers will award 25 percent of the total value of contracts to minority- and women-owned businesses, and that 20 percent of the residential units in the proposed mixed-use development will be classified as affordable housing. This CBA is the first of its kind in the state of Tennessee and could provide a model for equitable development in the city and state. As an increasingly international city, there will without doubt be fans to welcome soccer, the most popular sport in the world, to the Tennessee Fairgrounds. Nonetheless, with MLS ticket prices averaging $50 a game, questions remain with regard to whose interests are being prioritized in one of the city's most prized public spaces.

ABOUT THE AUTHORS

Odessa Kelly is a Nashville native and the executive director of Stand Up Nashville. **Amie Thurber** is a former Nashville resident.

NEARBY SITES OF INTEREST

The fourth weekend of each month, the Fairgrounds is home to the iconic **Nashville Flea Market,** which has been in operation since 1969.

4.5 CASA AZAFRÁN

2195 Nolensville Pike, Nashville, TN 37211

(615) 320-5152

As foreign-born residents begin their lives in the United States, they face significant social, cultural, and economic challenges. However, through the collective power of the immigrant population and the support of the local community, Nashville has been able to offer many opportunities for its international residents to meet and overcome those challenges. One way it does so is through Casa Azafrán.

While many people know *casa* to mean "home," *azafrán* (pronounced "ah-zah-frahn"), a Spanish word with Arabic roots, means "saffron." This spice, used across cultures and continents, symbolizes Casa Azafrán's vision to be a gathering place for people from all ethnic backgrounds. Located on Nolensville Pike, where much of Nashville's immigrant population is concentrated, Casa Azafrán serves as an event space, art gallery, business hub, and social service collaborative for the city's foreign-born residents. Conexión Américas, a nonprofit working in Nashville since 2002, founded Casa Azafrán in 2012

Figure 4.8. Artist Jairo Prado designed and installed the thirty-foot by twelve-foot mosaic mural titled *Migration*, representing the movement of all people across many lands, for Casa Azafrán. Photo courtesy of Conexión Américas

with the support of both private and public funds. Casa Azafrán houses numerous nonprofit organizations that offer educational, legal, healthcare, and other services to the international community. In addition to providing meeting and event space, Casa Azafrán features a commercial kitchen for immigrant-owned businesses and also hosts various visual, film, literary, and performing arts events from across Nashville.

In both name and in function, Casa Azafrán embodies the best of what Nashville has become—a vibrant, engaged home to people of diverse cultures and origins. It serves as a gateway for newcomers, to the city, and to the nation. It is not a wonder that in 2014, President Obama chose this Nashville site to deliver

a speech urging Congress to pass comprehensive immigration legislation. Despite continued needs within the immigrant population and a pervasive thread of anti-immigrant rhetoric across the nation, Casa Azafrán is a reflection of the welcoming spirit that has so often prevailed in Nashville, supporting immigrant ingenuity and creativity and amplifying opportunities for Nashville's foreign-born residents to transition and thrive.

As you visit Casa Azafrán, you can see for yourself what the place means to Nashville's immigrant community. Above the entrance shines a large, multicolored mosaic titled *Migration*, a symbol of diversity and hope. On any given day, the building is bustling with people from around the globe working to make

Nashville a more welcoming home for all. For more information about Casa Azafrán hours, programs, and events, visit www.casaazafran.org.

ABOUT THE AUTHOR

Anna Warren is a graduate of Vanderbilt University's Community Development and Action program.

NEARBY SITES OF INTEREST

Nolensville Pike: While you are in the area, there are numerous international markets and restaurants worth visiting.

4.6 CLAIRMONT APARTMENTS

1019 Patricia Dr.,
Nashville, TN 37217

A destructive collaboration between an absentee landlord, local law enforcement, and the US Immigration and Customs Enforcement (ICE) came to a head at this apartment complex in the heart of Nashville's immigrant community. In 2010, during the height of the mass deportation of over ten thousand Davidson County residents by Sheriff Daron Hall in collaboration with the Obama administration in an agreement called the 287(g) memorandum, many of the residents in this more than two-hundred-unit complex were immigrants. Although the apartments were notoriously poorly maintained—residents reported insect infestation, a lack of hot water, and broken windows—many of the families

living there appreciated living across the street from an elementary school, within walking distance to an international market, and close to public transit. Instead of investing in improving the complex, the absentee landlord collaborated with local police and ICE to remove residents.

On October 20, 2010, ICE agents broke into apartments, arrested more than twenty men and women at gunpoint, and separated parents from children. As reported in the *Tennessean*, one thirteen-year-old boy who remained shared, "They came and took my friends and their family members—people who take care of me after school and look out for me every day." The raid broke more than individual families; it ruptured a community that provided material, social, and emotional support to one another.

With legal help from the ACLU Immigrants' Rights Project, the ACLU of Tennessee, and two Nashville law firms, residents of Clairmont sued the apartment owner, Metro, and the federal government for constitutional violations. The city government, ICE, and apartment owners all settled the lawsuits, providing financial remediation to those targeted by the raid, while offering no admission of wrongdoing. Fortunately, none of those detained in the Clairmont raid were deported.

The Clairmont Apartments have changed hands several times since 2010, and as of 2020 it is currently under the ownership of Elmington Properties, a real-estate developer at the center of gentrification in Midtown and Southeast

Figure 4.9. Megan Macaraeg of the Tennessee Immigrant and Refugee Rights Coalition hugs a young boy after he gave a statement about a 2010 police raid at the Clairmont Apartments. Photo courtesy of the *Tennessean*

Nashville. The largely immigrant residents continue to complain of poor maintenance, including the flooding of entire buildings with raw sewage twice in 2019. In the years following the Clairmont immigration raid, a pro-immigrant movement successfully fought and defeated Sheriff Daron Hall's 287(g) program, and in a recent July 2019 victory, residents in Hermitage's Valley Grove neighborhood organized to resist and prevent ICE from arresting a father and his son who had been trapped in their driveway. The viral media story of the attempted arrest in Hermitage sparked a new round of public outcry that resulted in Sheriff Daron Hall announcing that he would no longer hold detainees arrested by ICE in the Davidson County jail. In the following months, ICE continued to make arrests with MNPD backup, including an incident where ICE agents shot a man and another where local police officers pepper-sprayed two mothers and a sixteen-year-old girl; a network of immigrant organizations continue to organize against ongoing collaboration between the Metro Nashville Police Department, the Davidson County Sheriff's Office, and ICE agents.

ABOUT THE AUTHOR

Tristan Call is a researcher, organizer, and urban farmer based at Nashville Greenlands in North Nashville.

NEARBY SITES OF INTEREST

Buchanan's Station and Cemetery (740 Massman Dr.): This two-hundred-year-old former fort and cemetery is also a site of Indigenous resistance to settler colonization.

4.7 THE BUDDHIST TEMPLE

99 Lyle Lane,
Nashville, TN 37210

(615) 271-1711

The oldest Buddhist Temple in Nashville sits in a small house tucked between two Baptist churches. The Temple began with a vision of providing a nonsectarian place of meditation and study for the city's diverse Buddhist populations. In the mid-1970s, Dr. Win Myint and his wife Patti opened Nashville's first Asian market (see section 5.16 for more about the Myint's International Market and Restaurant). As immigrants themselves—from Burma and Thailand respectively—the Myint's also felt compelled to offer the community a space for cultural and spiritual nourishment. An increasing number of Southeast Asian refugees and immigrants were relocating to Nashville, and the city's Buddhist population was in a period of rapid growth. Although some Buddhists began practicing together in apartments or houses, there was not a formal place for the community to gather. Working in collaboration with leaders from the city's diverse Asian communities and various Buddhist sects, in 1981 Dr. Myint bought the North Edgefield Baptist Church in East Nashville and converted it into the city's first Buddhist Temple.

The temple faced some initial difficulties in achieving its mission. Some refugees were resettled in Nashville through Catholic Charities and were reluctant to openly practice Buddhism for fear it would offend the agency that aided them. There was also initial conflict within the temple board regarding whether to maintain a non-sectarian temple, or to align with a particular sect of

Figure 4.10. The Buddhist Temple. Photo courtesy of Joseph Gutierrez

Buddhism. In 1982, the Sasana Council in Thailand sent thirty monks to Nashville in order to transform the temple into a monastery for the Dhammayuttika sect of Theravada Buddhism. Eager to build their presence in the United States, the monks offered substantial financial support to the temple, pledging to invest in the cost of renovations and building maintenance. This was an attractive proposition, but in a six-to-five vote, Dr. Myint cast the deciding vote against accepting this offer. The monks were dismissed, and the international, non-sectarian nature of the temple was preserved.

Indeed, the first three monks that took residency in the temple represented three different Buddhist traditions, from three different countries. In the early years of Nashville's growing Asian population, the temple became a cultural hub, bringing Buddhists from different traditions and countries of origin together. In these early years, the diverse nature of the temple enriched Buddhist thought in Nashville. However, as different ethnic groups became more firmly planted in the city, many had a desire to practice in their own languages, and a proliferation of temples resulted. Today, Nashville is home to a Cambodian temple in East Nashville, a Laotian temple in Antioch, and the Tibetan Dharma Center in the Berry Hill neighborhood, among others. In 1995, the original temple was sold, and in 2006, the Myints established a new Buddhist temple at this South Nashville location. Though the temple attendees are mostly of Burmese descent, Dr. Myint

continues to hold a vision for the temple as an international, non-sectarian space for all people to come and learn about Buddhism. The Buddhist Temple is located near the intersection of Gatlin Drive and Lyle Lane. Meditation events are open to all and held on Mondays at 7:30 p.m. and on Sundays at 9:00 a.m.

ABOUT THE AUTHORS

Joseph Gutierrez is a Vanderbilt graduate student and Antioch resident; he was assisted by **Dr. Myint**, a native of Burma and a retired mathematics professor at TSU.

NEARBY SITES OF INTEREST

Grandbury's Lunette (Polk Ave., between Hackworth St. and Fiber Glass Rd.): This was the site of a battle between the Confederate army and three Union brigades, including the 1st and 2nd Colored Brigade, on December 15, 1864. Hundreds of Black soldiers—most of whom were formerly enslaved and newly conscripted—lost their lives on that day, in a fight for their, and their descendants', freedom.

4.8 LA HACIENDA TAQUERIA Y SUPERMERCADO

2615 Nolensville Pike,
Nashville, TN 37211

(615) 256-6142
www.lahanashville.com

In March 2005, three Hispanic business owners in Middle Tennessee were killed within a span of eight days. One, Aureliano Ceja, was beaten to death by

Figure 4.11. La Hacienda. Photo courtesy of Learotha Williams Jr.

an intruder after being followed home from La Hacienda Taqueria y Super-Mercado, his family business. Known as the hub of Nashville's Hispanic community, La Hacienda has been a longtime symbol of success for the immigrant population. The restaurant and attached supermarket serve authentic foods and grocery items to Nashville's growing Hispanic population, and also provide traditional tortillas and other products to restaurants across seven states. The success of La Hacienda represents both the economic agency and cultural fortitude of Nashville's Hispanic community. Following Mr. Ceja's brutal murder and a number of robberies of Hispanic-owned businesses, many people believed that Hispanic residents were being targeted for crime. With political rhetoric

labeling undocumented immigrants as "illegal aliens" and making threats of deportation, some people assumed that Latinos would not report crimes to the police for fear of having their immigration status questioned, thus making them vulnerable to attack. There was some truth to this assumption; many in the immigrant community lived in increasing fear of their own victimization and did not feel it was safe to call law enforcement.

Within two weeks of Ceja's murder, the Nashville Area Hispanic Chamber of Commerce (NAHCC) delivered a letter to Police Chief Ronal Serpas. Signed by over one hundred Hispanic-owned businesses in Nashville, the letter requested that the Metro Police department ban immigration-related inquiries when

I've spent half of my life in Nashville. Since my first visit in 1992, I've been a tourist, a foreign student visa applicant, an unskilled factory worker, a cook, someone's neighbor with an accent, and occasionally an average José. By 2004 I was serving my first term as the chairman of the Nashville Area Hispanic Chamber of Commerce (NAHCC), an organization I continue to lead. It is a great honor to help represent small businesses and highlight the enormous contributions to the development of Nashville of those who trace their roots to Spanish-speaking countries. The journey of Hispanics in Nashville has made us proud residents of this city. As businesses such as La Hacienda provide economic and cultural sustenance for our population, they have also made us rich in friendships and more certain to call Nashville home.

On September 22, 2006, I became a US citizen. Despite seasonal storms, floods, economic downturns, and even more catastrophic episodes of local immigrant-phobia, our Hispanic community has been and always remained vibrant. And although I first came as a visitor, through my unexpected journey I have become a proud resident of this city.

Yuri Cunza

victims report crimes. Chief Serpas responded immediately, but cautioned that no formal policy would be adopted. In fact, the Metro city government was in the process of adopting a policy that did just the opposite. Under a collaborative agreement with Immigration and Customs Enforcement (ICE) called 287(g), in 2007 the federal government authorized Nashville Sheriff's Department to act as ICE agents, and the results were disastrous. Under this program, any person suspected of being undocumented was taken to jail and screened for immigration status. Regardless of whether there were any other charges, every undocumented immigrant was processed for deportation. After the agreement was created, more than ten thousand Nashvillians—almost exclusively Latino residents—were deported. Nearly 90 percent were charged with nothing but civil immigration violations.

In the face of mass deportations and continued political and physical attacks, Nashville's Hispanic community has grown and thrived, including at this popular restaurant on Nolensville Pike. Yet despite the success embodied by La Hacienda, the Hispanic community has long been portrayed as a community in need. It does in fact need many things: Respect. Appreciation. Cultural and political acknowledgment.

La Hacienda opens daily from 10 a.m. to 9 p.m., and Friday and Saturday until 10 p.m. The adjacent supermarket opens at 8 a.m. and closes with La Hacienda.

ABOUT THE AUTHORS

Yuri Cunza is president of the Nashville Area Hispanic Chamber of Commerce. **Anna Warren** is a graduate of Vanderbilt University's Community Development and Action program.

NEARBY SITES OF INTEREST

Nashville Cares (633 Thompson Ln.): The first and longest operating organization meeting the needs of Tennesseans living with HIV/AIDS.

4.9 WORKERS' DIGNITY

335 Whitsett Rd.,
Nashville, TN 37210

(615) 669-6679
workersdignity.nationbuilder.com

Figure 4.12. Workers Dignity marches to demand that the downtown Sheraton pay unpaid wages to more than thirty workers. Photo courtesy of Workers' Dignity

In 2016, Workers' Dignity bought a six-hundred-square foot house on Whitsett Road. After months of work parties to cut back overgrowth, tear out walls, install new wiring, and clean and paint, the small house now serves as an organizing base for more than four hundred members. Workers' Dignity began in April 2010 as a project designed to address abuses in the workplace. At first, workers arrived seeking help to recover stolen wages. People working in construction, restaurants, cleaning, and elsewhere reported that they were not being paid for their labor. In worker's rights trainings, workers learned how to seek recovery of their wages—from filling out forms about their cases, to writing letters requesting wages due, to planning public direct actions.

The workers who seek assistance from Workers' Dignity have experienced a wide range of workplace abuses, including unpaid overtime, sexual harassment, verbal abuse, discrimination, and modern-day slavery. Every day, more and more workers are speaking up: we're tired of being taken advantage of, and we're coming together to demand respect. As Fanny, a Workers' Dignity member and Sheraton housekeeper, said on one picket line: "We know that this injustice is not a one-time thing. We know this happens to other workers elsewhere. And we will continue standing up." Working together, workers have been able to recover over $1.2 million in stolen wages through direct action campaigns.

While much of the work of Workers' Dignity is in response to workplace abuse, the organization launched a campaign to proactively improve conditions for hospitality workers. Over the years, members learned that many women of color working in Nashville's hotels do so in hazardous and often unlawful conditions, are exposed to toxic cleaning chemicals, and are paid very low wages. These same hotels have received millions of dollars in incentives from the Nashville city government. Workers realized they needed a strategic and concentrated effort to win higher wages and safer workplaces.

In 2013, Workers' Dignity launched the Just Hospitality campaign. Over the course of a year, Workers' Dignity organized hotel workers to create the Cleaning Worker's Bill of Rights, which includes a $15 an hour minimum wage, two weeks of paid sick leave per year, and an end to all discrimination. Workers who united through the Just Hospitality campaign successfully won raises and improved benefits and forced the removal of unethical managers and contractors. From 2015 to 2019, cleaning workers at thirteen hotels, movie theaters, and department stores won over $888,000 in wage increases. Hotel housekeepers formed worker committees and took direct action to improve pay, reduce the number of hotel rooms they had to clean, remove abusive managers, and win back wages they said were stolen by exploitative cleaning agencies or the hotels directly.

The little house on Whitsett Avenue is the hub for all of Workers' Dignity campaigns and hosts other social justice groups as well. Thanks in part to the art- and drum-making workshops in advance of every action, Workers' Dignity is known for organizing some of the highest-energy actions in Nashville. In addition, Workers' Dignity is the home of WDYO 104.1FM, Music City's first-ever radio station owned and operated by low-wage workers. Dignity, onward! Onward with our struggle! Yes, we can!

ABOUT THE AUTHORS

Mariana López and **Kelly Waller** are former hotel workers and members of the Workers' Dignity steering committee. Mariana López is also one of the founders of Workers' Dignity.

NEARBY SITES OF INTEREST

La Parroquia Nuestra Señora de Guadalupe (3112 Nolensville Pike): This Catholic church is a key part of Nashville's Latinx community. The parish has its own priest, offers mass in Spanish, and provides many services to the community, including childcare, a food pantry, GED classes, and legal consultations.

4.10 GLOBAL MALL AT THE CROSSINGS
5252 Hickory Hollow Pkwy., Antioch, TN 37013

"Just more" was the slogan in the 1978 pamphlet for Tennessee's newest mall in Antioch, located southeast of downtown Nashville. For years, Hickory Hollow Mall *was* Antioch, anchoring the economic activity of the region. With a movie theater, dozens of restaurants, and the best department stores of the time, throughout the 1980s and '90s Hickory Hollow Mall was abuzz with social activity.

And yet, beginning in the early 2000s, Antioch became synonymous with delinquency. As its reputation worsened, several regional attractions in the area were abandoned, closed, and even razed to the ground. Harding Mall was demolished to make room for a new Walmart, Starwood

Figure 4.13. Southeast Branch of the Nashville Public Library. Designed by HBM Architects with Lose & Associates as architect of record. Photo courtesy of Tonda McKay

Aggarwal, the mall celebrates the diversity that once drew stigma to the community and is now filled with local entrepreneurs "representing Asian, African, Indian, Latino, and Middle Eastern culture." Nashville State Community College set up shop in the vacated Dillard's, the Nashville Public Library and Metro Parks opened a regional community center and a library branch where JCPenney once was, and the Ford Ice Center doubled the ice rinks available for public recreation in Nashville.

On any given day at` Global Mall at the Crossings, one can find moms in hijabs visiting as their kids play in the park, African American couples jogging with their dogs or strollers around the track, young college students heading to and from classes at Nashville State, and high-energy, multiethnic, and multigenerational Zumba classes. A new Antioch is emerging, embracing its diversity as a community asset, and learning to advocate for its interests. To get to the mall from downtown, take I-24 East to Exit 59, turn left on Bell Road, then turn left on Hickory Hollow Parkway. The mall entrance will be on the right. The mall is open 8 a.m. until 8 p.m., Monday through Saturday, and 12 p.m. to 6 p.m. on Sunday.

Amphitheatre was abandoned 2007, and by 2012, Hickory Hollow Mall was left hanging with only a handful of department stores. The perception of Nashville residents that Hickory Hollow and Antioch were dangerous was coupled with a growing immigrant population in the area. Local media outlets began streaming a steady flow of reports on crime in the area, and some enclaves within the Antioch region began to avoid associating with Antioch's now toxic name. Forming smaller communities called Cane Ridge, Brentioch, or just Southeast Nashville, the region was soon too disjointed to offer a counternarrative to the growing public sentiment that Antioch was a place to be feared and avoided. However, Hickory Hollow Mall may now be anchoring a new era in the region's history.

In 2013, the mall reopened with a new name, Global Mall at the Crossings. Created with the leadership of Middle Tennessee State University professor Rajesh

ABOUT THE AUTHORS

Dan Moranville is a youth programming consultant and has lived in South Nashville and Antioch for ten years. **Marcus Lyons** is a school counselor in Antioch, a featured speaker at conferences and workshops, and a gifted songwriter.

NEARBY SITES OF INTEREST

Antioch Community Center (5023 Blue Hole Rd.): The Center features the public art installation *Liquid 615*, consisting of 240 hand-blown glass drops which are illuminated at night. Constructed to honor the Antioch community's experience of the 2010 flood, the drops represent the floodwaters and the tears of the residents affected by the flood.

4.11 HANDS ON NASHVILLE URBAN FARM

361 Wimpole Dr.,
Nashville, TN 37211

(615) 298-1108

For years, volunteers arriving at the Hands On Nashville Urban Farm off of Murfreesboro Pike would be struck by the lush, tall grasses and trees, rows of growing fruits and vegetables, and the peaceful environment nestled between the single-family homes on Wimpole Drive. Only a stone's throw from I-24 and a couple of miles from the airport, the five-acre farm, owned by the Nashville Parks and Recreation Department, was operated by Hands On Nashville

Figure 4.14. Hands On Nashville Urban Farm. Photo courtesy of Learotha Williams Jr.

(HON), a nonprofit organization that connects volunteers to service opportunities. Public walkways, part of a city greenway system that leads to Mill Creek, wind through the fruit trees, garden beds, and a riparian buffer of tall grass.

The proximity of the farm to Mill Creek is actually the reason for its existence. Prior to the massive flood of 2010, homes stood here. The properties directly abutting the creek were completely destroyed by the flood, and a number of other homes were significantly damaged, condemned, and eventually purchased by the city. Through a partnership between the Mayor's Office, Nashville Parks and Recreation, Hands On Nashville, and hundreds of community volunteers, the empty lots were transformed into an urban farm. The riparian buffer, which supports runoff drainage through natural materials, was established to prevent future flooding from washing out the area again. Neighbors have noted that prior to the riparian buffer, flooding occurred annually, but since its installation the area has been flood-free.

For a decade, the Urban Farm served as a park, classroom, and nutritious food source for Nashville. Each year, hundreds of young people and adults visited the farm throughout the growing season, helping with maintenance while learning about urban agriculture and nutrition. The food grown on site was used for educational programs, and a portion of the crop was donated to the Nashville Food Project to provide healthy, local produce to Nashvillians with limited food access. The farm was one of several initiatives throughout Nashville working to promote healthy eating habits, combat food insecurity, and increase access to affordable and high-quality food. Though activities on this site were impacted by the 2020 tornado, HON coordinates volunteer opportunities at other local farms. To learn more, visit HON's website, www.hon.org.

ABOUT THE AUTHOR

Katie Goodman is a graduate of Vanderbilt University's Community Development and Action program and a former volunteer for the HON Urban Farm and Crop City Program.

NEARBY SITES OF INTEREST

Whitsett Park and Mill Creek Greenway
(375 Wimpole Dr.): Need to stretch your legs? Visit this park born out of the damaging 2010 flood, which connects to a 1.5-mile greenway that crosses Mills Creek.

4.12 SALAHADEEN CENTER

364 Elysian Fields Ct.,
Nashville, TN 37211

(615) 333-0530

The heart of Nashville's Kurdish community rests in an unassuming building off Nolensville Pike. Home to the largest Kurdish population outside of the Middle East, this area has earned the mantle "Little Kurdistan." The Kurdish people are a diverse ethnic group whose population, estimated at thirty-five million, primarily resides throughout Iraq, Iran, Syria, Turkey and Russia. Ethnic, religious, and political conflicts in the Middle East have left the Kurds vulnerable to attack, most significantly under Saddam Hussein's murderous reign, which killed over one hundred thousand Kurds in northern Iraq. Since the 1970s, more than three million Kurdish people have been displaced from their homelands. Approximately thirteen thousand of those have resettled in Nashville, choosing the city because of its relative affordability and its proximity to Fort Campbell, where many were received when they first came to America.

There have been several waves of Kurdish refugees to the city, most of them coming from Iraq. Indeed, the number of Iraqi refugees is so significant that the city hosts one of the few US voting sites in which Iraqi refugees are able to vote in Iraqi elections. While the earliest refugees came to Nashville with limited

Figure 4.15. Salahadeen Center. Photo courtesy of Joseph Gutierrez

English language skills or formal education, later refugees were educated professionals with experience working in humanitarian organizations in Iraq. Troubled by the lack of a community center, and particularly concerned about the needs of their elders, in 1998, a group came together to rent a space for the community to gather socially and spiritually. The refugees quickly outgrew the original building (now the home of the Mazi International Food Market), and within three years, they purchased the adjacent buildings and opened the Salahadeen Center. Center leaders credit their growth to both the commitment of the Kurdish people in Nashville and the generosity of allies.

Today the Center serves more than ten thousand people each year, providing a wide range of programs and services that include interfaith activities, educational programs, health clinics, civic education, dispute resolution, and assistance for new Kurdish arrivals to Nashville. The Center also offers daily prayer services, which are attended by Muslims of all backgrounds and nationalities. Established due to a concern for elders, the Salahadeen Center is now focused on addressing the needs of Kurdish youth. The Center owns eleven acres in Antioch where the community graveyard is located, as well as soccer fields and a small auxiliary community center. Plans are underway to open a multi-sport complex on the site.

The Salahdeen Center was founded with the belief that if opportunities are created for people to build community with one another—socially and spiritually—people will help one another thrive. With a strong community, people can address one another's needs and work through difficulties, and many problems fall away. Anyone is welcome to visit the Center, and the many Kurdish markets and restaurants nearby offer some of the best baklava and naan in the city. Little Kurdistan is one of many hidden gems that make Nashville such a thriving, diverse city.

ABOUT THE AUTHORS

Mohammed Kokoy has been in Nashville since 2003 and is a member of the Center's Education Committee. **Nawzad Hawrami** has been in Nashville since 1998, is a founding member of the Center, and serves as a board member and office administrator.

NEARBY SITES OF INTEREST

Little Kurdistan (the area of Nolensville Pike surrounding the Salahadeen Center): Follow your nose and visit the numerous Kurdish markets and restaurants, several of which feature traditional Tandoor ovens and serve up fresh breads and naan daily.

4.13 NASHVILLE ZOO AT GRASSMERE

3777 Nolensville Pike, Nashville, TN 37211

(615) 833-1534

The Nashville Zoo at Grassmere is a two-hundred-acre zoo and historic plantation farmhouse located six miles southeast of downtown Nashville. The Grassmere farmland and farmhouse were designated to be used for nature study by the last generation of Grassmere's owners, sisters Margaret and Elise Croft. The historic farmhouse was built in 1810 by enslaved people owned by Margaret and Elise's great-great-grandfather, Colonel Michael C. Dunn. Thereafter, Grassmere was passed down to the sisters through four generations. After the abolition of slavery, Margaret and Elise's mother and her three sisters ran the farm. One of their aunts, Leila Shute Tigert, managed the farm from the early 1900s until her death in 1952. Ms. Tigert was well known for her commitment to sustainable farming methods, paying farm workers a living wage, and ensuring safe working conditions.

After Ms. Tigert passed, Margaret and Elise Croft inherited the property and managed the farm with the assistance of the Morton family, tenant farmers, and descendants of the enslaved inhabitants of Grassmere Farm. In the early 1960s, at the height of urban development of former agricultural land in south Nashville, the city of Nashville attempted to negotiate the purchase of the property from the Croft sisters. Margaret and Elise Croft declined an offer from the city of over a million dollars for the three-hundred-acre property. Committed to the preservation of wildlife and a love of nature, in 1964 the sisters entered into an agreement with the Children's Museum of Nashville. The agreement stated that the museum would pay property taxes and assist with the upkeep of the home while

Figure 4.16. (above) The Nashville Zoo. Photo courtesy of Learotha Williams Jr.

Figure 4.17. (below) Marie spending quality time with female red kangaroos during her time as an interpreter in Kangaroo Kickabout at the Nashville Zoo. Photo courtesy of Marie Campbell

would be maintained as a "nature study center," preserved to educate the public about animals and the environment.

When Nashville Metro acquired the property in 1990, the city was bound by the will of the Croft sisters to preserve the property as a nature center. The Nashville Zoo opened on the Grassmere site in 1997. Today, the Nashville Zoo is a progressive and dynamic zoological park serving Middle Tennessee, southern Kentucky, and hundreds of thousands of tourists who travel to Nashville every year. The mission of Nashville Zoo is to inspire a culture of understanding and discovery of our natural world through conservation, innovation, and leadership. The zoo's experienced staff is actively involved in research, habitat protection, breeding programs, and education initiatives both onsite and around the world.

the sisters lived the remainder of their lives at Grassmere. The sisters placed one stipulation in their agreement with the museum: upon their death, the property

Staff are committed to carefully managing the breeding of species in order to maintain a healthy and self-sustaining captive population that is both genetically diverse and demographically stable. Now listed on the National Register of Historic Homes, the Grassmere Historic Home is open seasonally for guided tours to tell the story of Margaret and Elise Croft. Farm grounds include a three-tier heirloom garden, the family cemetery, a carriage barn, tool shed, livestock barn, slave cabin, and slave cemetery containing the remains of twenty African Americans who were enslaved by the Dune and Shute families. More information about the Nashville Zoo can be found at www.nashvillezoo.org.

ABOUT THE AUTHOR

Marie Campbell is a former educator at the Nashville Zoo.

NEARBY SITES OF INTEREST

Travellers Rest Plantation and Museum
(636 Farrell Pkwy.): This 1,050-acre plantation is best known as the former residence of the prominent Tennessee lawyer and judge John Overton. The lives of the approximately eighty enslaved persons who lived, and in many cases died, on site are less well known. Even less attention has been paid to the Indigenous people who first lived on the land.

5. SOUTHWEST

5.1 Capers Memorial Christian Methodist Episcopal Church   188

5.2 Local 257 American Federation of Musicians   190

5.3 Nashville Songwriters Association International   192

5.4 Music Row / Quonset Hut   194

5.5 Edgehill United Methodist Church   196

5.6 Edgehill Village   198

5.7 Scarritt Bennett Center   199

5.8 Roger Williams University   201

5.9 Vanderbilt Divinity School   202

5.10 Confederate Memorial Hall   205

5.11 Memorial Gymnasium   207

5.12 Vanderbilt Kirkland Hall / Occupy Vanderbilt   209

5.13 Centennial Park   211

5.14 The Parthenon   213

5.15 Fannie Mae Dees Park   215

5.16 International Market and Restaurant   217

5.17 Carver Food Park   218

5.18 CCA/CoreCivic   220

5.19 Glendale Baptist Church   222

5.20 Radnor Lake   224

5.21 Gordon Jewish Community Center   226

5.22 Aaittafama' Archeological Park   228

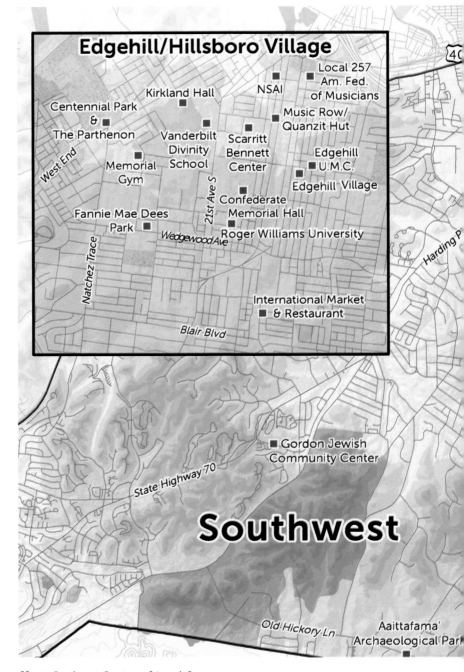

Map 7. Southwest. Courtesy of Joseph Speer

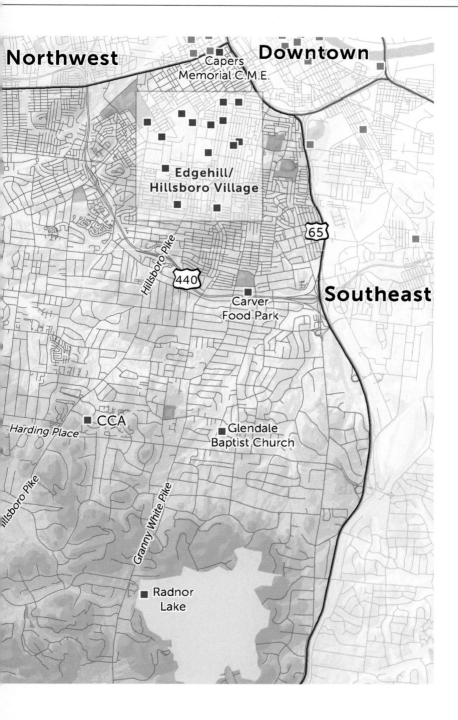

Northwest

Downtown

Capers
Memorial C.M.E.

Edgehill/
Hillsboro Village

Hillsboro Pike

65

440

Carver
Food Park

Southeast

CCA

Harding Place

Glendale
Baptist Church

Hillsboro Pike

Granny White Pike

Radnor
Lake

AN INTRODUCTION TO SOUTHWEST NASHVILLE

SOUTHWEST NASHVILLE IS DISTINGUISHED by some of the city's most starkly segregated neighborhoods, most prominent institutions, and most beloved recreation areas. Though this area is home to the historically Black neighborhood of Edgehill and borders the predominantly Black area of North Nashville, more than 80 percent of the region's residents are White, and Southwest Nashville is Davidson County's most affluent community. The region has been home to important preservation efforts as well as pilfering and profiteering. As a result of resident leadership, Southwest Nashville holds two of the county's most prized recreation areas, Percy Warner Park and Radnor Lake. Yet, while environmental conservation has been championed by some, cultural preservation has often been eschewed. Over the course of centuries prior to European contact, tens of thousands of prehistoric Indigenous people were buried in the territory referred to as Noel Cemetery, which surrounds the intersection of Harding Road and Granny White Pike. In a shockingly expansive act of grave robbing, in 1888, a wealthy Nashville businessman paid to have stone box graves dug up and burial offerings removed for his own collection. Within two years, an estimated four thousand graves were destroyed. As traced by a number of entries in this chapter, struggles for land justice continue in the current era, including efforts by Indigenous advocates to protect sacred sites and organizing by low-income tenants to protect affordable housing.

Over time, the region's most wealthy families have played a key role in shaping this region. Beyond the 440 Parkway are a number of suburban centers, including Green Hills, Sylvan Park, and Bellevue, and these

Figure 5.1. Full moon over Vanderbilt Medical Center. Photo courtesy of Sharon Shields

West Nashville, these lines enabled easy transportation for affluent Whites to move westward. The expansion of the West Nashville suburbs led to a greater demand for businesses, schools, parks, and elite clubs. Some of these new areas were elite enclaves by design; Belle Meade, for example, remains an independent city from Nashville. The growing belt of privilege in Southwest Nashville allowed wealthy White families to maintain distance from Black residential centers in the city (though these were also areas where Black residents lived, first as slaves), and simultaneously pushed poor White farmers closer to the county line. Later, as Nashville schools were forced by the courts to integrate, a proliferation of private schools spread through this region, supporting White flight from public education.

neighborhoods are also among the most affluent in Nashville. Much of the wealth derived here can be traced directly to slavery. One of the first European Americans to settle in Southwest Nashville was John Harding, who in 1806, bought 250 acres of land alongside Richland Creek. He eventually grew his farm into the Belle Meade Plantation, which still stands today. Harding was among Tennessee's largest slave owners during this period, and slave labor in trade, agricultural, and domestic work created enormous wealth for the Harding family. Travelling through this region, you will notice that Nashville celebrates many of its early slaveholders in street names such as Harding Pike.

The expansion of family-owned estates on the outskirts of Nashville was accelerated by the introduction of the streetcar in 1872. Connecting downtown to

Closer to the city, the Southwest region was shaped by powerful institutional anchors, many of which are profiled in this chapter. Residential neighborhoods formed around Belmont and Vanderbilt Universities, attracting professors and other White professionals, and by the 1940s, the nearby Edgehill neighborhood had also become home to middle

Figure 5.2. 1951 Construction on Edgehill at Twenty-First Avenue South. Photo courtesy of Nashville Metro Archives

income and professional Blacks. A Black business district once thrived in Edgehill. Here one could find a Black attorney, drug store, funeral home, and a rooming house for traveling musicians unable to stay at the segregated hotels downtown. As explored in this chapter, Edgehill soon faced encroachment from Music Row, the commercial heart of Nashville's music industry. Indeed, Edgehill has faced numerous threats, including urban renewal freeway construction and state-supported expansions of Music Row and the universities. Yet the neighborhood is also home to some of the most sustained resident-led Black organizing in the city, much of which has been and is still anchored by several historic religious institutions. These include Bethel African Methodist Episcopal (1866), Kayne Avenue Baptist (1882), Bass Street Baptist (1887), Lea Avenue Christian (1892), and Mt. Sinai Primitive Baptist (c. 1890) churches. The activism that emerged during the 1960s led to the founding of Edgehill United Methodist Church (1966), an institution that remains one of the most welcoming spaces in the Music City. For many years, the African American Church Publishing House was located at nearby 500 Eighth Avenue South, serving as a visible institutional anchor to this community.

Edgehill is a community whose history chronicles a persistent cultural and economic contest for space in Nashville. Early twentieth-century Edgehill emerged from the hopes and desires of African Americans who migrated to the city during the Civil War and the era of Jim Crow seeking better opportunities for their families and descendants. Some enjoyed spectacular success against long odds, while others struggled and sometimes collapsed under a city that was resolute in its commitment to racial inequality. Today the churches and schools referenced in the pages that follow stand as monuments to their struggle for equality for all Nashville's citizens, yet these institutions still fight to survive as they confront some of the most aggressive gentrification in the city. Notable examples include the effort by many in the community to protect the land around Fort Negley, a Civil War site recently designated as a UNESCO Site of Memory, from development. The workspace of Nashville's autodidactic sculptor, William Edmondson, who was a member of Nashville's first generation of African Americans who were not born under the curse of slavery, has also caught the eye of developers seeking to build on a property whose value seems to increase daily.

This chapter also features nearby Hillsboro Village, a predominantly White neighborhood that was also targeted by urban renewal, and also organized—with varying degrees of success—to protect their community. As entries in this chapter attest, the universities, churches, and Music Row businesses continue to be significant forces in this region, at times fostering intellectual, moral, cultural, and spiritual development, and at other moments deepening inequalities and fueling gentrification. We encourage you to explore the Southwest with all your senses—trekking through the region's stunning parks, enjoying the talents of area musicians, and reflecting on how patterns of wealth and privilege become concentrated in certain landscapes of the city.

ABOUT THE AUTHORS

Vanderbilt graduate students **Shea Davis, Dawn Harris, Bethany Hertrick, Fiona Hoehn, Katy Morgan, Elise Krews, Tilden Davis,** and **Janelle Wommer** contributed to this introduction.

5.1 CAPERS MEMORIAL CHRISTIAN METHODIST EPISCOPAL CHURCH

319 15th Ave. N., Nashville, TN 37203
(615) 329-2082

In a Bible Belt city like Nashville, one might easily stroll past Capers Memorial Christian Methodist Episcopal (CME) Church and assume it is simply one of many Nashville churches, rather than one of a kind. On any given Thursday, if you walk through a side door entrance to a basement fellowship hall, you will likely find Mrs. Fannie Hyde-Perry and Mrs. Terra Ridley kneeling and serving lunch to unhoused Nashvillians.

These walls tell the story of Capers Memorial: of humble beginnings,

Figure 5.3. Capers Memorial Christian Methodist Episcopal Church. Photo courtesy of Learotha Williams Jr.

resilience, and remarkable leadership. With ties to the earliest settlers in the region and roots in American Methodism itself, Capers began in 1832 as the "African Mission." On Christmas Day 1853, the African Mission congregation dedicated a church in honor of Methodist Episcopal bishop William C. Capers, a preacher and missionary responsible for establishing thirty slave missions across the region. After the turmoil of the Civil War, the church aligned with the newly cemented Colored Methodist Episcopal denomination, and in 1887, moved to a new site near present day Twelfth Avenue and Church Street.

A number of historic persons and events flowed through the church through the twentieth century. In 1911,

the Bethlehem Center began in the basement of Capers. This neighborhood-based community center provided a kindergarten, well-baby clinic, and recreation program for Nashville's impoverished African American population. When Capers moved to its current site in 1925, Bethlehem soon followed and set up directly across the street. The McKissack & McKissack Architectural Firm designed and built the 1925 location. The McKissacks, lifetime Capers members and descendants of liberated slaves, were the first licensed Black architects in the southeast. Capers Memorial Church was also the preaching home of Bishop Joseph A. Johnson Jr. In 1953, Vanderbilt University admitted Bishop Johnson as its first Black student, and in 1984 the University dedicated the Bishop Johnson Black Cultural Center in his name. Capers Memorial was also the site where Civil Rights leaders announced the lifting of the merchant boycott during the Nashville sit-ins of the early 1960s.

Caper's Memorial CME Church stands today as one of the Music City's most historic African American sites. While it remains a symbol of African American ingenuity and independence, it is also representative of the constant struggle between memory and marginalization. The historic site today holds the dubious distinction of being listed on Historic Nashville's Endangered Properties List. If substantive steps are not taken to preserve the site, the church is in danger of being demolished, risking the prospect of being erased from public memory. Visitors to the historic church are welcome. For more information, visit www.southeast1cme.church/capers-memorial-cma-church.

ABOUT THE AUTHOR

Reverend William Cole Sr. is the lead pastor of Capers Memorial CME Church. **Seth Gulsby** is a graduate of Vanderbilt University's Community Development and Action program.

NEARBY SITES OF INTEREST

Bethlehem Centers of Nashville (1417 Charlotte Ave.): This nonprofit family resource center serves the North Nashville community.

5.2 NASHVILLE MUSICIANS ASSOCIATION, AFM LOCAL 257

11 Music Circle N.,
Nashville, TN 37203

Tucked in an unassuming building on Music Row is the Nashville chapter of the American Federation of Musicians (AFM), the world's largest organization representing the interests of professional musicians. Though the physical space occupied by the union is not in and of itself a tourist destination, it would be hard to dismiss Local 257's influence throughout Nashville and to the city's most popular export—music. Nashville's Local 257 was established in 1902. For much of the twentieth century, the AFM did not welcome African Americans in the Union. As the intimacy experienced between Black musicians and White audiences created an environment abhorrent to many Southern segregationists, it was not until the 1960s that many chapters admitted Black members.

Today, the organization boasts over 2,200 members, making it the third largest AFM chapter in the United States, behind only Los Angeles and New York City. Local 257 creates wage standards for live, touring, and studio musicians. The local negotiates and administers the collective bargaining agreements of the musicians of the Nashville Symphony, the musicians who perform at the Grand Ole Opry, and those affiliated with the TV show *Nashville*, among others. In 2015,

Figure 5.4. Nashville Musicians Association, AFM Local 257 president Dave Pomeroy speaks on Capitol Hill in support of unified legislation to recognize performance rights for musicians and recording artists whose music is played on AM/FM radio. Photo courtesy of Music First Coalition

more than $11 million in scale wages were paid to musicians through Local 257.

Nashville is known worldwide for its incredible array of studios and session players, who have made many of the most well-known hit songs and albums in music history. In addition to many "star" members, Local 257 is home to an amazing creative community of working musicians whose names music fans may not recognize, but who excel in virtually every style of music from country to rock, blues, and orchestral work. Though the life of a working musician is sometimes perceived as glamorous, it is hard work, and the union's role is to promote respect and fair pay for these workers, whether in recording studios, clubs, or concert venues around the world.

Visitors may encounter working musicians in Lower Broadway's honky-tonks and bars, which serve as training grounds for new musicians. There is an oversupply of musicians willing to take these gigs. This results in "norms" that enable bar owners to pay musicians a very low nightly wage with the assumption this will be supplemented by tips. Local 257 has worked tirelessly to help the musicians of Lower Broadway with the day-to-day issues that make their jobs even harder. Tips are where these musicians make the most money, so offer what you can when you visit these venues.

On a larger scale, the AFM collaborates with local and federal governments and businesses to promote fair pay and better working conditions for musicians.

For example, AFM has lobbied Congress in Washington, DC, for royalties for musicians whose recordings are played on AM/FM radio, worked with the Metro Nashville government to create musician loading zones for the clubs on Lower Broadway, and established a formal policy with the Department of Transportation, the FAA, and airlines allowing musicians to store their instruments in the overhead bins when flying. Local 257's impact on Music City is felt every time music is recorded, sold, and performed in Nashville and around the world. The union's work in building a culture and infrastructure of respect and fair pay for musicians is essential to Nashville's creative community and the music industry.

While the AFM Local 257 is not equipped to host visitors, its location on Music Circle is an excellent place to start a self-guided walking tour of Music Row or view some of Nashville's public art. The best place to see the Local 257 in action is by visiting the many live music venues around Nashville.

ABOUT THE AUTHORS

Dave Pomeroy, president of AFM Local 257, is a bassist, writer, and producer; his website is www.davepomeroy.com. **Rachel Skaggs** is a Nashville native and sociologist who studies jobs in culture industries.

NEARBY SITES OF INTEREST

Musica (Roundabout at 16th Ave. S. and Division St.): You can't miss these nine nude, fifteen-foot dancers celebrating the musical soul of the city.

5.3 NASHVILLE SONGWRITERS ASSOCIATION INTERNATIONAL
1710 Roy Acuff Pl., Nashville, TN 37203

Songwriters are the farmers of the music industry; they feed the world's musical soul. You will find some of the most prolific and acclaimed songwriters at the Nashville Songwriters Association International (NSAI). NSAI is the world's largest not-for-profit songwriter's trade association. It was established in 1967, at a time when there were about eighty professional songwriters in Nashville. While famous artists and groups are the faces of the music industry familiar to the public, most songs are written by professional songwriters largely unknown outside of Nashville. These writers are the foundation of the music community. NSAI's motto is "It All Begins with a Song."

Over the past few years, the professional songwriting profession has been decimated. Songwriter royalties are governed by legislation, and in the streaming era, songwriter payments have declined to the point that there are now 90 percent fewer professional songwriters. While in the past, a songwriter's career could last a decade, now it may last but a few years. In response, NSAI is working to change restrictions imposed by the government on royalties.

Figure 5.5. The Music Mill, home of the Nashville Songwriters Association International (NSAI). Photo courtesy of Learotha Williams Jr.

James Madison wrote Article 1, Section 8 of the US Constitution—the copyright clause that provides authors and inventors with exclusive rights "to their respective writings and discoveries." Believing that the new nation would succeed based on ideas and intellectual creations, Madison understood that intellectual property had value. Yet regulations passed by Congress in 1909 and consent decrees imposed in 1941 undercut the intellectual property rights of songwriters. While a record label representing a recording artist can usually set the price for their product, songwriters are required to allow the use of their songs regardless of what they are paid. In other words, while a recording artist can "pull their songs from Spotify" or a similar service, a songwriter cannot, putting them at a disadvantage in the music marketplace. In response, NSAI has worked on hundreds of pieces of state and national legislation to enact laws to improve the viability of the songwriting profession.

Although NSAI began as an advocacy organization, it has expanded its services to help up-and-coming songwriters with their careers. NSAI introduces potential co-writers, organizes seminars on song-writing techniques and how to navigate the music industry, and helps international songwriters get visas to come to the United States. As a result of its advocacy and support services, NSAI has been instrumental in encouraging the careers of many successful songwriters.

NSAI is headquartered in Nashville's historic Music Mill building on Music Row. Built on the success of the country band Alabama, this building housed a publishing company, a label, and a recording studio, and helped launch the careers of KT Oslin, Reba McEntire, Toby Keith, Shania Twain, Billy Ray Cyrus, and the Kentucky Headhunters. The careers of America's future songwriters are still fostered in this building every single day.

ABOUT THE AUTHORS

Rachel Skaggs is a Nashville native and sociologist who studies jobs in culture industries. **Bart Herbison** is executive director of NSAI, and **Krista Darting** is director of development at NSAI.

NEARBY SITES OF INTEREST

Owen Bradley Park (1 Music Square E.): This small park is named after Owen Bradley, one of Nashville's most prominent country music producers.

5.4 MUSIC ROW / QUONSET HUT

34 Music Square E.,
Nashville, TN 37203

The section of Nashville known as Music Row has seen its fortunes rise and fall more than once. The area became popular when an electric streetcar line opened along what is now Sixteenth Avenue South in 1895 and White middle-class families were drawn to the area's large homes. By the early 1950s, property values had declined and many of the original homes were converted into boarding houses and apartments for students at nearby colleges.

Attracted by reasonable prices and the proximity to downtown, Owen and Harold Bradley moved their recording studio from nearby Hillsboro Village to a Victorian-era home located at 804 Sixteenth Avenue South, opening their doors in 1955. Country, rockabilly, bluegrass, and R&B recordings soon poured from the Quonset hut studio attached to the back of the house (a portion of the hut's arched roof is still visible from a rear parking lot).

Artists playing an important role in the Row's early days were not all male: Patsy Cline, Brenda Lee, and Loretta Lynn made number one recordings here. Nor were they all White: in the early 1960s country-soul singer Arthur Alexander wrote and recorded songs that were later covered by the Beatles. Charley Pride, the first Black country

star, recorded hits on Music Row, and co-owned Pi-Gem Music, one of the Row's most successful music publishers in the 1970s and '80s.

By the late 1960s, Music Row contained the most highly concentrated collection of music-related businesses in the world, but the area provided enough affordable space for startup businesses and residents, including entry-level musicians and songwriters. Yet music executives and city leaders almost destroyed it. Under an urban renewal proposal known as the Boulevard Plan, every building along the west side of Sixteenth Avenue South from Wedgewood to Division—stretching a solid mile—was slated by the city for demolition to make room for a six-lane, divided highway. Music Row corporations purchased real estate along the route and touted plans to replace the area's period historic homes and apartment buildings with new multistory buildings. After years of debate and fierce opposition by residents, including those living in the nearby historically Black neighborhood of Edgehill, the Boulevard Plan was dropped.

Since the early 2000s, the music industry has struggled with a loss of sales due to the growth of the Internet. Mergers, staff cuts, and vacancies on Music Row have increased. At the same time, a boom in Nashville's growth has intensified pressure to redevelop Music Row. From 2012 to 2015, thirty-five buildings on the Row were demolished for redevelopment projects. In 2014,

Figure 5.6. (above) New releases are promoted along Music Row. Photo courtesy of Amie Thurber
Figure 5.7. (left) Original Quonset. Image courtesy of the Grand Ole Opry Archives. Photo courtesy of Sid O'Berry

a pro-preservation group of artists and philanthropists barely saved RCA Victor Studio A from the wrecking ball. Nashville's Metro Council placed a moratorium on new building projects on the Row in 2016. Still, the question remains: in the face of increasing development pressures, will Music City be able to preserve the Row's historic buildings and legendary character as a music center?

For the time being, Music Row remains an anchor of the music industry in Nashville. To visit, stroll along Sixteenth and Seventeenth Avenues South between Wedgewood Avenue and Division Street. Take a tour of historic RCA Studio B and other recording studios where legendary artists made groundbreaking records. You'll be walking the same sidewalks as they did!

ABOUT THE AUTHOR

J. Hunter Moore is an active resident of the Hillsboro-West End neighborhood, a writer, musician, and Fulbright scholar.

NEARBY SITES OF INTEREST

RCA Studio B (1611 Roy Acuff Pl.): This iconic recording studio played a leading role in the development of the smooth subgenre of country music known as "the Nashville sound." Tours of the studio are run daily by the Country Music Hall of Fame.

5.5 EDGEHILL UNITED METHODIST CHURCH

1502 Edgehill Ave.,
Nashville, TN 37212

(615) 254-7628

Edgehill United Methodist Church (EUMC) was founded in 1966 in the community room at Gernert Apartments on Twelfth Avenue South. Troubled by the brutality of 1960s segregation in the urban South, Edgehill native and newly ordained Methodist pastor Bill Barnes envisioned an integrated, urban church that would serve as a place of healing, justice, and reconciliation in Nashville. What better place for the church than Edgehill, one of Nashville's first Black neighborhoods, adjacent to the historically White Vanderbilt and Belmont campuses? While Barnes' focus on racial integration was initially met with skepticism from both White and Black churchgoers, the congregation's wholehearted commitment to the struggles of

neighborhood residents bridged the racial divide. In 1967, the budding congregation moved into the house at 1502 Edgehill Avenue where it still resides today.

EUMC's founding came on the heels of urban renewal, a federal program designed to revitalize inner cities, usually with little, if any, input from the communities who lived in them. In Edgehill, many Black-owned homes and businesses were forcibly acquired through eminent domain and demolished when deemed substandard or inconsistent with the planned improvements. New freeways cut off the neighborhood from other parts of the city. As urban renewal ravaged Edgehill, residents moved out of the neighborhood and only a handful of local businesses survived.

The original Edgehill plan dealt with the loss of housing by concentrating low-income apartments in areas isolated from more desirable real estate. The result was a proposal to build almost seven hundred units of public housing right next to an existing low-income complex. While residents appreciated the need for affordable housing, many were outraged at this plan to appropriate land from Black communities, fearing it would tear apart the long-existing social fabric and isolate housing projects from shops, restaurants, and grocery stores.

EUMC played a key role in the fight to stop the damage to Edgehill. Rev. Barnes, Metro Councilor Mansfield Douglas, civil rights attorney Avon Williams, and other Edgehill residents filed a federal lawsuit

Figure 5.8. Early members of Edgehill United Methodist Church. Photo from the Edgehill United Methodist Church collection

House, South Nashville Youth Organization, HOPE Inc., Luke 14:12, Tennessee Hunger Coalition, Second Harvest Food Bank, Project Return, and Tennesseans for Fair Taxation are just a few of the organizations with roots in EUMC. The Brighter Days after-school and summer program, which started in the church sanctuary over twenty-five years ago, continues to be another vital contribution to the life of the church and the Edgehill community. The life and legacy of Edgehill United Methodist Church lies in the many acts of love and justice committed by its people.

against the proposal. Through swift and organized action, the Edgehill Committee (which later became the Organized Neighbors of Edgehill) pressured the housing authority to cancel plans for the project. Instead, the housing authority used a federal program called Turnkey III to build single-family, rent-to-own homes. Nevertheless, much harm had been done. Businesses in Edgehill had all but disappeared, and many residents had been displaced to neighborhoods further south.

Over the years, EUMC has been a hub of social activism, youth development, community organizing, and direct service for those in the Edgehill neighborhood and the city at large. In addition to being one of the earliest racially integrated Methodist congregations in Nashville, EUMC became one of the first churches in the city to openly welcome persons of all sexual and gender orientations. Organized Neighbors of Edgehill, Dialogue

ABOUT THE AUTHOR

Austin Sauerbrei is a former community organizer with the Edgehill Neighborhood Partnership and was assisted by the EUMC archives team and many congregants who contributed their memories of Edgehill past and present.

NEARBY SITES OF INTEREST

Edgehill Polar Bears (12th Ave. S. and Edgehill Ave.): These iconic polar bear statues have been around since the 1930s, although they were originally located elsewhere in the city.

Figure 5.9. Edgehill Village. Photo courtesy of Joseph Gutierrez

5.6 EDGEHILL VILLAGE

1202 Villa Pl.,
Nashville, TN 37212

Known by some as the "cafeteria for
Music Row," Edgehill Village plays the
role of both nighttime hot spot and a
manifestation of an increasingly changing neighborhood. Under the title of a
"mixed-used urban space," this nearly
sixty-thousand-square-foot former
steam laundry is often buzzing with activity. Edgehill Village is currently home
to about twenty different businesses
and restaurants that lease space across
eight buildings. At nearly any time of
day, these buildings are filled with both
locals and musicians from around the
globe, who stop for a quick bite to eat
while taking a break from recording on
Music Row.

Edgehill Vil-
lage also represents
a larger trend of
gentrification that
has transformed the
once predominantly
Black neighborhood
into a largely afflu-
ent, White space.
Built in the 1920s,
the building was
home to the his-
toric White Way
Cleaners, a Black-
owned steam laun-
dry that operated
for decades on the corner of Edgehill Ave.
and Villa Place. Opened at a time when
no one had dryers at home, White Way—
for much of its history only serving White
patrons—operated on the site into the
1990s. Although a number of concerns
have been raised in recent years regarding the impact of dry-cleaning toxins in
the area groundwater and soil, many still
mourn the loss of this and other Black-
owned businesses that long anchored the
neighborhood.

In the early 2000s, as the surrounding neighborhood began to gentrify, the
old White Way building was transformed
into a high-end commercial hub. In
recent years, the price of homes throughout the area has exploded as speculative
real estate investors buy up land, eager
to capitalize on Edgehill's close proximity to Vanderbilt University, Music
Row, and downtown. Between 1999 and

Figure 5.10. White Way Laundry serving the neighborhood in 1938. Image courtesy of Wisconsin Historical Society, image number Whi-26265

5.7 SCARRITT BENNETT CENTER

1008 19th Ave. S.,
Nashville, TN 37212

(615) 340-7500

2010, home values increased over 276 percent in Edgehill compared to an 86 percent county-wide average. As the neighborhood experiences a surge of capital investment and luxury development, many renters and homeowners are fighting desperately to ensure that Edgehill remains a community for middle- and working-class people of color.

ABOUT THE AUTHORS

Austin Sauerbrei is a community organizer with the Edgehill Neighborhood Partnership, a neighborhood organization started by EUMC in 2009. **Mike Thompson** is a graduate of Vanderbilt University's Community Development and Action program.

NEARBY SITES OF INTEREST

Reservoir Park (824 Argyle Ave.): A nice neighborhood park with a playground, sports courts, and picnic areas.

Scarritt Bennett Center's story is more than a century in the making, rich in cultural heritage, and deeply rooted in a commitment to social justice. Its history begins with Scarritt Bible and Training School, established by Southern women in 1892 in Kansas City, Missouri, with a mission of training young women missionaries. The school moved to Nashville in 1924 and became Scarritt College for Christian Workers, a fully accredited undergraduate college for women and men, which operated until its closure in 1988. Today, the Center is a nonprofit conference, retreat, and education center whose mission is to create space where groups and individuals can engage with one another to create a more just world.

Throughout its history, Scarritt fostered a cross-cultural and multiracial learning environment that encouraged its students and faculty to engage in rural, urban, and international work as agents of social change. Scarritt faculty, students, and alumni traveled to countries all over the world and throughout the US to learn about the needs of communities experiencing oppression and injustice, and to work alongside these communities as they struggled for justice. Many Scarritt alumni went on to play prominent leadership roles,

Figure 5.11. Scarritt Bennett Center. Photo courtesy of Learotha Williams Jr.

such as Bishop Abel Muzorewa, a Methodist bishop and nationalist leader who served as prime minister of Zimbabwe (Rhodesia), and Sue Thrasher, a civil rights activist instrumental in forming the Institute for Southern Studies with Julian Bond.

Located in Nashville, the school had a progressive voice and presence in the South, maintained close relationships with neighboring Peabody College and Vanderbilt University, and fostered connections with Fisk University and what was then Tennessee A & I during the segregation era. Scarritt was one of the first White private colleges in Tennessee to integrate. Although the school hosted international students of all races, it was not until 1952 that Lelia Robinson and DeLaris Johnson entered the college as the first full-time African American students. In 1957, Dr. Martin Luther King addressed hundreds of Southern religious leaders in Wightman Chapel during a three-day conference, which explored the role of southern religious organizations in alleviating racial tensions and racial segregation in the South. During the sixties, Scarritt held firm in the midst of backlash against the school's

integration. Notably, faculty and students were involved in the Civil Rights Movement and affiliated with Highlander Folk School, the Student Nonviolent Coordinating Committee (SNCC), and the Southern Student Organizing Committee (SSOC).

Today, Scarritt provides hospitality to groups meeting on campus as well as education for community members promoting the empowerment of women, the eradication of racism, cross-cultural dialogue, and spiritual formation. Visitors are welcome to tour the Scarritt grounds at any time. Built in 1928, the Wightman Chapel was featured in the PBS television series *Designed for Worship* as one of the finest sacred spaces in Nashville. The historic campus also features a labyrinth and outdoor sitting areas for reflection and conversation. Guests may use Parking Lot A or B, both off of Eighteenth Avenue South.

ABOUT THE AUTHOR

Marie Campbell is a former educator at Scarritt.

ADDITIONAL READING

Gregg Michel. *Struggle for a Better South: The Southern Student Organizing Committee, 1964–1969.* New York: Springer, 2004.
Penny Patch. *Deep in Our Hearts: Nine White Women in the Freedom Movement.* Athens: University of Georgia Press, 2000.

NEARBY SITES OF INTEREST

Presbyterian Campus Center (1112 19th Ave. S.): The former Presbyterian Campus Center was on the Scarritt campus and functioned as the center of feminist organizing in Nashville from the 1960s through the early 1970s.

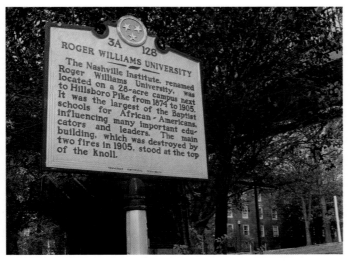

Figure 5.12. Roger Williams University historical marker, north of Hillsboro Village. Photo courtesy of Joseph Gutierrez

5.8 ROGER WILLIAMS UNIVERSITY

Peabody College, 21st Ave. S., Nashville, TN 37212

Vanderbilt University's Peabody College of Education occupies the former site of Roger Williams University (RWU), one of the four freedmen schools established in Nashville to educate Blacks after the Civil War. The almost forgotten story of RWU is a testament to the Black struggle for self-determination. Unfortunately, it is also a story of White paternalism and capitalist greed. RWU began in the home of Daniel W. Phillips, a White Baptist minister who moved to Nashville in 1864 seeking to educate freed Black ministers. As the school grew, it moved to several locations before settling in the estate of William Gordon on Hillsboro Pike in 1874, between the newly founded Vanderbilt University and the Belmont Mansion.

In 1883, the school incorporated as Roger Williams University. The new school educated both men and women, many of whom later played leadership roles throughout the country. Allen Allensworth, a RWU alum, became the first Black man to reach the rank of lieutenant colonel in the United States Army. Another alumna, Betty Hill, was an early twentieth-century activist for civil rights and women's rights in Southern California. RWU students were hungry for knowledge as well as self-determination, and many were willing to challenge the school on their own behalf.

In the winter of 1886–87, students led protests against T. E. Balch, RWU's White treasurer and superintendent of industrial work. The students claimed that Balch had insulted a female teacher and a female student and treated students unfairly, even when it came to campus finances. Student protests—including sending letters to the board and school walkouts—led to negative press, and eventually both Balch and then RWU president William Stifler were dismissed.

Over the next few years, this scandal continued to brew tensions between the local trustees and the school's executive board.

Roger Williams University's existence as a Black school in Jim Crow Nashville made it an attractive space and a potential target for racists. In 1904, unknown parties shot at the school's chapel and, later that year, at the university president's wife, Margaret Guernsey, at their home. On the night of January 24, 1905, Centennial Hall—RWU's main building—was destroyed by fire. Four months later, the girls' dormitory also burned down. Seizing the opportunity to capitalize on the fact that the school was "in a choice section of the city," the board closed the school, rather than make the needed repairs. With this decision, Blacks in Nashville lost one of the few institutions of higher learning available to them. Perhaps coincidentally, on the same day of the first fire, the trustees of the Peabody Education Fund allocated one million dollars for Peabody College. Five years later, the Peabody College trustees purchased the old RWU property.

Today, only a historical marker—which can be easily missed on Peabody's campus—provides a snapshot of the history and significance of RWU. You can see the marker from the sidewalk on Twenty-First Avenue South. It is near the north end of the Village at Vanderbilt Apartments.

ABOUT THE AUTHOR

Lee Hall-Perkins is an independent historian of African American religious history. He earned his bachelor's and master's degrees from Vanderbilt University.

ADDITIONAL READING

American Baptist Home Mission Society. 1906. *Annual Report.*

Tennessee Encyclopedia 3.0, s.v. "Roger Williams University," by Bobby L. Lovett. Last updated March 1, 2018. http://tennesseeencyclopedia.net/entry.php?rec=1147.

Eugene TeSelle. "The Nashville Institute and Roger Williams University: Benevolence, Paternalism, and Black Consciousness, 1867–1910." *Tennessee Historical Quarterly* 41, no. 1 (Spring 1982): 360–79.

NEARBY SITES OF INTEREST

Peabody Esplanade (off Magnolia Circle): While on campus, enjoy the shade of the more than a century old trees lining the esplanade.

5.9 VANDERBILT DIVINITY SCHOOL

411 21st Ave. S.,
Nashville, TN 37240
(615) 322-2776

A Southern, interdenominational, progressive, university-based divinity school, Vanderbilt Divinity School did not come by its descriptors easily or without struggle. Conflict has been an important part of the school's history. Established as a bible department with Vanderbilt University's founding in 1875, Vanderbilt

Figure 5.13. (above) Vanderbilt Divinity School, 1999. Photo by Gerald Holly, courtesy of Vanderbilt University Special Collections and University Archives
Figure 5.14. (right) Divinity students protesting the expulsion of James Lawson, 1960. Photo by Gerald Holly, courtesy of Vanderbilt University Special Collections and University Archives

played a key role in training clergy to lead congregations where progressive leaders in the New South could find church homes. Theological education at Vanderbilt thus took on a common label from the day, "school of the prophets," with a commitment to influence the culture around it.

Debates over academic freedom eventually led to Vanderbilt becoming a nonsectarian university in 1914. At this point, the School of Religion was established and became the first interdenominational theological school in the South. The 1915 school catalogue states that "its

doors are open not only to those preparing for the ministry, but to social and religious workers of all types, recognizing that those who are called to be co-workers in the kingdom of God will be mutually benefited by the close association during their years of preparation."

But it was not until 1953 that the divinity school admitted its first African American student, Joseph A. Johnson, who was also the first African American to enroll as a regular student at Vanderbilt University. In the decade to come, the Divinity School would earn its reputation as "the conscience of the university" while also incurring its ire. Before Johnson arrived on campus, the vice chancellor reminded the dean that a Tennessee state code declared it "unlawful for White and colored persons to attend the same school" noting that any teacher who violated the law was subject to a penalty of fifty dollars and imprisonment up to six months. When Johnson arrived on campus, he was instructed that he had to confine himself to the School of Religion and could not take meals in the dining room or live in the dormitory.

In many ways, the faculty's decision to enroll Johnson, and Johnson's courage to attend, set the groundwork for an even bolder stand that occurred with the expulsion of another student. By the time James Lawson arrived on campus in 1958, the School of Religion had changed its name to the Divinity School. Before his arrival, Lawson had worked with the Fellowship of Reconciliation and led workshops on nonviolence throughout the South. After his arrival in Nashville, he continued to serve as the field secretary for Fellowship of Reconciliation and began to work with local ministers to desegregate Nashville using nonviolent tactics. Impressed with his resolve and dedication, Kelly Miller Smith invited Lawson to conduct a training at his Nashville church under the auspices of the Nashville Christian Leadership Council. This meeting would lead to the sit-ins

that occurred in Nashville in February 1960. As a result of his community organizing activities, the Vanderbilt Board of Trust expelled Lawson on March 3, 1960.

The majority of the faculty and the dean of the Divinity School protested Lawson's expulsion and submitted letters of resignation when he was not readmitted. Their action made the national news and has had a lasting impact on Vanderbilt Divinity School: continually prompting serious reflection and action by faculty and student body alike, resulting in the drafting and periodic revisions of the Commitments Statement combatting racism, sexism, homophobia, environmental destruction, poverty, and anti-Semitism, and embracing religious plurality. These commitments guide Vanderbilt Divinity School's behavior, individually and institutionally, as it continues its historic mission of educating progressive Christian clergy, and nonprofit, activist, and religious leaders. In 2006, Vanderbilt publicly apologized for its treatment of James Lawson during the Nashville Student Movement and hired him as a professor from 2006 to 2009.

ABOUT THE AUTHOR

Dr. C. Melissa Snarr is associate professor of ethics and society at Vanderbilt Divinity School.

ADDITIONAL READING

Dale A. Johnson. *Vanderbilt Divinity School: Education, Contest, and Change.* Nashville, TN: Vanderbilt University Press, 2001.

Figure 5.15. Faculty member John Hill speaking during the dedication of Confederate Memorial Hall, June 1, 1935. Photo courtesy of Vanderbilt University Special Collections and University Archives

NEARBY SITES OF INTEREST

Benton Chapel (411 21st Ave. S.): Located next to the University's main library, the Divinity School also shares space with the university's Benton Chapel, which is open daily from 7 a.m. to 7 p.m. during academic sessions.

5.10 CONFEDERATE MEMORIAL HALL

18th Ave. S. and Horton Ave., Nashville TN 37212

Today, there is no evidence of the decades-long controversy that surrounds this building. The dispute traces back to the years following the Civil War, when a number of women from the states of the former Confederacy founded the United Daughters of the Confederacy. One of their primary goals

was to influence the teaching of the history of slavery and the Civil War for future generations. In 1933, the Tennessee Chapter of the Daughters of the Confederacy presented a gift of $50,000 to the George Peabody College for Teachers. The donation was earmarked to create a dormitory for the female student descendants of Confederate soldiers who fought in the Civil War. Two years after the donation, construction of the dormitory was completed. Ironically, the new building sat on the site where Roger Williams University, a school established for the education of the descendants of formerly enslaved, existed during the late nineteenth and early twentieth centuries. Above the large wood front doors were inscribed the words Confederate Memorial Hall.

Nearly thirty years later, Vanderbilt University acquired Peabody College and Confederate Memorial Hall. It was not long until Vanderbilt students began protesting the dormitory's inclusion of *Confederate* in the title. In 1988, following a large student protest, the University placed a plaque outside the dorm intended to contextualize the building's name. The plaque, however, did little to quell the frustration of some students and faculty. A major effort to remove *Confederate* from the name came in 2002, when newly appointed university chancellor Gordon Gee attempted to unilaterally change the name. Upon hearing this, the Daughters of the Confederacy swiftly filed legal suit, claiming that the terms of the original donation mandated that the name remain on the building. Vanderbilt initially won the lawsuit, but lost the resulting appeal, which ordered that, prior to removing the name, Vanderbilt must repay the Daughters the amount of the original gift plus interest. Vanderbilt did not repay the Daughters and while the building name remained the same, the university began referring to the dormitory as Memorial Hall in all official documents, maps, and public discourse. While protests and efforts to remove the title continued, Confederate Memorial Hall was added to the National Register of Historic Places in 2011.

After the 2015 massacre at Emanuel African Methodist Episcopal Church in Charleston, South Carolina, and other nationwide events of racial unrest and protest, Vanderbilt students led various campus dialogues pressuring the university to remove the title. In the fall of 2015, the university installed a second plaque, this time explaining how it had lost the case in the court of appeals. A number of student groups objected, continuing to seek the name's removal. Many in the Vanderbilt administration agreed; at one campus forum associate counsel James Floyd

stated that the name was, "at best, offensive, and at worst, a total affront to a free and open society." Yet as conversations on campus continued, others expressed concern as to whether it was appropriate to pay over a million dollars to an organization the community was fundamentally and ideologically opposed to.

The dilemma was resolved in 2016, when an anonymous donor gave Vanderbilt $1.2 million to pay back the present-day value of the initial $50,000 donation. That summer, the Vanderbilt Board of Trust authorized Chancellor Zeppos to officially remove the name, which was completed in August 2016. In addition, Zeppos announced that Vanderbilt would work to "establish a major annual conference on race, reconciliation, and reunion." Interestingly, with the removal of the name, the plaques describing the history of the building and the naming controversy were also removed, scrubbing the campus of any visible sign of this Confederate history.

ABOUT THE AUTHORS

Dr. Kevin Leander is a Vanderbilt professor and former faculty head of Memorial Hall. **Mike Thompson** graduated with a MEd in Community Development from Vanderbilt.

NEARBY SITES OF INTEREST

Vanderbilt University Cohen Memorial Fine Arts Gallery (1220 21st Ave. S.): This university gallery features collections from around the world, as well as contemporary exhibitions, and is free to the public.

My most vivid memory of Memorial Gymnasium is what happened there on the evening of April 5, 1968—the day after Martin Luther King Jr. was shot and killed in Memphis. Rock-throwing violence erupted in North Nashville, injuring Metro's assistant police chief and triggering the activation of the National Guard. Mayor Beverly Briley imposed a dusk-to-dawn curfew. From my dorm room window on Vanderbilt's campus overlooking West End Avenue, I could see armored personnel carriers, jeeps, trucks loaded with troops, and tanks rolling down the empty street. Troops bivouacked in Centennial Park and fires burned in dumpsters.

That night, Julian Bond (the African American social activist and civil rights leader, then a member of the Georgia House of Representatives) was scheduled to speak on campus as part of a student-led symposium. The Metropolitan Government granted Vanderbilt an exception from the curfew, and I remember sitting on the tarpaulin covering the basketball court when Mr. Bond slowly approached the podium, then stood and waited silently. When Memorial Gymnasium got so quiet you could hear a pin drop, Mr. Bond softly and slowly spoke: "nonviolence died last night in Memphis." I don't remember anything else that was said that evening, but I still feel a chill up my spine whenever I remember hearing those words.

James Berry, Vanderbilt University, Class of 1971

5.11 MEMORIAL GYMNASIUM

210 25th Ave. S.,
Nashville, TN 37240

In the heart of Vanderbilt University stands a historic symbol of the power of both words and sport to promote racial equality. Memorial Gymnasium, designed by architect Edwin Keeble and dedicated to all Vanderbilt men and women who served in World War II, has been home to the Vanderbilt Commodores basketball team since December 6, 1952. Two events in 1967, however, gave this sporting landmark an even deeper social significance. The first occurred on April 7 and 8, 1967, and had nothing to do with basketball. In the fourth year of Vanderbilt's historic, student-organized Impact Symposium series, thousands of Nashvillians gathered in the gym to hear the Rev. Dr. Martin Luther King Jr. give a speech titled "The Future of Integration." Other featured speakers were US senator Strom Thurmond, with his speech, "Conservative Individualism," the poet Allen Ginsberg reading from his works in a talk entitled "The Individual in American Society," and Stokely Carmichael, whose speech "The Individual and Black Power" received a standing ovation from the mostly White Vanderbilt audience. Following the speeches, sporadic outbreaks of violence occurred throughout the city. Most members of the local press blamed the unrest on Carmichael's "more inflammatory" speeches at Fisk and Tennessee State Universities, two Nashville HBCUs whose students could cite a history of mistreatment from the police during Jim Crow.

Figure 5.16. Martin Luther King Jr. and Stokely Carmichael at the 1967 Impact Symposium in Memorial Gymnasium. Photo courtesy of Vanderbilt University Special Collections and University Archives

The second significant event at Memorial Gymnasium occurred in the fall of 1967, when Perry Wallace, a Vanderbilt basketball player, broke the color barrier by becoming the first African American athlete to play in the Southeastern Conference (SEC). Bishop Joseph A. Johnson integrated Vanderbilt in 1953, and the first Black undergraduates arrived in 1964. But until Wallace, the Commodores remained all White. A Nashville native and Pearl High School basketball standout, many assumed Wallace would attend a historically Black school, like Tennessee State University, or a Northern university. After numerous scholarship offers, Wallace chose to stay in his hometown, to play for Vanderbilt University and desegregate the SEC.

Despite having been recruited by Vanderbilt, many on campus were openly hostile toward Wallace. Indeed, his years on campus were marked by social isolation, and his time playing basketball in the SEC was clouded by racism. The University of Mississippi opted to cancel its scheduled game rather than play against an integrated Vanderbilt team. Wallace endured and ultimately prevailed, graduating with many honors, including All-SEC and NABC Silver Anniversary All-America Team. He was inducted into both the Tennessee and Vanderbilt Sports Halls of Fame and was voted "most outstanding engineering student" as well as "most outstanding undergraduate student."

Wallace went on to get a law degree from Columbia University and work for the US Department of Justice, and became a law professor at American University in Washington, DC. Vanderbilt Athletic Director David Williams declared that Wallace's strength could be reflected in the brick walls of Memorial Gymnasium and that "Perry Wallace was the Jackie Robinson of basketball in the SEC. There are not a lot of people that could have endured what he did during that time." He continues, "It is amazing to think that it all happened in Nashville, Vanderbilt University's Memorial Gym represents a key place of change and equality." Wallace's jersey was retired in 2004. After Wallace's death in 2017, Vanderbilt University and Nashville Metro Council collaborated to rename the portion of Twenty-Fifth Avenue South that passes through campus and in front of Memorial Gym "Perry Wallace Way."

Memorial Gymnasium's location is unchanged, and it has become one of Vanderbilt's proudest attractions. Known as having a certain "Memorial Magic," the spirit of equality and feelings of accomplishment can be experienced, appreciated, and radiated throughout all of Nashville.

ABOUT THE AUTHORS

Ashley Vega was a defender/midfielder for the Vanderbilt Women's Soccer team (2011–2015), and graduated from Vanderbilt's Community Development and Action program. **Douglas D. Perkins** is a professor and director of the PhD program in Community Research and Action at Vanderbilt University and played basketball at Swarthmore College (1976–1980).

ADDITIONAL READING

Andrew Maraniss. *Strong Inside: Perry Wallace and the Collision of Race and Sports in the South.* Nashville, TN: Vanderbilt University Press, 2014.

NEARBY SITES OF INTEREST

Bishop Johnson Black Cultural Center (off West Side Row): Named in honor of the first African American graduate of Vanderbilt University, this center serves as a cultural hub of Black life on campus.

5.12 VANDERBILT KIRKLAND HALL / OCCUPY VANDERBILT

2201 West End Ave., Nashville, TN 37235

The most visible arm of Vanderbilt's first student-led divestment campaign was a sustained action on the lawn of Kirkland Hall, the administrative hub of Vanderbilt University. In 2011, as the United States was experiencing its worst recession since the Great Depression, the "Occupy" movement sprang up in hundreds of urban centers around the country, including Nashville. Aiming to challenge the political control of the wealthiest 1 percent of the population, Occupy was a social movement against inequality and unrealized democracy.

Figure 5.17. Site of the Occupy Vanderbilt protest. Photo © Al Levenson

Influenced by visits to and media coverage of Occupy Wall Street in New York, and the two-month occupation of Legislative Plaza in downtown Nashville, student activists at Vanderbilt University chose to escalate two major campus campaigns. Occupy Vanderbilt culminated in a forty-five-day long encampment outside Kirkland Hall from March to May 2012, and involved hundreds of students and dozens of faculty who, as a show of support, taught their classes at the encampment.

Occupy Vanderbilt grew primarily out of a network of students who spent the previous several years building support for the struggle of unionized dining, grounds, and housekeeping workers at Vanderbilt seeking a living wage. Using the Living Wage campaign to train each other in community organizing and direct-action tactics, students eventually focused their demands on summer employment for the dining workers, who were laid off each summer but denied unemployment insurance by the university. The students' slogan became "End poverty at Vanderbilt," drawing attention to the economic inequality within Nashville's largest employer: most dining workers made well below the poverty line, while seven of the ten highest-paid university employees in the nation were Vanderbilt administrators. Occupy Vanderbilt's second issue was a campaign to get Vanderbilt to divest its endowment funds from a London-based hedge fund at the center of a land-grab scandal involving the use of private equity funds to dispossess land owned by peasants in

Sub-Saharan Africa. After the *Guardian* newspaper revealed that Vanderbilt was among a group of universities invested in the hedge fund, students began organizing a campaign to pressure the Vanderbilt Office of Investments, and the Board of Trust, to pull out. The "No Land Grabs" campaign transformed into a larger 'Responsible Endowment Campaign' to reform all Vanderbilt investing policies.

The campaign formally began on March 19, 2012, with a rally attended by over one hundred students outside Kirkland Hall. In tents donated from Occupy Harvard (and later sent to Occupy Memphis), a group of over a hundred students took turns sleeping at and maintaining the encampment outside of Kirkland Hall. Occupiers used the encampment as an organizing hub from which to stage direct actions elsewhere on campus and in Nashville. On March 21, the students disrupted the National Association of College and University Food Services annual Southern regional conference, hosted at Vanderbilt, to call attention to the massive income gaps between food service workers and the CEOs of these companies. The students filled a tent with helium balloons and marched with the tent flying overhead from the Vanderbilt campus to Legislative Plaza in support of the Rally for the Right to Exist, which protested new legislation criminalizing unauthorized camping and creating rules directed at both Nashville's homeless population and the occupy movements. The forty-five-day long effort ended with a final rally outside Kirkland Hall on May 1.

The Occupy Vanderbilt movement drew support across the student body, including from the editorial board of the student newspaper, the *Hustler*, a typically conservative paper. Occupy Vanderbilt activists forged strong relationships with rank-and-file leaders in the university dining halls and continued to support the struggle against poverty and for summer employment in subsequent contract negotiations. Occupy's most impressive victory occurred when Vanderbilt ultimately withdrew its $26 million investment in EMVest, and, for the first time, Vanderbilt students at Vanderbilt declared success in an endowment divestment campaign.

ABOUT THE AUTHORS

Kate Goodman is a graduate of Vanderbilt University's Community Development and Action program. **Tristan Call** is an eighth-year anthropology student and adjunct faculty at Vanderbilt who slept very little from March to May 2012.

NEARBY SITES OF INTEREST

K. C. Potter Center (312 West Side Row): Vanderbilt's center for LGBTQI life—visitors welcome.

5.13 CENTENNIAL PARK

2500 West End Ave., Nashville, TN 37203
(615) 862-8400

While the large urban park west of downtown is most well-known for its full-scale model of the Parthenon built

As the school year of 1960/61 drew to an end, Matthew Walker and I—both college students and civil rights activists—were back in Nashville together. After devoting most of the previous year to lunch counter sit-ins, freedom rides, seminars on nonviolence, marches, and rallies, in addition to school at TSU and Fisk, our current project was to desegregate the HG Hills supermarkets in town. We were physically tired, but spiritually energized. Our experience with sometimes dangerous but inspiring civil rights work was starting to convince us that, by working with other dedicated people, we might be able to change the world.

But on a hot summer day in July 1961, Matthew and I were thinking that, since we'd helped integrate Nashville's segregated lunch counters and survived hostile Alabama sheriffs and highly unpleasant Mississippi jails and prisons, we could certainly gain entrance to a public pool right in our own home town. So we brought our towels and the twenty-five-cent admission fee to the lady at the entrance of the Centennial Park pool and told her politely that we'd like to go swimming. A little rattled, she explained that the pool was for Whites only (not for "niggers"). Schooled in nonviolent tactics, we calmly repeated that we'd like to go swimming. Not knowing exactly how to handle this situation, she called her boss, who phoned the head of the Parks Department, who ultimately called the mayor. Little did we know that the city would rather prohibit all of Nashville from swimming than let us swim that day.

Kwame Lillard

Figure 5.18. Centennial Park Pool before being closed. Photo courtesy of Nashville Metro Archives

for the Tennessee Centennial Exposition, it is also an important site in the struggle to integrate public accommodations. In pre–air conditioning Nashville, community pools were spread across the city in local parks. In 1961, the premier public pool was in the lovely but segregated Centennial Park. During the Christmas season, African Americans were allowed to drive through the park to observe the nativity scene from their cars, but at any other time of the year, Black people risked arrest or worse for walking on the lawns of the lovely green island across from Vanderbilt University. During Nashville's humid and steamy summers, no one questioned that the Centennial Park swimming pool was off limits to anyone who was not White.

On a hot summer day in July 1961, two young Black civil rights activists sought admission to the pool (see sidebar). Not only were they denied admittance, but when the news quickly spread the city's Board of Parks commissioners ordered that the Centennial Park pool, along with the city's twenty-six other pools, be immediately closed, citing "financial reasons." Many Nashvillians, however, believed the board acted under Mayor Ben West's orders despite his denials of having received prior notification about their intended actions. With the certainty of eventual integration at the national level in mind, and hoping to avoid the horror of Blacks and Whites swimming in the same water, Nashville city government permanently closed the Centennial Park pool in 1963, and by 1966, all of the city's public pools had been drained and filled with concrete, so neither Whites nor Blacks could swim in a public pool in Nashville. Today, the Centennial Park pool site is home to the Centennial Park Arts Center.

Thousands of people visit Centennial Park each year to take in the iconic Parthenon and accompanying museum, stroll along the walking trail and gardens, participate in activities in the Centennial Art Center, or attend one of the many concerts and festivals. What they will not find is reference to the civil rights struggles that took place here; there are no plaques or markers describing its important history.

ABOUT THE AUTHORS

Kwame Lillard was one of the organizers of the student movement, later serving as a Metro councilman and community leader.
Barbara Clinton served as director of the Vanderbilt Center for Health Services and is a public health consultant.

NEARBY SITES OF INTEREST

Tennessee Woman Suffrage Monument (Centennial Park): This statue by Alan LeQuire was installed in the park in 2016. Women gathered in Centennial Park as early as 1848 to advocate for voting rights.

5.14   THE PARTHENON
2500 West End Ave., Nashville, TN 37203

The Parthenon of Ancient Greece was a temple erected to worship and honor Athena—the Greek goddess of wisdom, artistry, and warfare. Viewed as the protector of the city, Athena was admired for her calmness and her commitment to only fight for just causes. In 1897, as part of the state's one hundredth anniversary, Nashville erected a full-scale replica of the Parthenon in Centennial Park. The city would later complete the work by adding a four-story statue of the goddess Athena.

The city is still known as the "Athens of the South," largely in reference to the abundance of colleges and universities based in Nashville. However, not all Nashville residents have equal access to higher education in Music City. Undocumented students in Tennessee, no matter how long they have lived or studied in the state, must pay more than three times as much as their peers to enroll in Tennessee's public colleges and universities—putting college out of reach for many of Nashville's undocumented graduates.

On May 19, 2012, as high school graduations were taking place across Nashville, undocumented students and educator allies gathered on the steps of the Parthenon to launch their campaign for tuition equality in Tennessee. Graduating high school seniors, clad in caps and gowns, shared their stories with their fellow students, parents, educators,

Figure 5.19. (above) Tuition Equality Now 2015 Rally. Photo courtesy of TIRRC

Figure 5.20. (left) At 41' 10" tall, *Athena Parthenos* by Alan LeQuire is the largest freestanding interior statue in the Western world. Photo courtesy of Dean Dixon

community members, and members of the media present for the demonstration. The students spoke with passion about their desire to pursue higher education, their aspirations for life and careers after college, and the unjust tuition policies that prevented them from following their dreams. The graduating students vowed to change tuition policies so that future graduating classes would walk across the stage with greater opportunity.

In the five years since the campaign's launch, undocumented students in

Tennessee have been sharing their stories and building a powerful coalition in support of tuition equality. Although the policy has yet to change, the students have come closer than many thought possible. In 2015, the tuition equality bill passed the conservative state senate by a vote of 21 to 2 and came within a single vote of passing the House of Representatives. Nearly every legislator who supported the bill credited a conversation with an undocumented student for their decision. Over time, the campaign has shifted public perceptions of undocumented students and tuition equality. In 2017, a Vanderbilt poll found that two thirds of Tennessee voters supported the policy change.

Whether fighting for tuition equality, to stop deportations, or for immigration reform, undocumented youth in Nashville and across the country have been at the forefront of the immigrant rights movement. In 2009, after campaigning for the DREAM Act, undocumented youth formed Jovenes Unido por un Mejor Presente (JUMP), a youth group affiliated with the Tennessee Immigrant and Refugee Rights Coalition (TIRRC). Since then, JUMP has led the campaign for tuition equality and inspired undocumented youth across the state to join the movement for immigrant rights.

ABOUT THE AUTHORS

Jewlz Davis is a graduate of Vanderbilt University's Community Development and Action program. **Jazmin Ramirez** is studying social justice at Trevecca Nazarene University.

NEARBY SITES OF INTEREST

Thread (28th/31st Avenue Connector Bridge): This connector bridge linking formerly separated neighborhoods also features public art reflecting the use of space. The 150 steel panels, featuring different sewing motifs, were gathered from community workshops and form a quilt-like pattern across the bridge.

5.15 FANNIE MAE DEES PARK
2400 Blakemore Ave., Nashville, TN 37212

Fannie Mae Dees Park, a popular recreational space for Nashville families, is better known as Dragon Park for the large mosaic sculpture that sits at its center. Most visitors do not know that the park is the former site of homes that were demolished under a 1960s urban renewal plan. Hillsboro-West End Neighborhood (HWEN), where the park is located, began as a streetcar suburb when electric trolley lines were extended out West End Avenue and Twenty-First Avenue South. Today, the neighborhood is popular for its proximity to downtown and the large number of early twentieth century homes, which have earned the neighborhood a spot on the National Register of Historic Places.

By the mid-1960s, HWEN was an urban neighborhood facing competition with newer, more spacious suburbs. Deferred maintenance, the perception of higher crime, and restricted financing from lenders created pressure from

Figure 5.21. Fannie Mae Dees and her mother protesting Urban Renewal and Vanderbilt University expansion in 1965. Photo courtesy of the *Tennessean*

more than six hundred families and fifty businesses were forced to relocate. Not all residents went peacefully. One of the most outspoken, Fannie Mae Dees, protested by putting large hand-painted signs on her porch and a coffin in her yard. Today, the Metro park located on the south side of Blakemore Avenue bears her name.

developers to convert residential properties to commercial use. Things came to a head in 1967, when Nashville's Metro Council adopted an urban renewal plan based upon new federal legislation. With matching funds provided by Vanderbilt University, several blocks of homes and businesses to the south and west of the campus were targeted for purchase and demolition. In response, a group of neighbors organized the United Neighborhood Association and filed a lawsuit to stop the action. The case proceeded to the federal appeals court level but was ultimately unsuccessful. However, public sentiment eventually turned against the project, and resident organizing saved much of the neighborhood. While many Black neighborhoods were completely bulldozed during the urban renewal years, the fact that HWEN was a predominantly White neighborhood likely helped to curtail demolition efforts. Even so,

The sculpture in Fannie Mae Dees Park, completed in 1980, was an effort to bring the community together following the fractious urban renewal project. Designed by artist Pedro de Silva and formally titled *Sea Serpents* (a second smaller serpent was added one year later), the images that form the serpent's "skin" are made of thousands of ceramic tiles, the work of dozens of volunteers including HWEN residents and students who created the designs themselves.

Drawing inspiration from Dees and her fellow neighbors' activism, HWEN residents have continued to mobilize for their community. Other efforts include fighting the construction of Interstate 440, which runs through the neighborhood. Though unable to stop the interstate's construction entirely, residents worked with other affected neighborhoods to force a number of concessions resulting in a smaller and less obtrusive design. HWEN's residents also organized crime watches, made lending easier to obtain for neighborhood homes, and led Nashville's recycling efforts.

Today, HWEN's focus has shifted to preserving homes through two widely supported conservation overlays. Fannie Mae Dees Park remains at its center, as a reminder of neighbors coming together.

ABOUT THE AUTHOR

J. Hunter Moore is an active resident of the Hillsboro-West End neighborhood, a writer, musician, and Fulbright scholar.

NEARBY SITES OF INTEREST

Belcourt Theatre (2102 Belcourt Ave.): Check out the offerings at Nashville's historic and only independent movie house.

5.16 INTERNATIONAL MARKET AND RESTAURANT

2010 Belmont Blvd.,
Nashville, TN 37212

(615) 297-4453

For forty-four years, the first Asian grocery store in Nashville operated from a small, unassuming building near Belmont University. Started in 1975, the establishment offered a wide variety of Asian goods and served Southeast Asian cuisine. Patti Myint, affectionately known as Ms. Patti, recalls that when she first came to Nashville as a student from Thailand, the city's Asian population numbered fewer than a thousand

Figure 5.22. Win and Patti Myint look out the window of the International Market on Belmont Boulevard, February 16, 1976. Photo by Jack Corn, courtesy of the Tennessean

people. Shortly after marrying her husband, Dr. Win Myint (a Burmese immigrant and professor and lecturer at Tennessee State University), they opened the market to provide Nashville with Asian foods and ingredients that could not be found in the city. The Myints initially specialized in wholesaling rice to the small Asian community and the two area Asian restaurants. The first year was difficult: the market was robbed twice, and Ms. Patti was once held at gunpoint. But within that first year, the Myints added a dining section to the market. They hoped the increased traffic would make the store safer for when Ms.

Patti was working alone, and they also wanted to show their growing customer base what they could create with the market's ingredients.

The market quickly grew from a store and restaurant into a hub for Nashville's growing Southeast Asian population. Immigrants from Cambodia, Thailand, Laos, and Vietnam came to the city in the seventies and eighties. Many came as refugees, escaping the violent military rule in Burma, fleeing Pol Pot and the Khmer Rouge in Cambodia, and leaving behind the aftermath of the Vietnam War. As the city's de-facto community center for Asian immigrants, the market was often contacted by local hospitals looking for help with translations or performing Buddhist ceremonial rites (for more about the Myints role in the oldest Buddhist temple in Nashville, see section 4.7). The Myints also helped many new immigrants settle in Nashville; many Southeast Asian immigrants found their first job in the US working alongside Ms. Patti.

Ms. Patti's love of food was inherited by her son, Arnold Myint, who has served as the executive chef at several Nashville restaurants. After Ms. Patti died in 2018, the Myint family prepared to move the market and restaurant across the street to 2013 Belmont Blvd., the site of one of Arnold Mynt's restaurants. The original location was purchased and demolished by Belmont University to make way for a performance center.

ABOUT THE AUTHOR

Joseph Gutierrez is a graduate of Vanderbilt University's Community Development and Action program; he was assisted by **Ms. Patti Myint** in her final years working at the International Market.

NEARBY SITES OF INTEREST

Belmont University (1900 Belmont Blvd.): This private Christian university is also home to the historic Belmont Mansion.

5.17 CARVER FOOD PARK

1001 Gale Lane,
Nashville, TN 37204

For nearly twenty years, the Carver Food Park provided food and compost from an unused stretch of land between the Interstate and the surrounding neighborhood. The story of Carver Food Park's 2011 destruction marks the unassailable transformation of one of Nashville's most visibly changed neighborhoods, 12 South. Historically, the neighborhood was populated by working-class Black families. However, 12 South is experiencing a rapid increase in real estate prices and businesses. As 12 South has gentrified, many smaller, older homes have been demolished to make way for larger, more expensive houses, and the population is becoming increasingly affluent and White.

Carver Food Park was founded on the precipice of these changes. Named after George Washington Carver (the famous African American agriculturalist

Figure 5.23. Demolition of Carver Food Park. Photo courtesy of Kim Green

recognized for developing many uses for the peanut), the four-acre community garden and leaf composting operation began in 1991 through the efforts of two local organizations: Recycle! Nashville and EarthMatters. Taking advantage of unused land owned by the Tennessee Department of Transportation (TDOT) near Interstate 440, the organizers envisioned a citywide competition encouraging people to "rescue" leaves before disposal into landfills. The organizers converted the land into a "food park," where nature could feed the community and the community could feed nature. The park grew to include more than thirty garden beds, a green house, and a tool bank.

Organizers and community volunteers incorporated art into the project, planting 250 rose bushes and creating earthworks sculptures. For many neighborhood residents, Carver Food Park fostered a sense of unity through nourishment. Over twenty years, hundreds of volunteers participated in composting and gardening activities, including many people from the neighborhood, as well as members of the United Methodist Church, Women's Leadership Conference, Unitarian Universalists, Mennonites, and area fraternities and sororities.

Some of the neighborhood's newer residents disliked the park and began complaining about noise, odor, and what they perceived as an unappealing aesthetic. In early 2011, growing tension led a group of thirteen residents to complain about the park to TDOT, describing it as a "gypsy camp" and "eyesore." After his appointment, TDOT commissioner John Schroer demanded that the park comply with Metro codes rather than the state regulations it had been following. The new codes prohibited composting, tools, or vehicles on the site. On April 8, 2011, bulldozers from TDOT arrived and destroyed 90 percent of Carver Park. In a scathing article in the *Nashville Scene*, Stephen George wrote that, "a new and aggressive TDOT commissioner who says he didn't need to know the site's history to take action" paired with a campaign by the new residents "is what ultimately doomed Carver Food Park."

Though you can no longer visit Carver Food Park, it inspired generations of environmental justice advocates, and similar projects have since been established

throughout Nashville, including the
Nashville Food Project and Sow Nashville.

ABOUT THE AUTHOR

Nicola Koepnick is a student of human rights,
and **Sizwe Herring** is the director of Earth-
Matters Tennessee and founder and former
director of the Carver Food Park.

NEARBY SITES OF INTEREST

Islamic Center of Nashville (2515 12th Ave.
S.): Nashville's first mosque, started in 1978
by a small group of Bangladeshi and Egyptian
immigrants with support from Yusuf Islam, the
musician formerly known as Cat Stevens.

5.18 CCA/CORECIVIC

10 Burton Hills Blvd.,
Nashville, TN 37215

Just a few blocks beyond the iconic Bluebird Café, nestled among retirement
villages and real estate companies, is
the original corporate headquarters of
the nation's largest private prison company, Corrections Corporation of America (CCA). In the 1980s, the Tennessee
prison system was experiencing overcrowding and intolerable living conditions, provoking prison riots and a class
action lawsuit. It was precisely at this
moment of crisis that CCA emerged as
a capitalist "solution" to the problem
of systemic Eighth Amendment violations in Tennessee prisons. In the words
of one of CCA's founders: "We knew
the era of big government was over. We

could sell privatization as a solution, you
sell it just like you were selling cars, or
real estate, or hamburgers."

CCA was founded in 1983 by three
men: Thomas W. Beasley, Doctor R.
Crants, and T. Don Hutto. From the
beginning, CCA relied on political connections to secure its financial interests,
with the understanding that its only "clients" would be governments with the
authority to sanction punishment and
captivity. During law school, Beasley
rented an apartment from Lamar Alexander, who would later become governor of Tennessee and a supporter of
CCA's bid to take over the entire Tennessee prison system. His wife, Honey Alexander, was an early investor in CCA, as
was Vanderbilt University, Hospital Corporation of America, and the Tennessee
Valley Authority. The third partner, Don
Hutto, was the only member of the team
with relevant experience, having served
as director of corrections in Virginia and
Arkansas.

Today, CCA headquarters are in Brentwood, and it operates more than sixty-
five prisons, jails, and detention centers
across the US, seven of which are in Tennessee. The company made nearly $1.7
billion in annual gross revenue in 2013,
including an annual payment of $96 mil-
lion from Tennessee tax dollars. Between
1993 and 2013, five Tennessee politicians—
including Lamar Alexander and former
governor Bill Haslam—were among the
top ten individuals who received the
most in political contributions from CCA

Figure 5.24. 2016 annual protest during the CCA's shareholder's meeting. Photo © Al Levenson

the corporation's civic virtue. Every year in mid-May, protesters gathered at 10 Burton Hills Boulevard for the annual shareholders' meeting to support Alex Friedmann and other activist-shareholders in their attempts to hold CCA/Core-Civic accountable for neglect, mis-management, and sexual violence at its facilities. Incarcerated in a CCA prison for six years in the 1990s, Friedmann is now the associate director of the Human Rights Defense Center and the managing editor of *Prison Legal News*. Friedmann owns just enough stock to propose shareholder resolutions to address issues of prison rape and medical neglect. Each year, Friedmann is joined by other activists and faith leaders who are committed to ending for-profit prisons and reforming or abolishing the prison industrial complex.

employees, their family members, and the CCA political action committee.

CCA's profitability relies on high rates of incarceration, long prison sentences, and the absence or marginalization of restorative and transformative justice. It profits from the confinement and control of those who have been "duly convicted of a crime," and does so even if the "crime" results from policies that criminalize addiction or immigration status, and causes no injury. Indeed, during the Trump administration's 2019 surge in detaining immigrants—including the devastating raid of a chicken processing plant in Mississippi that arrested nearly seven hundred workers on their children's first day back to school—the company began operating new for-profit immigration detention centers in the South.

In 2016, CCA rebranded itself as Core-Civic, but not everyone is convinced of

ABOUT THE AUTHOR

Lisa Guenther is Queen's National Scholar in Critical Prison Studies at Queen's University in Canada. An expanded version of this article was published as "Prison Beds and Compensated Man-Days: The Spatio-Temporal Order of Carceral Neoliberalism" in *Social Justice* (Spring 2018).

Figure 5.25. Glendale Baptist Church. Photo courtesy of Learotha Williams Jr.

ADDITIONAL READING

Donna Selman and Paul Leighton. *Punishment for Sale: Private Prisons, Big Business, and the Incarceration Binge*. Lanham, MD: Rowman & Littlefield Publishers, 2010.

NEARBY SITES OF INTEREST

Bluebird Café (4104 Hillsboro Pike): You might not expect to find one of the most famous listening rooms in the world tucked in a Nashville strip mall, but the Bluebird Cafe has packed more than thirty years of history, legacy, and great music into its space. Check its website for shows and tickets.

Parnassus Books (3900 Hillsboro Pike #14): An independent bookstore co-owned by novelist Ann Patchett and featuring a large collection of local works.

5.19 GLENDALE BAPTIST CHURCH

1021 Glendale Lane, Nashville, TN 37204
(615) 269-0926

Set atop a hill with its red brick and white columns, Glendale Baptist Church looks like a "typical Southern Baptist church," which it was until the early 1970s with the arrival of a new pastor, Richard Smith. Under his leadership, the church began to seriously consider Christian responses to the disturbing realities of war, racism, and economic injustice. This church's attention to justice came into sharper focus in 1971 during the debates over the desegregation of Nashville's public schools.

Smith's public support for desegregation led many members to leave Glendale for more traditional churches. Rejecting the security of traditional Baptist leadership practices, remaining and new members proclaimed a strong belief in God's grace and mercy and held that his disciples should work as agents for change in the world. As early as 1972, the church embraced gender equality, with both women and men serving as deacons and in leadership positions.

Under the subsequent leadership of pastor Mark Caldwell, Glendale developed its identity as a caring community of equality and grace. Glendale continued its involvement in community ministries as one of the founding members of both Room in the Inn and Tying Nashville Together, a justice-focused community-organizing group. In 2000, the church developed a partnership with a church in Santa Clara, Cuba, a partnership that continues to thrive today.

In 2002, Glendale called April Baker as its first associate pastor to support its Christian Education ministry. The calling of a woman pastor led to a parting of the ways between Glendale and the Nashville Baptist Association and the Tennessee Baptist Convention. The church stood firm in honoring Baptist autonomy as well as the inclusion of LGBTQ individuals, families, and ministers. When Pastor Caldwell retired in 2003, Glendale began a discernment process regarding leadership, theology, and the congregation's values. The process led the church to adopt a new model of pastoral leadership. In 2004, the church called April Baker and Amy Mears to serve as co-pastors, adopting a leadership model reflecting the church's commitment to shared ministry.

Today Glendale Baptist Church continues its commitment to gender equality, radical inclusion, and social justice. It has partnered with the Alliance of Baptists, the Association of Welcoming and Affirming Baptists, the Baptist Peace Fellowship of North America/Bautistas por la Paz, and the Cooperative Baptist Fellowship. Its members come from many denominations, and the church opens its doors to all who wish to worship and work for peace and justice in Nashville and beyond. Though Glendale is not the "typical" Baptist church on the hill, it remains proud of the positions it has taken, and its members offer themselves to Nashville as a caring community of equality and grace. Come join us for worship at 10:30 a.m. every Sunday morning!

ABOUT THE AUTHOR

Martha Jo Berry has been a member of Glendale Baptist Church since 1974.

NEARBY SITES OF INTEREST

Battle of Nashville Monument Park (Battlefield Dr. and Granny White Pike): Honors the soldiers on both sides of the Civil War as well as the American soldiers who fought in World War I. It is also the site of the Noel Cemetery, where tens of thousands of Indigenous people are buried.

Figure 5.26. Aerial view of Radnor Lake. Photo courtesy of Special Collections Division, Nashville Public Library

5.20 RADNOR LAKE

1160 Otter Creek Rd.,
Nashville, TN 37220

Travelers on Franklin and Granny White Pikes south of downtown Nashville might not have a clue it is there, yet between those two well-trod arteries lies the most visited place in Tennessee's state parks system. Each year a million people find sanctuary in the beauty and tranquility of Nashville's unique 1,332-acre urban wilderness: Radnor Lake State Natural Area. Through the heroic efforts of dedicated citizens, Radnor was spared from becoming just another residential development.

In 1914, needing a reliable source of water for its massive Radnor Yard, the Louisville & Nashville Railroad (L&N) acquired the forested bowl-shaped headwaters of Otter Creek and built an earthen dam to create a lake. The resulting eighty-acre lake, nestled among Davidson County's tallest ridges, quickly attracted waterfowl and other wildlife. In the 1920s, Albert Ganier, a founder of the Tennessee Ornithological Society, convinced the L&N to maintain the lake and adjacent land as a nature preserve. As development encircled the ridges holding Radnor Lake, the Otter Creek basin remained unspoiled.

With the demise of steam locomotives, the railroad no longer needed the lake. In 1971, real-estate developers acquired an option on the property and submitted plans for a massive project that would have obliterated the pristine area's natural character. But to make it work financially, the developers needed a zoning change. Alarmed over losing Radnor, thousands of citizens signed a petition opposing the change, defeating the proposal. The success of the petition was but a stop-gap solution, though, as Radnor needed permanent protection.

The price tag for state acquisition of the area was $3.4 million, and the developers gave the state a deadline of July 1, 1973, to secure funding. Through some masterful maneuvering, Governor Winfield Dunn and US representative Richard Fulton secured some, but not enough, state and federal funds. The developers extended the deadline to August 16. What followed was a massive grassroots fundraising effort led by state senator Douglas Henry. Fundraising events—such as bake sales and lemonade stands—were sponsored by a local radio station, Boy and Girl Scout troops, and other adults and children. Vanderbilt and Lipscomb Universities kicked in funds. Local McDonald's gave away meals in exchange for Radnor donations. Thousands of ordinary citizens contributed, including Radnor's owner, who had granted the option to the developers, and, in the end, the developers even made a contribution. During the months of July and August 1973, all of Nashville seemed to be in an uproar over saving Radnor Lake. The effort succeeded, and Radnor Lake became the first area acquired under Tennessee's Natural Areas Act.

Citizen action not only saved Radnor; it has continued with the park's expansion. Since its original acquisition, under the leadership and fundraising efforts of the Friends of Radnor Lake the amount of protected land has nearly doubled, and most of the hollows and ridges that make up Otter Creek's headwaters are now permanently protected. The Friends also raise funds for maintenance and improvements at Radnor and coordinate the recruitment of volunteers who provide much of the labor required to maintain six miles of trails, wildlife-viewing platforms, and a host of other amenities.

"The preservation and continued expansion of the Radnor is a perfect example of what dedicated citizen action can accomplish," said Ann Tidwell, a long-time Radnor advocate. "Starting with Mr. Ganier back in the 1920s and right through today, Radnor has been saved and improved through the efforts of countless ordinary citizens." Visitors can access this stunning state park off Otter Creek Road, which intersects with Franklin Pike (US 31) on the east and Granny White Pike on the west. It is open daily from 6 a.m. to sunset. For information about wildlife and interpretative programs, visit tnstateparks.com/parks/about/radnor-lake.

ABOUT THE AUTHOR

Robert Brandt is a Tennessee native, active conservationist and nature writer, and a retired judge and attorney.

NEARBY SITES OF INTEREST

The Grave of Granny White (1186 Travelers Ridge Dr.): Pay tribute to the woman who left North Carolina with two children in the 1780s—widowed and impoverished—and went on to build an inn and tavern so popular the Granny White Turnpike Company was incorporated in her name.

Figure 5.27. Holocaust Memorial at the Gordon Jewish Community Center. Photo courtesy of Amie Thurber

5.21 GORDON JEWISH COMMUNITY CENTER

801 Percy Warner Blvd., Nashville, TN 37205

(615) 356-7170

Nine miles from the throbbing core of downtown Nashville one finds a place of serenity: the Gordon Jewish Community Center (GJCC). Founded as the Young Men's Hebrew Association (YMHA) on the last day of 1902, the Center emerged in response to the exclusionary bias of the Young Men's Christian Association, which denied membership status to Jews. The YMHA mandate was to establish a place where young Jewish men could improve themselves "mentally, morally and physically." The YMHA quickly became the center of Jewish life and grew from its first rented space on Cherry Street (now Fourth Avenue) to a permanent home on Union Street. Although conceived as an association for men, it was not long before Jewish women rose up and stamped their own identity on the association. In 1924, the name was graciously changed to the YM-YWHA.

In the era of urban renewal after World War II, the association moved to a West End location where I-440 crosses under West End. The name was changed to the Jewish Community Center, and many non-Jewish members joined the well-equipped, conveniently located center, which included a bowling alley. On a quiet Sunday evening in 1958, a bomb exploded at the Center's entrance. Civic and church groups condemned the criminal act of violence. While the crime was never solved, many assumed correctly that it was in retaliation for the Jewish community's engagement in Nashville's desegregation struggle. During this era, several Jewish physicians integrated their waiting rooms, many of Vanderbilt University's Jewish staff resigned when James Lawson was expelled from Vanderbilt's Divinity School, and at least two high profile rabbis joined in the Civil Rights Movement. Rabbi William Silverman exchanged pulpits with Black clergy, and Rabbi Randall Falk assisted with training young people for lunch counter sit-ins and organized a march of clergymen on city hall to protest segregation and demand equality for city workers.

In 1981, White supremacists in the Nashville area plotted to bomb a number of businesses owned by Jewish people, as well as the Temple, a prominent synagogue in the city. The attacks were organized by members of the KKK and

American Nazi Party; six people were ultimately indicted in the planned attacks.

In 1984, the Gordon Jewish Community Center moved to its current location. Perched on fifty-two acres of wooded hillside, the facility serves as a community and recreation center, and a key gathering place for community meetings addressing issues of local government, family matters, race relations, environmental concerns, and health issues. The Center also serves as a central educational space for learning about the Jewish Holocaust.

As part of their training, Metro Nashville police officers spend a day at the GJCC and visit the Nashville Holocaust Memorial, which is located on site. Opened in 2006, the memorial serves as an abiding tribute to those Nashville families and Holocaust survivors who directly experienced the genocide. The interactive site includes a memorial wall inscribed with the names of deceased Holocaust survivors and victims, an eternal flame, a symbolic sculpture inspired by a survivor, and a reflection area with seating. The Memorial is open to the public and accessible to people with disabilities.

Today, the Gordon Jewish Community Center is a vibrant place for people of all ages, faiths, and family configurations to come together in peace and understanding to strengthen minds, bodies, and spirits. The GJCC offers a full spectrum of fitness and wellness programs, senior and youth activities, art classes and showings, and a film festival. The Center is open daily. For hours and information, visit their website at www.nashvillejcc.org. For more about the Holocaust Memorial, visit www.nashvilleholocaustmemorial.org.

ABOUT THE AUTHORS

Jean Roseman is the author of *From Y to J: The Hundred-Year History of Nashville's Jewish Community Center*, and has called Nashville home for forty-nine years.

ADDITIONAL READING

Jean Roseman. *From Y to J: The Hundred-Year History of Nashville's Jewish Community Center*. Self-published, 2004.

Janette Silverman. "Three More than a Minyan: The First 150 Years of the Jewish Community in Nashville, Tennessee." *Tennessee Historical Quarterly* 75, no. 2 (2016): 126–41.

NEARBY SITES OF INTEREST

Edwin and Percy Warner Parks (the intersection of Hwy 100 and Old Hickory Blvd.): One of Nashville's most beloved park systems, these three thousand acres are home to more than four hundred species of plants and animals, including trees estimated to be over four hundred years old.

Cheekwood Estate and Gardens (1200 Forrest Park Dr.): A stunning fifty-five-acre botanical garden, historical estate, and art museum, with live outdoor events throughout the year. Check the website for ticket prices and events.

Belle Meade Plantation (5025 Harding Pike): For those wanting to learn more about Nashville's plantation past, there's much history here. Check website for admission and hours.

Figure 5.28. Site drawing for Aaittafama' Archeological Park, courtesy of HDLA Landscape Architects

5.22 AAITTAFAMA' ARCHEOLOGICAL PARK

Intersection of Hillsboro Rd. and Old Hickory Blvd.

Unbeknownst to many, there is a prehistoric village buried near the intersection of Hillsboro Road and Old Hickory Boulevard. The seven-acre meadow, dotted with hackberry and cedar trees, will soon become an archeological park, thanks to a ten-year struggle by Indigenous activists to preserve the area. Dating back to the 1400s, the site is believed to be the largest late-prehistoric Indigenous village remaining in Davidson County. Indeed, with more than five hundred graves buried beneath the soil,

this is one of the largest undisturbed Mississippian-era Native American villages in the United States. In 2017, the site's name was legally changed to Aaittafama' (ah-IT-tah-fah-mah), meaning "a place for meeting together" in the Chickasaw Muskegon language.

The site became a legal battleground in the 1990s when the Tennessee Department of Transportation attempted to widen Old Hickory Blvd. After graves were unearthed by construction, Native American activists immediately organized and filed a lawsuit against the state to protect the burial grounds. Construction stalled for ten years, during which time a full archeological survey was completed. Archeologists discovered parts of homes and buildings, simple tools, and food remains spanning a much larger geographic area than was first believed. Legal battles continued as the owner of the land, a commercial development company, sought to develop the property. Pat Cummins, president of the Tennessee-based Native History Association, led preservation efforts, and eventually, a broader coalition formed, including the Land Trust for Tennessee, Middle Tennessee State University, the Tennessee Historical Commission, and the City of Forest Hills (an incorporated city within Davidson County). A local nonprofit group, now called Friends of Aaittafama', raised $400,000 to preserve the site, and in 2014, the City of Nashville provided the remaining funds needed to purchase the property. Master planning for the park is underway. Preliminary designs include an interpretive Mississippian Culture Plaza, native vegetation, a rain garden, and access to area greenways.

In spite of ten years of litigation to stop the road expansion on Old Hickory Boulevard, the Tennessee Department of Transportation ultimately won, widening the road and paving over the burial grounds. However, given how many graves have been removed by development in recent years, Indigenous activists such as Cummins are grateful the burial site remained intact. Other sites were not so lucky. Despite Indigenous protests and attempts at litigation, the Brentwood Library was built over a Mississippian Village site, and 160 stone box graves were removed during construction of the Walmart on Charlotte Pike.

As reported by the *Tennessean* in December 2014, the preservation of the burial site has great significance to Cummins, who reflected: "I'm just overwhelmed standing here. We have deep ties to this land. Our ancestors weren't given a choice when settlement came to Middle Tennessee and we weren't given a chance to claim our burial grounds—until today." Cummins hopes that, true to its name, Aaittafama' Archeological Park will serve as a place for people to come together far into the future, learning both about the Indigenous roots of Nashville as well as the contemporary struggles to protect Indigenous sites.

ABOUT THE AUTHOR

Amie Thurber is a former resident of East Nashville.

NEARBY SITES OF INTEREST

Percy Warner Park (7311 TN-100, Nashville, TN 37221): One of Nashville's public gems, this forest and green space offers abundant hiking and equestrian trails, bicycle routes, and athletic fields.

6. ON THE ROAD

6.1   Promise Land   237

6.2   Wessyngton Plantation   239

6.3   Coal Creek Miners Museum   241

6.4   Highlander Research and Education Center   243

6.5   Islamic Center of Murfreesboro   245

6.6   The Town of Old Jefferson   247

6.7   The Farm   249

6.8   Giles County Trail of Tears Interpretive Center   251

6.9   Walnut Street Bridge, Chattanooga   253

6.10   Mound Bottom   254

6.11   Fayette County Courthouse   256

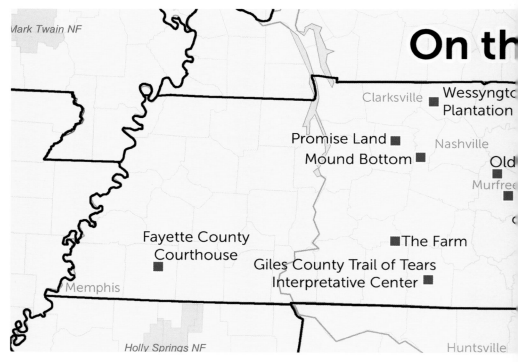

Map 8. On the Road. Courtesy of Joseph Speer

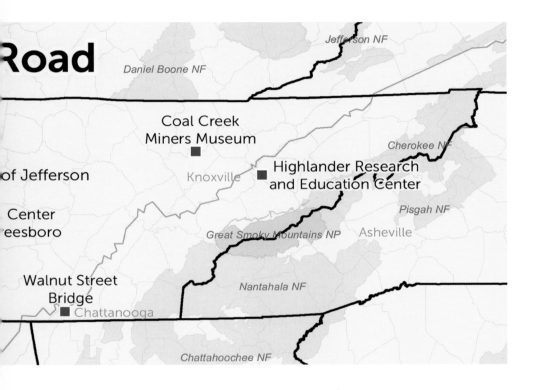

Road

Daniel Boone NF

Jefferson NF

Coal Creek
Miners Museum

of Jefferson

Knoxville

Cherokee NF

Highlander Research
and Education Center

Center
eesboro

Pisgah NF

Great Smoky Mountains NP   Asheville

Walnut Street
Bridge

Nantahala NF

Chattanooga

Chattahoochee NF

INTRODUCTION

STRUGGLES FOR SOCIAL JUSTICE do not take place in isolation. In this chapter we highlight extra-local events that were triggered by Nashville policies—such as the decision to raze the town of Old Jefferson to create a recreation area for Nashvillians' enjoyment—as well as events originating outside the city whose significance inspired hope, and sometimes terror, in Nashville. Although there are important regional distinctions across the state, this chapter underscores the through lines that connect places and periods in Tennessee history, exploring some of the places beyond Nashville's city limits that are nonetheless significant to understanding Nashville's history, culture, and context. Memphis and Knoxville, the state's two most populated cities after Nashville, carry their own robust traditions of organizing and warrant guides of their own. We focus here on sites in rural and less populated areas that might otherwise be missed. While not intended to provide an exhaustive list, this chapter flags some places you might consider visiting either as day trips from Nashville or as part of a larger exploration of Tennessee.

For example, many people travel east to explore the Great Smokey Mountains. En route, there are fascinating places to visit, including the famed Highlander Institute, which served as a central organizing and training center during the Civil Rights Movement. There is an intimate bond between the teaching of nonviolent protest at Highlander and in Nashville, and Highlander continues as a catalyst for social justice movement building across the South. Nearby is the lesser-known Coal Creek Miner's Museum, where visitors can consider the historic struggle for labor and prisoners' rights.

Those interested in tracing Civil Rights Movement history might also travel three hours south to Birmingham, home of the Birmingham

Figure 6.1. (above) Located at 115 Huling Avenue (near the National Civil Rights Museum), this mural was created by artists Nelson Gutierrez, a Bogota, Columbia, native who now works out of Memphis, and Cedar Nordbye, an associate professor at the University of Memphis and founder of the Memphis Mural Brigade. Photo courtesy of Amie Thurber
Figure 6.2. (left) View from the Highlander Center. Photo courtesy of Amie Thurber

Civil Rights Institute, a large interpretive museum, and a citywide walking tour of the Birmingham Civil Rights Movement. Along the way, you will pass a twenty-five-foot tall statue of early Ku Klux Klan leader and Confederate general Nathan Bedford Forrest, located on private land and clearly visible from Interstate 65. The neo-Confederate sculpture is the work of Jack Kershaw, the former Nashville attorney and White supremacist whom the Southern Poverty Law Center described as being "one of the most iconic American White segregationists of the 20th century." He explained the monument by offering, "Somebody needs to say a good word for slavery." Continuing south, you might stop in Pulaski, a town reckoning with its role in the formation of the KKK, and the Farm, the largest and longest lasting intentional community in the United States.

Many outdoor enthusiasts travel southeast to Chattanooga, dubbed by *Outside* magazine the "Best Town Ever" for its access to a wide range of outdoor recreational activities. On the way, you can visit the impressive Islamic Center of Murfreesboro, as well as remains of the town of Old Jefferson, razed during the creation of the Percy Priest recreation area. As you take in all that the burgeoning downtown Chattanooga has to offer, you might visit the walking bridge and pay homage to Alfred Blount and Ed Johnson, two African American men who lost their lives there as a result of lynching.

Many people are drawn to Memphis—just three hours west of Nashville—to experience the National Civil Rights Museum at the Lorraine Motel, where Reverend Dr. Martin Luther King Jr. was assassinated. In route, you will drive near the Mound Bottom archeological area—the site of a prehistoric Indigenous city—and might also visit the rural town of Promise Land, settled by free Blacks. Less than an hour outside Memphis, you'll find the Fayette County courthouse, which figures prominently in the struggle for civil rights in the Volunteer State. As you explore beyond Nashville, we encourage you to look for connections between people and places, to consider how ideas and movements travel across the state, and to reflect on the ways that history is bound up in the present struggles for justice.

6.1 PROMISE LAND

707 Promise Land Rd.,
Charlotte, TN 37036

Promise Land is a small, rural community located in Charlotte, Dickson County, Tennessee, which was settled

shortly after the Civil War by former enslaved men, women, and children from nearby farms and the ironworks town of Cumberland Furnace. Among the settlers were at least five men who had served with the United States Colored Troops (USCT) during the war: Clark Garrett, Landin Williams, Ed Vanleer, and brothers John and Arch Nesbitt. Their purchase and settlement of the area exemplified the hopes and aspirations of generations of enslaved Black men and women, which equated independence with land ownership. At the start of the Civil War, only seven of the 2,208 African Americans who called Dickson County home were free. This new settlement, aptly named Promise Land, consisted of approximately one thousand acres on which fifty families would quickly become a self-sufficient village with three churches, two stores, and a school.

Although much of the original settlement no longer exists, the Promise Land church and school still stand as testaments to the early settlers' fortitude and perseverance through the post-Civil War period and the Jim Crow era. John Nesbitt, who served faithfully in the Union Army during the Civil War, led the way in creating a school to educate the descendants of the first settlers. In 1880, Nesbitt received retroactive compensation from the Department of the Army for injuries he sustained during the war, and with some of these funds, he purchased land on which a school was built. Nesbitt and his wife deeded the school to the county in 1889, where it

Figure 6.3. Promise Land in fall. Photo courtesy of Learotha Williams Jr.

in Nashville where they would emerge to become award-winning educators in Dickson County. The musical talent that was both nourished and cultivated in Promise Land also had a tremendous impact on Nashville's music scene throughout the twentieth century. Famed Nashville guitarist James "Nick" Nixon, a musician whose guitar and entertaining voice became a fixture of Jefferson Street and the Nashville music scene for over half a century, had deep roots in the Promise Land community.

served as a county elementary school for Black students until closing in 1957.

Although many of its original families migrated to the Midwest during the twentieth century, Promise Land still occupies a special place in the hearts and minds of African Americans in Middle Tennessee. Promise Land symbolizes the commitment African Americans had to freedom, with many of its residents saving to purchase land in order to become independent farmers. One historian of Dickson County remembered the members of Promise Land as being fiercely independent, noting that its residents were not interested in working for anyone but themselves. A story that still resonates in the area today describes the men of the community having to take weapons to the polls during Reconstruction to protect their newly gained right to vote. During the era of Jim Crow, Promise Land would send its most exceptional students and members of the community to college

In 2007, Promise Land's remaining built environment was placed on the National Register of Historic Places. Today, it and other remnants of the once thriving community make up the Promise Land Historic Site and are open to the public. Thanks to the dedication and persistent efforts of Promise Land residents Essie Van Leer Gilbert and Betty Ruth Edmonson, the community retains, chronicles, and celebrates its remarkable history each year. An annual community festival takes place at the site each June, featuring historic exhibitions, reunion activities, and musical performances. The Promise Land Heritage Association—a nonprofit organization dedicated to preserving the legacy of strength,

Figure 6.4. Memorial monument in the African American Cemetery on Wessyngton Plantation. Photo courtesy of John F. Baker Jr.

courage, and fortitude at Promise Land—oversees the site, organizes the annual festival, and coordinates interpretive tours and re-enactments. For more information visit www.promiselandtn.org.

ABOUT THE AUTHOR

Serina K. Gilbert is the executive director of the Promise Land Heritage Association and a direct descendant of William Gilbert, Nathan Bowen, and George Washington Van Leer, three of Promise Land's original inhabitants.

NEARBY SITES OF INTEREST

Country View Amish Market (3380 Hwy. 48 N., Charlotte, TN): This family owned and operated business sells bulk staples as well as homemade spreads, salads, jellies, and farm fresh milk and butter.

6.2 WESSYNGTON PLANTATION

3021 Wessyngton Rd.,
Cedar Hill, TN 37032

In 2015, more than two hundred descendants of slaves and slaveholders gathered at the African American Cemetery at Wessyngton Plantation to honor the memory of those once enslaved on the grounds. They came together to dedicate a memorial—a fourteen-foot-by-six-foot granite monument with the names and dates of birth and death of all the African Americans known to have been enslaved on the plantation. This comprehensive information makes this monument and space unique and significant in the history of African Americans.

Wessyngton Plantation in Robertson County, Tennessee, was founded in 1796 by Joseph Washington (1770–1848), who came from Southampton County, Virginia, bringing with him enslaved Africans and African Americans. Joseph named the estate Wessyngton, the English version of his family surname dating back to the twelfth century. The African American Cemetery was established around 1798 as a burial ground for the plantation slaves. The graves were marked with rough fieldstones, roses, and wildflowers.

In 1812, Joseph Washington married Mary Cheatham (1796–1865), whose father owned a nearby plantation. The Wessyngton mansion was constructed between 1815 and 1819. The couple's only surviving child, George Augustine Washington (1815–1892), joined his father in purchasing land until the plantation encompassed 13,100 acres. In 1860, the enslaved population of 274 individuals was the largest in Tennessee, and they collectively produced 250,000 pounds of dark-fired tobacco, making it the largest producer in the United States and the second largest in the world. From 1796 to 1865, more than 446 African Americans were enslaved at Wessyngton.

During the Civil War, at least eleven men from the plantation enlisted in the United States Colored Troops. After 1865, many African American families moved to Nashville, the North, and the West, while other freedmen returned to "Washington," as they called Wessyngton. Today

tens of thousands of their descendants—Washingtons, Blows, Cheathams, Greens, Gardners, Terrys, Whites, Scotts, Lewises, and many others—reside throughout the United States.

After George A. Washington's death, the plantation was divided among his children. His son, Joseph Edwin Washington (1851–1915), inherited the mansion and the vast lands around it. The plantation was placed on the National Register of Historic Places in 1971. Wessyngton was the largest farm in America owned by direct descendants of its founder until it was sold in 1983.

Wessyngton slaves and some of their descendants were buried in the African American Cemetery until 1928. A ground-penetrating radar survey has located nearly two hundred graves, and historical research has identified the names of one hundred men, women, and children buried in this sacred place. State highway 257 through Cedar Hill, Tennessee, passes by the plantation land. If one has ancestors from Wessyngton Plantation or is interested in its history, contact John F. Baker Jr. through the website, www.wessyngton.com, for more information.

ABOUT THE AUTHOR

John F. Baker Jr. is a direct descendant of African Americans enslaved on Wessyngton Plantation.

ADDITIONAL READING

John F. Baker. *The Washingtons of Wessyngton Plantation: Stories of My Family's*

Journey to Freedom. New York: Simon & Schuster, 2009.

NEARBY SITES OF INTEREST

Fort Defiance (120 A St., Clarksville, TN): Those interested in Civil War history may enjoy touring the earthen fort, walking trails, and interpretative center here.

6.3 COAL CREEK MINERS MUSEUM

201 S. Main St.,
Rocky Top, TN 37769

(865) 340-3269

Tucked in the mountains of East Tennessee lies a museum paying tribute to one of the most important labor rebellions in Tennessee history. Now called Rocky Top, Coal Creek was founded in the late 1800s as a small mining town where early miners earned decent wages and most could afford a plot of land after working but a couple of years. The town became the site of conflict in April 1891, when miners believed that the Tennessee Coal Mining Company (TCMC) was shorting wages. At the time, a miner's wage was determined by the weight of the coal handed in each day. The company refused the miners' request to elect a checkweighman, the person designated to weigh the coal. After months of wage cuts, the Coal Creek miners went on strike.

In response, TCMC hired contracted prison labor and brought twenty-four prisoners to Coal Creek with instructions to tear down existing company housing and build stockades for their housing. As this was occurring, three hundred armed miners descended upon the stockade, forcing the guards to surrender. After putting the convicts and guards on a train bound for Knoxville, the miners sent a telegram to Tennessee governor John Buchanan defending their actions as a "necessary step in the defense of our families from starvation and our properties from ruin." The next day, Buchanan and the Tennessee National Guard travelled to Coal Creek where they were met by roughly six hundred miners. Although a self-proclaimed "champion of labor," Buchanan ordered the National Guard to return the contracted convicts to work and to guard them against the miners.

The use of contracted prison labor hurt miners and prisoners alike. The Tennessee Convict Leasing Law of 1866 essentially perpetuated recently abolished slavery. At the time, over 60 percent of the convicts were African Americans who now found themselves in a condition some argued was worse than slavery. Convicts feared for their own safety—and were ten times more likely to die in the mines than miners. Convicts typically only lived for ten years working in the leasing system and were subject to intense neglect and abuse by guards and employers.

As the conflict escalated, troops and miners resorted to guerilla warfare. Reports emerged of snipers in the hills shooting mining company officials, convicts, and guards while state militia fired

Figure 6.5. Miners at the Fraterville Mine in Coal Creek in the late 1890s. Photo from the Coal Creek Miner's Museum Collection

on civilians. Bolstered by miners from Kentucky and surrounding areas, the miners' numbers grew into the thousands. For protection, the National Guard built Fort Anderson, a fortress on a hill overlooking the Coal Creek mine. In the end, dozens of miners and soldiers were killed. As the conflict was reported across the country, the miners gained sympathy from the general public, and public opinion began shifting against convict leasing. Despite this, Governor Buchanan failed to push the state assembly to change the leasing legislation.

The state militia put down the rebellion in August, 1892. Hundreds of miners were arrested, including their leaders. While over three hundred miners were indicted, only two were convicted for conspiracy. As a result of this conflict, Governor Buchanan's career was damaged and he was soon defeated by Governor Pete Turney, who, in 1896, abolished the convict lease system and restored the miners to their jobs.

To this day, Tennessee continues to wrestle with labor and prisoners' rights. Tennessee is a "right to work" state, rendering unions uncommon and laborers prone to abuse. Tennessee is also home to the largest private prison corporation in the country, CoreCivic, formerly Corrections Corporation America (CCA), which some believe employs modern day convict labor practices. To learn more about the miner's rebellion, visit the Coal

Creek Miners Museum, which opened in 2016 and features photographs, video, labor songs, and other artifacts related to the mining history of Coal Creek. For hours visit the website, www.coalcreekminersmuseum.com.

ABOUT THE AUTHOR

Kate Goodman is a graduate of Vanderbilt University's Community Development and Action program.

NEARBY SITES OF INTEREST

Fort Anderson on Militia Hill (Intersection of Vowell Mountain Ln. and Beech Grove Rd., Lake City, TN): Historical marker of the fort built during the Coal Creek War.

6.4 HIGHLANDER RESEARCH AND EDUCATION CENTER

1959 Highlander Way, New Market, TN 37820

(865) 933-3443

On a 186-acre farm about twenty-five miles east of Knoxville, you will find Highlander, one of the most significant sites of learning for grassroots organizing and movement building in the South. Highlander's first name was "Highlander Folk School," and it opened its doors in Grundy County, Tennessee (in Summerfield, near Monteagle) in 1932, after receiving generous support from Dr. Lilian Johnson, who provided the land for the school. Myles Horton was a founder and the longest-serving school administrator, and he was joined in Highlander's early years by Don West, Jim Dombrowski, Elizabeth Hawes, and others.

Inspired by the Social Gospel Movement, Danish folk schools, and their own experiences witnessing the exploitation of land and people during the Great Depression and in the Jim Crow South, Highlander's founders started the school with a profoundly simple idea: people are their own best teachers. According to the founders, those most impacted by problems are the ones who should design the solutions. As a result, Highlander has strived to be a place where people can share their experiences, learn together, research together, sing together, eat together, rest together, and envision a better world together.

In its earliest years, Highlander focused on organizing unemployed and working people. By the late 1930s, Highlander was serving as the de facto Congress of Industrial Organizations education center for the region, training union organizers and leaders in eleven Southern states. During this period, Highlander also fought segregation in the labor movement, holding its first integrated workshop in 1944.

During the 1950s and 1960s, Highlander became an important meeting place for leaders of the Civil Rights Movement. Workshops and training sessions helped give shape to the movement's most important moments and initiatives, including the Montgomery bus boycott, the Citizenship Schools, and the founding of the Student Nonviolent Coordinating Committee (SNCC).

Figure 6.6. Desegregation workshop at Highlander. Rosa Parks is at the end of the table. Six months later, her actions sparked the Montgomery Bus Boycott. Photo from the Highlander Research and Education Center Collection

In 1961, after years of red-baiting and several government investigations, the State of Tennessee revoked Highlander's charter and seized its land and buildings in Summerfield. Highlander reopened the next day as the Highlander Research and Education Center. From 1961 to 1971, Highlander was based in Knoxville, and in 1972 it moved to its current location near New Market, Tennessee.

In the late 1960s and 1970s, Highlander played a vital role fostering organizing in Appalachia, supporting anti-stripmining and worker health and safety struggles, among other efforts. In the 1980s and 1990s, Highlander expanded its work to support grassroots groups fighting pollution and toxic dumping and supported the emerging anti-globalization movement by sponsoring workshops on economic human rights and trade and globalization issues and by forging connections with international activists and organizers.

In the twenty-first century, Highlander plays the same role in social movements as it has since its inception in 1932. People come to Highlander to learn together and strategize together. Highlander's staff has made significant contributions to supporting leadership development and cultural organizing at the intersection of key movements in the South and in Appalachia, such as the immigrant and refugee rights movement and local and regional struggles for economic democracy.

On March 29, 2019, a fire destroyed the center's main office building. Authorities suspect that a White supremacist group bears responsibility for the fire after finding a symbol associated with a known hate group spray painted on the asphalt. Despite this most recent attack, Highlander remains vigilant in its struggle for equality.

To learn more about Highlander's legacy of supporting movements, its current role in movement work, or to check out its incredible library, archives, and bookstore, visit its website, www.highlandercenter.org. Newcomers to Highlander may want to keep an eye out for its annual homecoming (usually in September) or other open-call workshops that staff organize throughout the year.

ABOUT THE AUTHOR

Reverend Allyn Maxfield-Steele is a pastor, educator-organizer, and, with **Ash-Lee Woodard Henderson**, the co-executive director of Highlander.

NEARBY SITES OF INTEREST

Dollywood (2700 Dollywood Parks Blvd., Pigeon Forge, TN): Dolly Parton's theme park . . . with rides, shows, restaurants, and more.

6.5 ISLAMIC CENTER OF MURFREESBORO

2605 Veals Rd.,
Murfreesboro, TN 37127

(615) 890-1551

The seeds of the Islamic Center of Murfreesboro (ICM) were planted in 1982. Essam Fathy, a physical therapist originally from Egypt, yearned for a place of worship in Murfreesboro, Tennessee, home at the time to a modest number of Muslims. Fathy rented a one-bedroom apartment where he and local Muslims gathered for the weekly Friday prayer. As Rutherford County grew, so too did its Muslim community. Fathy's group expanded to a two-bedroom apartment, and then a four-suite building, before beginning plans for a full-scale community center.

In November 2009, the ICM board members purchased land on the outskirts of the city and submitted a proposal to the Regional Planning Commission of Rutherford County to build an Islamic center. The site plan was unanimously approved. However, anti-Islamic activists strongly opposed the construction of the new center and filed lawsuits against the county and mayor. Rival demonstrations were held in favor of and in opposition to the building. After a short period of construction, the site was subject to severe arson, which led to an FBI investigation. Vandalism followed, and soon ICM became a topic of national discussion. In

Figure 6.7. Islamic Center of Murfreesboro. Photo courtesy of Sarah Imran

response to the controversy, the county court refused to issue a certificate of occupancy to ICM. In 2012, the US federal court lifted this prohibition. The center was allowed to open for the month of Ramadan, August of 2012. Appeals and lawsuits continued to arise, but in June 2014, all lawsuits were finally dismissed.

While the Muslim community in Murfreesboro went through a stressful time during this three-year process, many ICM members believe that the media overemphasized the controversy. In spite of loud opposition from a select few, ICM garnered strong support from many non-Muslims and leaders of other houses of worship. More than one hundred local religious leaders signed a letter of support for the mosque, and a group of lawyers represented ICM free of charge. Over the years of conflict, the supporters of ICM far outnumbered the protesters.

ICM has come a long way from the one-bedroom apartment where people once came together in prayer. While continuing as a place of worship, the eight hundred members of ICM participate in social celebrations, weddings, and educational interfaith conferences. ICM also offers an Islamic school on the weekends with classes in Arabic studies, Islamic studies, and the Quran. ICM has an open-door policy, and the beautiful new building is worth a visit. Anyone is welcome to attend gatherings, religious sermons, congregational prayers, or other events of interest. One can call ahead to (615) 890-1551 and schedule a guided tour of the Center.

ABOUT THE AUTHORS

Dr. Saleh Sbenaty, originally from Syria, is a professor of engineering technology at MTSU and a board member of ICM. **Sarah Imran** is a graduate of Vanderbilt University's Community Development and Action program.

Murfree Spring Wetlands (460 SE Broad St., Murfreesboro, TN): This former water treatment site is now a twenty-five-acre park that features trails, raised boardwalks, and interpretive signs to educate the public about the role of wetlands.

6.6 THE TOWN OF OLD JEFFERSON

5798 Central Valley Rd., Murfreesboro, TN 37129

Just forty minutes southeast of Nashville lies the remains of a town razed to make way for others to "recreate." While the purposes of dam construction were traditionally tied to hydroelectric power and flood control, these were secondary concerns to the US Army Corps of Engineers when the Corps sought and gained authorization for Stewarts Ferry Reservoir, later renamed J. Percy Priest Lake. The original proposal calculated the anticipated benefits for the project as follows: recreation, 56 percent; flood control, 30 percent; and power, 14 percent. To construct the reservoir, the Corps acquired 33,210 acres of land through eminent domain. Several small towns were razed and subsequently flooded by the lake in their entirety—or so it was reported by news outlets well after the dam's dedication in 1968. In fact, at the water's highest, 19,011 acres

of the acquired land were not inundated by Percy Priest. One demolished town, remaining well above water, is Old Jefferson.

Situated at the confluence of the east and west forks of the Stones River, Old Jefferson was once a small yet busy riverboat town. Thomas Bedford and Robert Weakley first surveyed the area in 1802. Recognized as a key location for trade, in 1803 Old Jefferson became the seat of the newly formed Rutherford County. As river transportation slowed, and the county seat moved to Murfreesboro in 1811, businesses and homes developed along the main road, Jefferson Pike.

This particular road was also one of several detours taken from the main route of the Trail of Tears in order to avoid tolls. The US military marched four detachments of Cherokees—numbering more than four thousand travelers—through Old Jefferson. Later, during the Civil War, the town was a site of conflict between Union and Confederate troops, and in 1864, it was briefly a recruiting station for the United States Colored Troops. Old Jefferson Church of Christ was founded around 1900, and St. Paul's, a Black church and school, also made its home in Old Jefferson. Eades Grocery was the last of many businesses which operated in the town during its more than 160-year history.

The construction of the J. Percy Priest Dam was a trying, stressful time for residents up and down the Stones River, and those from Old Jefferson live with the knowledge that had they remained, their

Figure 6.8. Sampson Wesley Keeble, the first African American elected to the Tennessee General Assembly, was once enslaved here as a child. The house was one of many razed. Photo taken by Jimmy Francis, former Old Jefferson resident

foundations, cellars, and 1960s-era Coca-Cola bottles left behind by patrons of Eades Grocery—all evidence of life before the lake. While the J. Percy Priest Dam has in many ways fulfilled its intended purposes, Old Jefferson, the riverboat town, offers a lasting reminder of what was lost en route. For more information about historic Jefferson, visit www.rutherfordtnhistory.org. For illustrated, turn-by-turn driving and hiking directions, visit www.nativehistoryassociation.org/old_jefferson.

homes would not have been inundated by the lake as the US Army Corps of Engineers projected. Some former residents resent the Corps for taking their homes and farms unnecessarily, while others welcome the greater level of flood control in the area. Among the many houses and historic landmarks lost was the Keeble home, also called Stoney Lonesome, where Sampson Wesley Keeble, the first African American elected to the Tennessee General Assembly, was enslaved as a child.

Visitors can explore the remains of Old Jefferson individually or on walking tours alongside former residents, who will likely point to where they were baptized in the river, where their homes stood, and where they went to church. A young forest now stands in place of the historic town, and along the narrow horse trail that was once Jefferson Pike, one can find

ABOUT THE AUTHORS

Lauren Marlar is a graduate of Vanderbilt University's Community Development and Action program, and completed this in conversation with **Toby Francis**, an Old Jefferson native and Rutherford County historian.

NEARBY SITES OF INTEREST

Poole Knobs Recreational Area (493 Jones Mill Rd., LaVergne, TN): This is one of many recreation areas on the reservoir. Poole Knob features campsites, an archery trail, and access to fishing, hunting, picnicking, boating, canoeing, hiking, horseback riding, and wildlife viewing.

Figure 6.9. Stephen Gaskin at the Farm in 1971. Photo courtesy of Special Collections Division, Nashville Public Library

6.7 THE FARM

100 Farm Rd.,
Summertown, TN 38483

Tucked in the rolling hills just seventy miles south of Nashville is the largest and longest functioning commune in the United States. In 1971, at the height of protests against the Vietnam War, "The Farm" was founded as a self-sufficient, intentional community with a mission to save the world. Led by Steven and Ina Gaskin, The Farm's founding members loaded into school buses in the San Francisco Bay area and drove east, settling on this land outside Summertown, Tennessee. The community pooled resources, took a vow of poverty, and committed to a nonviolent and collective existence dedicated to humanitarian work across the globe.

The Farm was completely vegan, eschewed hard drugs and alcohol, and had an unmistakable influence on Middle Tennessee, the Nashville area, and the world. Beyond the size—numbering 1500 residents at its height in the late seventies—and duration—operating as a commune for more than fifteen years and continuing to this day as an intentional community—The Farm is well known for advancing vegan nutrition and natural childbirth. Several vegan cookbooks were created and published on the Farm, and the midwifery-led natural childbirth approach is world-renowned today.

Of the 2,844 pregnant women accepted for care at The Farm Between 1970 and 2010, 95 percent delivered their babies as home births, including breech babies and twins, and the cesarean rate over this same period was 1.7 percent, far below the 2014 US national average of 32 percent. Teachings of The Farm midwives have been widely shared through books, instructional videos, and workshops in medical settings. Ina Gaskin became a leading authority on midwifery, helping to set up numerous midwifery centers, including the one within Vanderbilt University Medical Center. The efforts of The Farm midwives helped to normalize childbirth and ultimately contributed to improving women's health.

The Farm is also known for its humanitarian work. In the early 1970s, The Farm founded Plenty International, a not-for-profit charitable organization that continues to promote economic self-sufficiency, cultural integrity, and environmental responsibility. Projects include establishing soy dairies in developing countries as a way to address hunger, implementing a free ambulance in the South Bronx in the early 1980s when first responders were unable or unwilling to go into the then-troubled neighborhood, and more recently, helping non-federally

I was born and raised on The Farm and consider myself very fortunate to have been raised in such an incredibly strong community with a commitment to doing justice in the world. The Farm has shaped me in so many ways, especially in my career as an activist. I started out as a Farm- and apprentice-trained midwife, committed to ensuring women had safe choices in how, where, and when they gave birth. My experience supporting women through birth informed my early work in feminist activism and continues to inform my work as a social justice activist living and working in Washington, DC, on national policy to make the world a more just place.

Kate Kahan

recognized tribes in Louisiana in the aftermath of Hurricane Katrina. The Farm is particularly committed to supporting Indigenous communities' fight for their land and water rights—especially in regions that have been used as dumping grounds for nuclear and other toxic waste—and maintains many relationships across the country and the globe to fight such environmental racism.

Over the years of its existence, hundreds of children have been raised on The Farm. Whether they stayed on The Farm or moved elsewhere, these children have gone on to contribute to making the world a better place as community builders, healers, midwives, social justice activists, and artists.

The Farm continues today as an intentional community rooted in the principles of nonviolence and sustainable living. Approximately 250 people live on the four thousand acres, and thousands of people visit each year to give birth in The Farm Midwifery Center or to attend educational workshops on topics such as midwifery, organic gardening, and sustainable building. In addition to seeing examples of innovative energy production and cooperative living, as you pass through The Farm today, you can spot some of the original school busses in which the founding families caravanned to Tennessee, now built into hillsides and homes. The Farm is open to visitors every day 9 a.m. to 7 p.m., and a variety of guest accommodations are available. Visit the website for directions and to make reservations: thefarmcommunity.com.

ABOUT THE AUTHOR

Kate Kahan was born and raised on The Farm, and is the legislative director for Community Change.

NEARBY SITES OF INTEREST

Franklin Farmers Market (230 Franklin Rd., Franklin, TN): If you visit The Farm on a Saturday, consider stopping here on the way. Open every Saturday (8 a.m.–1 p.m.) year-round for farm fresh meats, dairy, produce, fruits, berries, honey, eggs, breads and baked goods, jams, jellies, flowers, trees, shrubs, dog treats, art, crafts, jewelry, mosaics, rain barrels, composters, organic soils, prepared foods, live entertainment, and so much more . . .

Figure 6.10. Giles County Trail of Tears Interpretive Center. Photo courtesy of Amie Thurber

6.8 GILES COUNTY TRAIL OF TEARS INTERPRETIVE CENTER

220 Stadium St.,
Pulaski, TN 38478

From the Trail of Tears Interpretive Center to the historical marker outside the law offices where the Ku Klux Klan (KKK) was founded, the small town of Pulaski offers an opportunity to bear witness to the legacy of racial injustice in Tennessee, while also experiencing how residents are wrestling with this legacy and reshaping the identity of their town.

In the autumn of 1838, approximately 1,800 Cherokee were marched through Pulaski as part of their forced removal and relocation to Oklahoma. It is estimated that hundreds of Cherokee perished along the eight-hundred-mile journey. Known as the Trail of Tears, the relocation followed a number of routes, with Cherokee traveling in detachments of about one thousand men, women, and children. Two of these routes passed through Pulaski.

Pulaski also has the notorious history of having served as the birthplace of the KKK. Following the Civil War, the newly elected Tennessee legislature enacted laws that conferred citizenship to African Americans, including allowing them to hold public office. During the same period, laws were passed that denied ex-Confederate soldiers the right to vote. Many ex-Confederates were concerned about their lack of representation and the high taxes imposed on their communities. In addition, most were fervently opposed to the rise of freed Blacks' political power and manifested that opposition violently toward African Americans. These tensions—and the fact that local governments appeared unwilling to protect Blacks from attacks—gave rise to the KKK. Within a few short years, the KKK had expanded to almost every Southern state. The corresponding rise of violence and lawlessness led to federal involvement to help suppress Klan activities, and to the passage of Jim Crow laws that reversed some of the greatest gains toward racial equity during

Reconstruction. By 1870, the original Pulaski KKK had disbanded, and much of the movement went underground. In 1915, the KKK was revived by a group in Georgia concerned about Jewish and Catholic immigration, and its ranks quickly swelled to more than four million people nationwide. It arose again in the 1960s to oppose the Civil Rights Movement. Though exact numbers remain unknown, the KKK is responsible for thousands of acts of intimidation, terror, and murder. Today, the Southern Poverty Law Center estimates there are between five thousand and eight thousand Klan members in the US.

Pulaski has long wrestled with how to address its legacy of racial injustice, particularly as the contemporary KKK still considers Pulaski its birthplace. Much to the outrage of many in Giles County, since the 1980s, the KKK has staged annual "homecoming" celebrations in Pulaski. In 1989, Mayor Dan Speer organized a citywide opposition to a Klan rally. All businesses closed their doors in protest, and city leaders draped the square in orange banners, the international color of brotherhood. More recently, the city helped launch the Heroes Project, a series of murals and portraits portraying everyday people in Pulaski who have fought for human rights and social justice. These murals include portraits of Matt and Henrietta Gardner, born into slavery, who—after being freed following the Civil War—financed public schools for Black children throughout Giles County.

In another effort to address the region's legacy of injustice, Giles County residents raised $900,000 to build a Trail of Tears Memorial and Interpretive Center. During your visit to Pulaski, you can walk down the side street off the city square to see the law office where six ex-Confederate soldiers first met to form the KKK (205 W. Madison St., Pulaski, TN 38478). The historical marker at the site has been turned face-in, reportedly to stop White supremacists from posing for pictures. You can visit the Gardner murals at the Giles County Department of Tourism and Chamber of Commerce, and find a complete listing of Heroes Project murals and locations at gilescoheroes.org.

ABOUT THE AUTHOR

Bernice Davidson is an associate professor of art at the Martin Methodist College and the artist and founder of the Heroes Project.

NEARBY SITES OF INTEREST

Law Office of Judge Thomas M. Jones (205 W. Madison St., Pulaski, TN): The location where six ex-Confederate soldiers first met to form the KKK

Matt Gardner Museum (110 Dixon Town Rd., Elkton, TN): Just fifteen miles away, learn more about this incredible Tennessean. Visit mattgardnerhomestead.org.

Figure 6.11. Walnut Street Bridge. Photo courtesy of Learotha Williams Jr.

6.9 WALNUT STREET BRIDGE, CHATTANOOGA

1 Walnut St.,
Chattanooga, TN 37403

Chattanooga's Walnut Street Bridge is arguably one of the most aesthetically pleasing features of the city's built environment. Built in 1890, the 2,376-foot bridge spans the Tennessee River, providing city residents and visitors a serene and visually stimulating path from downtown Chattanooga to the North Shore area. Holding the distinction as being one of the Volunteer State's longest pedestrian bridges, the Walnut Street Bridge symbolizes the city's transformation from a town once referred to as being the "Doorway to the Deep South" to a bustling New South City. In recent years, Chattanooga has boasted a "downtown renaissance," replete with new parks, upscale shops, art museums, and an outdoor climbing wall. But the downtown renaissance has come at a cost. Between 1990 and 2013, there has

been a 36 percent decline in Black residents as rising land values pushed out working-class people of color. A striking one third of the city's Black residents live in poverty—more than double the rate of their White counterparts. Black residents are more likely to be uninsured, live in higher crime areas, attend lower quality schools, and live in neighborhoods marked by disinvestment.

For many of Chattanooga's Black residents the bridge has a somewhat dubious past, one which has caused them to eschew the exercise, relaxation, and sense of community it provides for its travelers. Some Blacks still remember stories of the Walnut Street Bridge being the site of the lynchings of two Black men, Alfred Blount and Ed Johnson. These crimes, committed in 1893 and 1906 respectively, created a collective, trans-generational trauma among the city's residents, a condition which still resonates today.

Alfred Blount was the first to be lynched on the bridge, during a horrific period in the nation's history when Blacks were being lynched roughly once every three days. However, it is the lynching of Ed Johnson that has become most closely associated with the bridge's dark past. The narrative of the Johnson lynching closely resembled that of sixty-two other Black men and women murdered that year.

In 1906, Nevada Taylor, a twenty-one-year-old White woman, accused Ed Johnson of rape. Although the prosecution offered very flimsy evidence in the case, an all-White jury quickly convicted

Johnson and condemned him to death. Johnson's lawyers appealed the verdict and successfully gained a stay of execution from the Supreme Court. The stay would not be sufficient to save Johnson's life, however. The following day, a mob abducted Johnson from his cell in Chattanooga. The sheriff at the time, Joseph F. Shipp, sat quietly in an unlocked bathroom while the mob carried Johnson away.

Upon reaching the Walnut Street Bridge, the mob hung Johnson from one of its steel girders. When he did not succumb to strangulation immediately, the participants opened fire on him while he dangled from the rope. An errant shot, however, severed the rope, causing Johnson to fall on the bridge. Finally, a member of the mob completed the act by firing five shots into Johnson's head. The US Supreme Court quickly responded, charging the sheriff, several other law enforcement officials, and known members of the lynch mob with contempt of court and aiding and abetting Johnson's murder. In an act that was unprecedented in its 110-year history, the court held a criminal trial and found Shipp and the other defendants guilty of the charges filed against them and of being complicit in the murder of Ed Johnson.

Though a Hamilton County judge overturned Johnson's rape conviction in 2000, the event still elicits deep emotions from many in the city and state. Absent a historical marker to commemorate the lives and deaths of Alfred Blount and Ed Johnson, for many the Walnut Street Bridge represents access, possibility, and adventure. But for those who carry the knowledge of its past, the bridge conjures feelings of risk and vulnerability, and it is a vivid example of the intractability of racial amnesia in a city where racial disparities still run deep.

ABOUT THE AUTHOR

Learotha Williams Jr. is an associate professor of African American and Public History and coordinator of the North Nashville Heritage Project at Tennessee State University.

NEARBY SITES OF INTEREST

Chattanooga Organized for Action (1918 Union Ave.): Organizing to achieve social, economic, and environmental justice. Search on Facebook for upcoming trainings, events, and actions!

6.10   MOUND BOTTOM
Near intersection of Cedar Creek Rd. and Mound Creek Rd., Kingston Springs, TN 37082

Located in a large horseshoe bend in the Harpeth River just thirty minutes west of Nashville, Mound Bottom stands as a powerful testament to the continued significance of prehistoric Indigenous sites. Covering over five hundred acres of land, the area once contained nearly thirty large flat-topped earthen mounds dating back to the Mississippian era. Currently, the site is a state-designated archeological area under the management of Harpeth River State Park. The park covers one hundred acres and contains twelve mounds.

Figure 6.12. Mound Bottom. Photo courtesy of Melba Eads

The largest mound is twenty-five feet high and overlooks the others.

It is believed that in 950 CE, Mound Bottom served as the economic, social, and political epicenter of one of the most complex civilizations of the Mississippian era. Artifacts found in Mound Bottom match those found in Cahokia, the largest known Mississippian site in the United States, now a National Historic Landmark in Illinois. Mound Bottom functioned as a central hub in a trade network that reached north to the Great Lakes and south to the Gulf Coast. Once home to thousands, Mound Bottom experienced its decline as a booming Native American city around 1300 CE, likely due to increasing competition from other rising metropoles.

Little is known about the Mound Bottom site from the time of its decline to its ownership by the Taylors, a local farming family who acquired the land in 1919. The owners initially allowed no disturbances

to the area, but permitted an excavation by the Smithsonian Institute in the early 1920s. Artifacts from this excavation are now located at the University of Tennessee in Knoxville. However, the Taylor family quickly returned to the no disturbance order, leaving many more artifacts buried to this day. Over the years, the site was plowed and farmed; watermelons once grew atop the great mound.

In 1971 the State of Tennessee purchased the land, adding it to the Harpeth River State Park. In an effort to preserve the site, the State initially kept the area closed to the public. In 2012, the Harpeth River State Park began offering ranger-led hikes through the prehistoric site. On June 23, 2012, a Muscogee (Creek) Citizens Gathering took place at the Mound. Three generations of Muscogee visited the mound that day, connecting to their ancestors, "the people of One Fire," through the sacred mound. Although the Muscogee (Creek) Nation is now based in Oklahoma, the tribe's ancestral homeland includes land in Tennessee, and Nashville has a Muscogee citizen group with over fifty tribal members.

Indigenous leaders are pleased Mound Bottom is being preserved and are advocating for an interpretive center to be added to the Harpeth River State Park where visitors can learn more about the lives, culture, and achievements of the earliest inhabitants of Mound Bottom. In the meantime, guided tours of Mound Bottom are offered by reservation October through March, and the mounds can be viewed from the Mace Bluff Trail located across the river and directly north of Mound Bottom. This trail is unmarked; for more information or a to reserve a tour, call (615) 952-2099.

ABOUT THE AUTHOR

Melba Checote-Eads is an enrolled member of the Muscogee Creek Nation of Oklahoma and is the great-great-granddaughter of Principal Chief Samuel Checote who walked the Trail of Tears as a child from Fort Mitchell, Alabama. She advocates for preservation of sacred sites and commemorates the Trail of Tears.

NEARBY SITES OF INTEREST

Narrows of the Harpeth (1640 Cedar Hill Rd., Kingston Springs, TN): While Mound Bottom is not always accessible, this is a beautiful spot for hiking, swimming, kayaking, and more. The waterfall was created by enslaved Blacks for Nashville entrepreneur Montgomery Bell.

6.11 FAYETTE COUNTY COURTHOUSE

1 Court Square, #101,
Somerville, TN 38068

A less well-known but significant struggle in the Civil Rights Movement took place in rural Fayette County, fifty miles east of Memphis, Tennessee. In 1959, civil rights activists from the Fayette County Civic and Welfare League (FCCWL) began organizing Black voters. The first project undertaken by the league was a voter-registration drive, which, coupled with a rise in voter-suppression tactics targeting African Americans, forced the US Department of Justice (DOJ) to send monitors to the region. On November 16, 1959, a federal lawsuit was filed against the Fayette County Democratic Executive Committee claiming that it prevented African Americans from registering to vote. Within six months, the DOJ entered into a consent decree allowing Blacks to register in the county. This became the first voting rights case brought under the 1957 Civil Rights Act to be settled by negotiation.

Two months after signing the consent decree, Fayette County election officials erected new barriers to prevent African Americans from voting. While Blacks were allowed to register, they could do so only one day a week, and all of their applications were processed by one county official. On Wednesdays, in the hot summer months, hundreds of Black registrants were forced to stand in long lines and denied the ability to sit or stand on the courthouse lawn. Courthouse workers showered African American registrants with hot coffee, spit, red pepper, and paint. And election officials moved registration to the inside of the courthouse, where registrants could not use the segregated restrooms. Despite these suppression tactics, by September 1960, approximately one thousand Blacks had registered to vote.

Figure 6.13. Tent City brochure. Photo courtesy of Special Collections Division, Nashville Public Library

Civil rights activists, labor and faith-based leaders, and government agencies rallied to assist African Americans in Fayette and neighboring Haywood County, where a similar voting rights movement was occurring. In 1962, consent decrees were negotiated in Fayette and Haywood counties to address the issues. These consent decrees were a watershed moment in the history of the US voting rights movement. Though reprisals continued against voting rights advocates, within a couple of years, thousands of Blacks in Fayette County had been added to the voter registration rolls, ultimately resulting in the election of Blacks to local offices. More importantly, the Tent City movement provided a model of how to build a locally led resistance movement that prioritized the interests of working-class African Americans.

African Americans faced other reprisals for registering to vote. Members of the White Citizens' Council created a blacklist targeting Blacks and White voting rights advocates. Grocers, drug stores, and gas companies refused to sell them food, medicine, and fuel. Some Blacks were denied access to the hospitals, others lost their teaching jobs. The White power structure further intensified its attacks by evicting hundreds of Black sharecroppers and tenant farmers from their homes. The evicted farmers set up makeshift tents for temporary housing—leading to the moniker in rural west Tennessee of Tent City—where they were targets of shootings by Ku Klux Klan and White Citizens' Council members.

ABOUT THE AUTHOR

Linda T. Wynn is the assistant director for state programs at the Tennessee Historical Commission and on faculty at Fisk University in the Department of History and Political Science. A version of this essay appeared as "Toward a Perfect Democracy: The Struggle of African Americans in Fayette County, Tennessee," *Tennessee Historical Quarterly* 55, no. 3 (Fall 1996): 202–22.

NEARBY SITES OF INTEREST

Slave Haven Underground Railroad Museum (826 N. 2nd St., Memphis, TN): Visit a stop along the Underground Railroad. The home now serves as a museum, and starting point of a tour of more than thirty historical sites in the area. Check the website, slavehavenmemphis.com, for details.

7. THEMATIC TOURS

7.1 "It City"   264
7.2 Athens of the South   270
7.3 Music City   276
7.4 Southern Hospitality   280

FOR THOSE WISHING TO explore the city thematically, this chapter includes four tours that follow the themes introduced in the introductory chapter: It City, Athens of the South, Music City, and Southern Hospitality. Though designed as full-day tours most easily undertaken by car, each can also be completed, in part, by bicycle or bus. For those looking to rent a bike for the day, Nashville has a number of local vendors as well as Nashville B-cycle, a bike share program. For a station map and fares, visit nashville.bcycle.com. Each tour provides point-to-point driving directions. Frequently, in addition to main sites of interest to visit, we suggest nearby restaurants for a good meal.

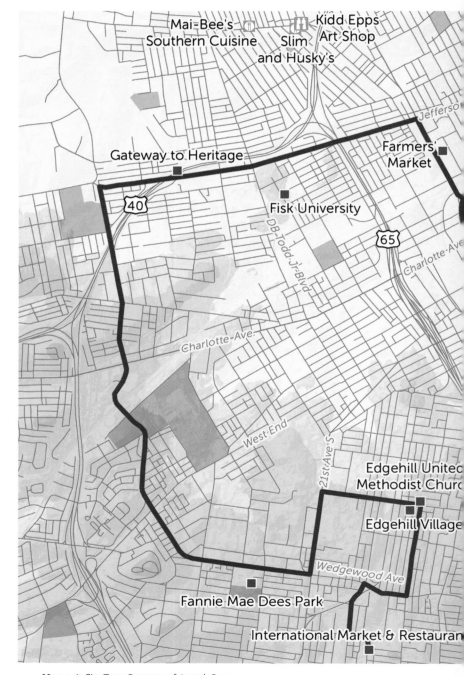

Map 9. It City Tour. Courtesy of Joseph Speer

"It City" Tour

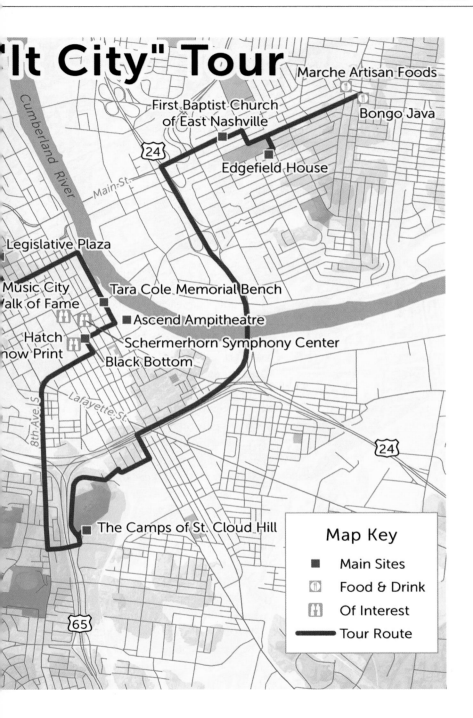

Marche Artisan Foods

First Baptist Church
of East Nashville

Bongo Java

{24}

Main St.

Edgefield House

Legislative Plaza

Music City
Walk of Fame

Tara Cole Memorial Bench

■ Ascend Ampitheatre

Hatch
now Print

Schermerhorn Symphony Center

Black Bottom

Lafayette St.

8th Ave S

{24}

The Camps of St. Cloud Hill

{65}

Map Key

■ Main Sites

Food & Drink

Of Interest

—— Tour Route

Cumberland River

Figure 7.1. Five Points during the annual Tomato Arts Festival. Photo courtesy of Solar Cabin Studios/Tomato Art Festival

7.1 "IT CITY"

This tour traces historic and present-day tensions around development in the city, taking you through neighborhoods that have experienced the greatest transformations over history, with particular attention to the effects of urban renewal, modern day development, and gentrification.

We begin the tour in one of the city's most rapidly gentrifying areas—East Nashville's 5 Points District (the corner of Woodland and 11th St.). After grabbing a coffee at Bongo Java or having a proper breakfast at Marche Artisan Foods, you can learn about past and current struggles to preserve community in the midst of development at several sites within walking distance, including the Edgefield House (3.3, 714 Russell St.) and First Baptist Church of East Nashville (3.7, 601 Main St.). From Five Points, drive west on Woodland Street toward Interstate 24 E / 40 W, and enter the interstate headed south. At the highway split, stay right on I-40 W/65 S, then get off immediately at the 4th St. exit. Turn left at the exit intersection, and after passing under the Interstate, turn right onto Oak St. Continue along Oak Street until you reach the parking lot for the Fort Negley Visitor Center, where you can tour The Camps of St. Cloud Hill (4.2, 1100 Fort Negley Blvd.) and learn more about the struggles for housing and labor justice in the city. The Fort Negley Visitors Center is worth a visit; it is open noon to 4 p.m. on weekdays, and 9 a.m. to 4 p.m. on Saturdays. Fort Negley Park is open each day from dawn to dusk.

From Fort Negley, head to the area once known as Black Bottom (1.7. 299 4th Ave. S.). Travel northwest out of the parking lot, turning left onto Fort Negley Blvd. and then right on Chestnut St. Turn right again on 8th Ave. S., enter the traffic circle, and take the second exit onto Korean Veterans Blvd. After turning left on 4th Ave., you will be in the heart of today's tourist district, and what was once known as Black Bottom. Though you will find little remnant of the area's history as a Black urban neighborhood, there is plenty to see,

Figure 7.2. Fort Negley in winter. Photo courtesy of Learotha Williams Jr.

including Hatch Show Print (224 5th Ave. S.), the Music City Walk of Fame (121 4th Ave. S.), and the Schermerhorn Symphony Center (1 Symphony Place).

Another site noteworthy for what is no longer present on the landscape is the Incinerator/Ascend Amphitheater (1.8, 301 1st Ave. S.), transformed through resident activism. To visit, walk or drive left onto Molloy St., and then left down 1st St. The amphitheater will be on your left and has a large open park, greenway, and fenced dog park to enjoy. To pay tribute to the unhoused, visit the Tara Cole Memorial Bench (1.6, 106 1st Ave. S). Continue north along the riverfront walk for .2 miles on 1st St., and the Memorial Bench will be on your right.

As Nashvillians fight for an "It City" that serves us all, Legislative Plaza (1.15, 301 6th Ave. N.) remains a key site of protest. From Tara Cole Memorial Bench, head up Church St., and take a right when you reach 6th St. N. Legislative Plaza is located .2 miles ahead on the left. The Plaza is immediately in front of the State Capital, which has regular free tours between 9 a.m. and 4 p.m. on weekdays.

In the current moment, the Nashville Farmers Market (1.19, 900 Rosa L. Parks Blvd.) is one of the city's most contested sites related to the intended beneficiaries of redevelopment. To explore, continue on 6th Ave. N., turning left when you get to Martin Luther King Jr. Blvd. Turn left again onto Rosa L. Parks Blvd. and

Figure 7.3. Ascend Amphitheater. Photo courtesy of Mike Thompson

Figure 7.4. Southern V is located at the site of the iconic Mai-Bee's, which has closed. Photo courtesy of Joseph Gutierrez

continue until you reach the Farmers Market, which will be on your left. While at the market, consider lunch at the Jamaica Way restaurant, which has authentic Jamaican cuisine and catering options.

From the Farmers Market, travel to North Nashville to explore the impact of urban renewal and contemporary redevelopment efforts on North Nashville. To reach the Gateway to Heritage (2.1, 2412 Jefferson St.), head north on Rosa L. Parks to Jefferson St., and turn left. Continue down Jefferson about 3 miles until reaching the Interstate 40 underpass. The Gateway to Heritage is a pedestrian plaza chronicling the history of Jefferson Street—before and after urban renewal—and contains both murals and photographs. If you wish to explore North Nashville while you are in the area, Fisk University, Meharry Medical College, and Tennessee State University are just a few blocks away, as is the Buchanan Street area. Although development is contested in the neighborhood, there is a wave of Black-owned businesses in the area committed to hiring and serving neighbors. These include Southern V, a family-owned and -operated vegan soul food restaurant (1200 Buchanan St.); Slim & Husky's (911 Buchanan St.), a pizza-and-beer place run by three Tennessee State University graduates; and Kidd Epps Art Shop (906 Buchanan St.), a handcrafted furniture store.

Continue your exploration of urban renewal at Fannie Mae Dees Park (5.15, 2400 Blakemore Ave.), another area shaped by highway construction, and home to a popular park. Continue west along Jefferson St. until you reach 28th Ave. N. Turn left onto 28th which crosses Charlotte Ave. and turns into 31st Ave. N. After crossing Natchez Trace, 31st Ave. N. turns into Blakemore Ave. Fannie Mae Dees Park will be on your right at the intersection of Blakemore and 24th Ave. S. Round out your visit by touring the Edgehill neighborhood, a short drive or pleasant twenty-five-minute walk through Vanderbilt University. Here you can see Edgehill United Methodist Church (5.5, 1502 Edgehill Ave.)—a center for organizing against the harms of urban renewal—and the rapidly gentrifying Edgehill Village (5.6, 1200 Villa Pl.)—once an anchor Black-owned business in the neighborhood. If you are ready for dinner, there are plenty of places to eat here.

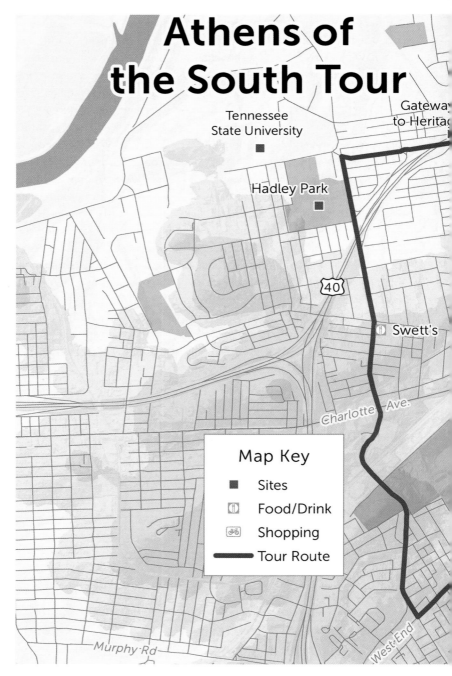

Map 10. Athens of the South Tour. Courtesy of Joseph Speer

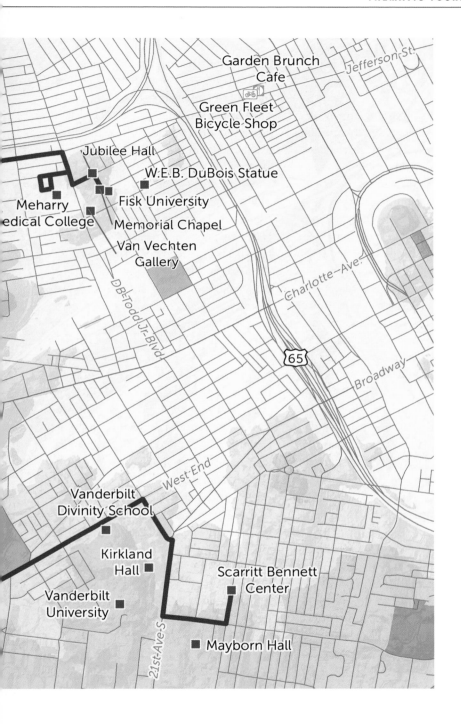

Garden Brunch
Cafe

Jefferson St.

Green Fleet
Bicycle Shop

Jubilee Hall

W.E.B. DuBois Statue

Meharry
edical College

Fisk University

Memorial Chapel

Van Vechten
Gallery

DB Todd Jr. Blvd

Charlotte Ave.

65

Broadway

West End

Vanderbilt
Divinity School

Kirkland
Hall

Scarritt Bennett
Center

Vanderbilt
University

21st Ave S

Mayborn Hall

7.2 ATHENS OF THE SOUTH

This tour takes you through many of the important educational institutions of the city. If you are starting the day hungry, stop in to Silver Sands Cafe (937 Locklayer St.), where you can enjoy a soulful meal accompanied by soulful tunes.If you feel adventurous, stop by Green Fleet Bikes (934 Jefferson St., adjacent to the Garden Brunch Café) and rent a bike for this part of the tour. Green Fleet is open Monday through Saturday, from 10 a.m. to 6 p.m. By car or bike, head west down Jefferson St. and make a right onto 17th Ave. N. Continue one block, make a left onto Meharry Boulevard and on the right, you will find parking and a circular drive (also known as 17th Ave. N.).

Start your tour at Fisk University (2.4, 1000 17th Ave. N.), Nashville's premiere private historically Black university. Learn more about the history of the school at Jubilee Hall (2.5, corner of 17th Ave. N. and Meharry Blvd.), which became a National Historic Landmark in 1974. This Victorian Gothic building, completed in 1876, was named after the famed Fisk Jubilee Singers, who are commemorated inside the building with a floor-to-ceiling painting given by Queen Victoria after their 1873 tour to England. From there head toward the W. E. B. Du Bois statue on campus (1500 Jackson St.). After his graduation from Fisk University in 1888,

Du Bois became one of America's premier intellectuals and the co-founder of the National Association for the Advancement of Colored People (NAACP).

While at Fisk University, you might also stop by the Memorial Chapel (17th Ave. N. and Phillips St.) and see where Dr. Martin Luther King Jr. and author Langston Hughes both visited over the past century. To get a look at chapel events and happenings, see the chapel's Facebook page. Next head to Fisk University Galleries, also known as the Carl Van Vechten Gallery (on the corner of Dr. D.B. Todd Jr. Blvd. and Jackson St.; open Monday through Friday from 10 a.m. to 5 p.m.). There you will find paintings in the Alfred Stieglitz Collection of Modern Art (shared biannually with another gallery, so check in advance for current exhibits) including works by Georgia O'Keeffe, one of the most significant American artists of the twentieth century. In addition to the permanent art collections, the Fisk University Gallery shows a variety of traveling exhibitions.

The next stop is Meharry Medical College (2.8, 1005 Dr. D. B. Todd Jr. Blvd.), the oldest medical college for African Americans, located across the street from Fisk on Dr. D. B. Todd Jr. Blvd. (between Albion St. and Meharry Blvd.). Meharry is one of the leading producers of African American doctors, dentists, and biomedical scientists in the United States. Then head toward Jefferson St. from Dr. D. B. Todd Jr. Blvd. and make a left to travel toward the third HBCU in North

Figure 7.5. (above) Jubilee Hall at Fisk University. Photo courtesy of Learotha Williams Jr.

Figure 7.6. (left) Benton Chapel at the Vanderbilt University Divinity School. Photo courtesy of Sharon Shields

Figure 7.7. Griggs Hall at American Baptist College. Photo courtesy of Learotha Williams Jr.

Nashville, Tennessee State University (2.6, 3500 John A. Merritt Blvd.). En route, you might stop at the overpass of Interstate 40 (on the right side of the street) to visit the Gateway to Heritage (2.1, 2412 Jefferson St.), a pocket park beneath the freeway commemorating historic Jefferson Street.

Continue heading down Jefferson St. until you reach 28th Ave. N., where Jefferson St. turns into John A. Merritt Blvd. and leads you into Tennessee State University, the largest and only state-funded historically Black university in Tennessee. If you feel like enjoying the outdoors, you will find Hadley Park to your left (2.7, 1037 28th Ave. N.) or continue on John A. Merritt Blvd. until you get to the center of campus, where

you can tour the grounds. Look for the six-story dormitory dedicated to gold medal Olympian and TSU alumna Wilma G. Rudolph, and TSU's Olympic statue. When leaving Tennessee State University, head down 28th Ave. N. (Edmondson Turnpike) on route to Vanderbilt University. If you are ready for lunch, stop by the famous family-owned Swett's (2725 Clinton Ave.) for home-cooked Southern food served cafeteria style.

To travel to Vanderbilt's campus, continue down 28th. Crossing Charlotte, the road becomes 31st. Turn left on West End and look for parking as you near the campus. The campus has been designated an arboretum, making it a pleasure to experience. You can find a campus map on Vanderbilt's website, and maps of the university are posted along major walkways. On this campus, you will find a number of sites significant to movements for social justice, including Kirkland Hall (5.12, 2201 West End Ave.), a site of contemporary student organizing, as well as the Vanderbilt Divinity School (5.9, 411 21st Ave. S.), which has long served as the university's moral compass. Benton Chapel is worth a visit; the beautiful gathering place was named after Dean Benton, who was instrumental in the university's 1952 decision to accept African American students.

From Benton Chapel, follow the walkway over the 21st Ave. S. pedestrian bridge to the Peabody campus of the university. Formerly home to Roger Williams University, one of the four freedmen schools established to educate Blacks after the Civil War, Peabody College now houses the Department of Human and Organizational Development's Community, Research, and Action doctoral program and the Community, Development, and Action master's program. Since the turn of the twenty-first century these programs, which were founded with the mission of promoting social justice, have been producing scholar activists. The Mayborn Building, completed in 1914, is the oldest building on the Peabody campus. As you walk past Mayborn on Magnolia Circle, exit the campus down 19th Ave. S. for a block until you reach the Scarritt Bennett Center (5.7, 1008 19th Ave. S.). Over time, the campus has been host to numerous

social justice speakers, including Dr. Martin Luther King Jr., who during the civil rights era delivered a speech at Wightman Chapel. After visiting Scarritt Bennett, return to 21st Ave. S. a few blocks away for nourishment before returning to your car.

There are other significant universities in Nashville, including the American Baptist College in North Nashville (2.2, 1800 Baptist World Center Dr.), a school that produced many of the leaders of the Nashville Movement during the 1960s, and Trevecca Nazarene University in the Southeast (333 Murfreesboro Pike, Nashville, TN 37210). While these are a little farther away, they both provide opportunities to see how Nashville deserves its reputation as the Athens of the South.

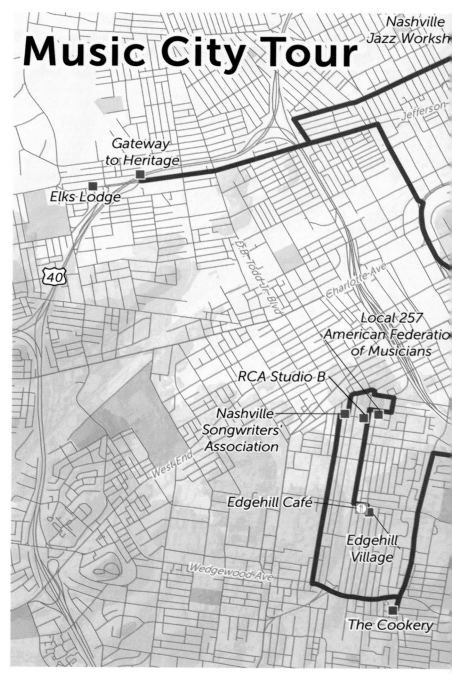

Map 11. Music City Tour. Courtesy of Joseph Speer

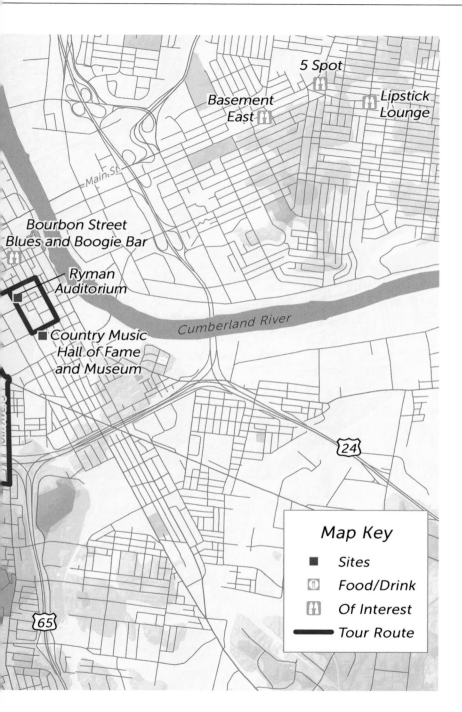

5 Spot

Basement
East

Lipstick
Lounge

Main St.

Bourbon Street
Blues and Boogie Bar

Ryman
Auditorium

Cumberland River

Country Music
Hall of Fame
and Museum

24

65

Map Key

- ■ Sites
- 🍴 Food/Drink
- 🚹 Of Interest
- ▬▬ Tour Route

7.3 MUSIC CITY

Explore Nashville's diverse musical past and present on this tour through the city. Start near Edgehill Village (5.6, 1200 Villa Pl.), perhaps grabbing coffee or breakfast at Edgehill Café. From here you can explore Music Row by foot, learning about the role Local 257 American Federation of Musicians (5.2, 11 Music Circle N.) and the Nashville Songwriters Association International (5.3, 1710 Roy Acuff Pl.) play in supporting Nashville's artists and strolling past dozens of record companies, recording studios, and publishing houses on the mile-long stretch up 16th Ave. S. You can also take a tour at RCA Studio B (1161 Roy Acuff Pl.).

If you are ready for a late breakfast or for lunch, head to the Cookery (1827 12th Ave. S.). This full-service restaurant trains and employs previously homeless and incarcerated Nashvillians and operates multiple programs hoping to alleviate hunger. From here, head downtown, where the Nashville Public Library has the best parking rates. To get there, travel north on 12th Ave. S., turn right on South Ave., and left on 8th Ave. S. Turn right on Church St. and make an immediate right on 6th Ave. N. to park in the library's garage. Walking from the garage, turn left onto Commerce St. and then right on 5th Ave. N. On the left, you will see the Mother Church of Country Music, the Ryman Auditorium (1.5, 116 5th Ave. N.). Go inside for a tour (from 9 a.m. to 4 p.m. daily, $20 for adults, $15 for children under 11) or grab a snack at the Lula C. Nuff café.

For a deeper dive into music history, head two blocks south on 5th to the Country Music Hall of Fame and Museum (222 5th Ave. S.). Check its website for exhibits, and leave yourself a couple of hours to explore this site, one of the world's largest American music museums. While downtown, follow the sound of the honky-tonks to explore Lower Broadway, observe the original buildings of downtown Nashville, and learn about some of the venues that are no longer present, such as Juanita's (1.4, Commerce St. and 4th Ave.).

The Music City Tour would not be complete without a trip to North Nashville to learn about a different era of Nashville's music history. From the library parking garage, head southeast on 6th, take your first right on to Commerce, and a right on Rosa L. Parks Blvd. Follow Rosa Parks for a half mile, then take a left on Jefferson St. Once on Jefferson you are on "Black Broadway," the heart of North Nashville, which was once a vibrant music scene. Find street parking near where the I-40 overpass meets Jefferson Street and then explore the Gateway to Heritage Plaza (2.1, 2412 Jefferson St.) located under the overpass. To learn about the area's history, the changes that occurred with the construction of I-40, and the music performed there, consider following the "digital spatial story line" introduced at the start of Chapter 2. Continue walking or driving Jefferson St., until you reach the Elks Lodge (2614 Jefferson St.), which features a large mural commemorating the infamous guitar battle between a young Jimi Hendrix and the great

Figure 7.8. *Musica* by Alan LeQuire. At forty feet high, *Musica* is the largest bronze figure group in America. Photo by Dean Dixon

Nashville bluesman Johnny Jones, when the site was formerly Club Baron.

Head back East on Jefferson St. and turn left onto 11th Ave. N. Soon, turn right on Monroe St. crossing Rosa L. Parks Blvd. into Germantown. Monroe St. turns left and becomes Adams St. The Nashville Jazz Workshop (1319 Adams St.) is a jazz community center that connects Nashville to its history as a vibrant jazz scene. In addition to hosting periodic free jazz performances, the NJW offers education programs for new musicians.

As you consider sites for live music to end your day, you will have problems of abundance. The famous Bluebird Café (4104 Hillsboro Pike) is an excellent venue known for cultivating an intimate listening environment and famous open mic events. The Bluebird Café is open most days starting at 5 p.m. Tickets are available online and sold one week in advance. Shows for Friday and Saturday go on sale on Mondays at 8 a.m., and Sunday and Monday nights are first come, first serve

(make sure to get there early to beat the line). Cover ranges from nothing to $15, and there is a $10 per person food or drink minimum.

If you are hoping to dance, the Bourbon Street Blues & Boogie Bar (220 Printers Alley) delivers a great downtown option, and the Basement East (917 Woodland St., home to QDP [3.5], the first Saturday of the month) and the 5 Spot (1006 Forrest Ave., home to Sunday Night Soul [3.4], the second and fourth Saturdays of the month,) are excellent east-side locations for live music. If you are looking for something more laid back, check out the Lipstick Lounge (1400 Woodland St.), Nashville's only lesbian bar, featuring a friendly neighborhood vibe, good food, and nightly karaoke.

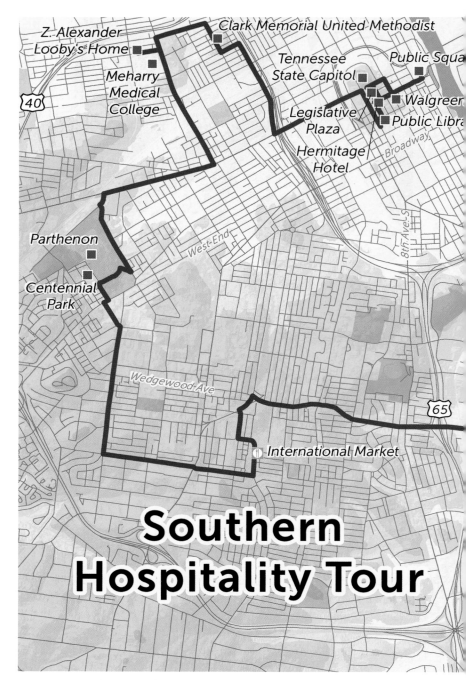

Map 12. Southern Hospitality Tour. Courtesy of Joseph Speer

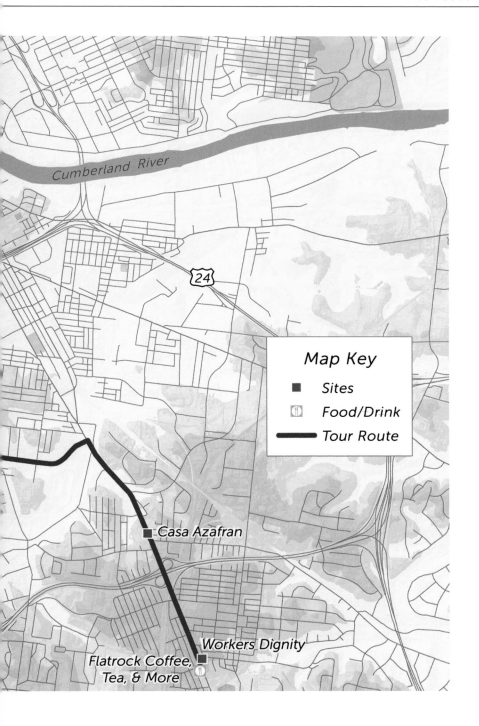

7.4 SOUTHERN HOSPITALITY

This tour explores the contested terrain of hospitality in Nashville, traveling through sites where residents at different points in time have fought to be valued as welcome members of Nashville's community. Start your day at Sam & Zoe's (525 Heather Place), which claims to be the second oldest coffee shop in Nashville. Pop over to Workers' Dignity (4.9, 335 Whitsett Rd.) to learn more about this immigrant-led worker center, and then continue north on Nolensville Pike to Casa Azafrán (4.5, 2195 Nolensville Pike), a hub for immigrant and refugee-serving organizations and organizing groups in Nashville.

Stop at any of the delicious spots to eat on Nolensville Pike, or head to the next stop, Centennial Park (5.13, 2500 West End Ave.) for a picnic. Segregated until 1964, this park hosts many public events, festivals, and protests, including a 2012 protest led by undocumented youth for tuition equality, held on the steps of the park's most notable feature—an exact replica of the Parthenon (5.14) in Greece.

Next, drive to North Nashville to continue to explore Southern Hospitality through the lens of the Civil Rights Movement. From the park, turn left onto 25th Ave. N. Turn right to stay on 25th Ave. N. and then right into Charlotte Ave. In .7 miles, turn left onto Dr. D. B. Todd Jr. Blvd. In a little less than a mile, turn left onto Meharry Blvd. There, you will find

the site of civil rights attorney Z. Alexander Looby's home (2.15, 2012 Meharry Blvd.), which was bombed with twenty-one sticks of dynamite on April 19, 1960, prompting the historic march to Legislative Plaza later that day.

Drive or walk along Meharry Blvd., past Meharry Medical College. Turn left onto Dr. D. B. Todd Jr. Blvd., then right onto Jefferson St., and then right onto 14th Ave. N. On the left is Clark Memorial United Methodist Church (2.3, 1014 14th Ave.), one of the oldest Black churches in Nashville and a primary gathering and training space during the Civil Rights Movement.

From Clark Memorial UMC, head downtown for a final collection of sites exploring Southern Hospitality. Turn left onto Jackson St. from 14th Ave. N., then right onto 12th Ave. N., which turns into Frontage Rd. Turn left onto Martin Luther King Jr. Blvd. for half a mile. Turn right onto 7th Ave. N. and then left into the Nashville Public Library parking garage. The Nashville Public Library (1.11, 615 Church St.) contains the Civil Rights Room, which is a curated space that tells the history of the Civil Rights Movement in Nashville. The Civil Rights Room is open every day (9 a.m. to 6 p.m. Monday through Friday; 9 a.m. to 5 p.m. Saturdays; 2 p.m. to 5 p.m. Sundays).

Exiting the library onto Church St., proceed across the street onto Anne Dallas Dudley Blvd. Turn right onto Union St. and right again onto 6th Ave. N. The Hermitage Hotel (1.14, 231 6th Ave. N.) is a Nashville landmark and played a key role in the

Figure 7.10. (left) Worker's Dignity headquarters. Photo courtesy of Workers' Dignity

Figure 7.11. (above) The Parthenon. Photo courtesy of Joseph Gutierrez

women's suffrage movement in Tennessee. Turn left onto 6th Ave. N. and right back onto Union St. and right onto 5th Ave. N. Walgreens (1.12, 226 5th Ave. N.) is one of the last remaining site of the Nashville sit-ins during the Civil Rights Movement. The student-led movement was one of the first sit-in movements in the South and led to the desegregation of many public and commercial spaces in the city.

Walk north on 5th Ave. N. and turn left onto Martin Luther King Jr. Blvd. The Tennessee State Capitol (1.13, 600 MLK Jr. Blvd.) will be on your right and Legislative Plaza (1.15) on the left. The capitol building is home to the Tennessee General Assembly and the site of numerous historic moments in the state's policy history. The capitol is open to visitors Monday through Friday from 8 a.m. to 4 p.m. and there are free tours. Across the street, Legislative Plaza is the primary spot for rallies and protests in the city. Finally, from the Plaza turn right onto 6th Ave. N. and left onto Union St. Across from 2nd Ave. N. off Union is Public Square (1.2, 300 Union St.), home to the public artwork *Witness Walls* and also the annual Nashville Pride Festival. From here you can continue to explore downtown, or return to the Library to pick up your car.

RECOMMENDED READING

Adkinson, Tom. *100 Things to Do in Nashville before You Die.* St. Louis, MO: Reedy Press, 2018.

Baptist, Edward. *The Half That's Never Been Told: Slavery and the Making of American Capitalism.* New York: Basic Books, 2014.

Bertrand, Michael T. "Night Train to Nashville: Music City Rhythm & Blues, 1945–1970." *Journal of American History* 92, no. 1 (2005): 175–77.

Bockman, Guy A. *Madison Station.* Franklin, TN: Hillsboro Press, 1997.

Bucy, Carole Stanford. "'The Thrill of History Making': Suffrage Memories of Abby Crawford Milton." *Tennessee Historical Quarterly* 55, no. 3 (1996): 224.

Burt, Jesse Clifton. *Nashville, Its Life and Times.* Nashville: Tennessee Book Company, 1959.

Cartwright, Joseph H. *The Triumph of Jim Crow: Tennessee Race Relations in the 1880s.* Knoxville: University of Tennessee Press, 1976.

Davis, Kenneth Penn. "The Cherokee Removal, 1835–1838." *Tennessee Historical Quarterly* 32, no. 4 (1973): 311–31.

Dorman, Lee. *Nashville's Jewish Community.* Charleston, SC: Arcadia Publishing, 2010.

Douglas, Mason. *Now You Know Nashville: The Ultimate Guide to the Pop Culture Sights and Sounds That Made Music City.* Nashville: Wild Cataclysm Press, 2013.

Doyle, Don H. *Nashville in the New South, 1880–1930.* Knoxville: University of Tennessee Press, 1985.

Eaves, Yvonne, and Doug Eckert. *Nashville's Sylvan Park.* Charleston, SC: Arcadia Publishing, 2011.

Egerton, John. *Nashville: The Faces of Two Centuries, 1780–1980.* Nashville, TN: Plus Media, 1979.

Egerton, John. "Walking into History: The Beginning of School Desegregation in Nashville." *Southern Spaces*, May 4, 2009.

Egerton, John, and E. Thomas Wood, eds. *Nashville: An American Self-Portrait.* Knoxville: University of Tennessee Press, 2005.

Ellis, John Joseph. *Belle Meade: Development of a Southern Upper-Class Suburb, 1905–1938.* Nashville, TN: Vanderbilt University Press, 1983.

Erickson, Ansley T. *Making the Unequal Metropolis: School Desegregation and Its Limits*. Chicago: University of Chicago Press, 2016.

Farris, W. L. *A Chronology of Old Hickory, Tennessee, 1750–1983*. Old Hickory, TN: W.L. Farris, 1984.

Fleenor, E. Michael. *East Nashville*. Charleston, SC: Arcadia Publishing, 1998.

Foster, Dave. *Tennessee: Territory to Statehood*. Johnson City, TN: Overmountain Press, 2002.

Franklin, John Hope, and Loren Schweninger. *In Search of the Promised Land: A Slave Family in the Old South*. New York: Oxford University Press, 2005.

Franklin, Sekou, ed. *The State of Blacks in Middle Tennessee*. Nashville: Urban League of Middle Tennessee, 2010.

Gelbert, Doug. *A Walking Tour of Nashville, Tennessee*. Nashville, TN: Doug Gelbert, 2011.

Goodstein, Anita Shafar. *Nashville, 1780–1860*. Gainesville: University of Florida Press, 1989.

Graves, John P. *Northwest Davidson County: The Land, Its People: Historical Sketches of Bordeaux, Jordonia, Scottsboro, Bell's Bend, Joelton, White's Creek, Union Hill, Lickton, Bull Run and Marrowbone*. Nashville, TN: Graves, 1975.

Haugen, Ashley Driggs, and Bob Grannis. *Historic Photos of Nashville in the 50s, 60s, and 70s*. Nashville, TN: Turner Publishing Company, 2009.

Haywood, John. *The Natural and Aboriginal History of Tennessee up to the First Settlements therein by the White People in the Year 1768*. Jackson, TN: McCowat-Mercer Press, 1959.

Hill Jones, Crystal, Naomi C. Manning, and Melanie J. Meadows. *Nashville's Inglewood*. Charleston, SC: Arcadia Publishing, 2009.

Hogan, Wesley C. *Many Minds, One Heart: SNCC's Dream for a New America*. Chapel Hill: University of North Carolina Press, 2007.

Hoobler, James A. *A Guide to Historic Nashville, Tennessee*. Charleston, SC: History Press, 2008.

Horn, Stanley F. *The Decisive Battle of Nashville*. Baton Rouge: Louisiana State University Press, 1956.

Houston, Benjamin. *The Nashville Way: Racial Etiquette and the Struggle for Social Justice in a Southern City*. Athens: University of Georgia Press, 2012.

Johnson, Charles W. *The Spirit of a Place Called Meharry: The Strength of Its Past to Shape the Future*. Franklin, TN: Hillsboro Press, 2000.

Kelley, Sarah Foster. *West Nashville: Its People and Environs*. Nashville, TN: S.F. Kelley, 1987.

Klein, Maury. *History of the Louisville & Nashville Railroad*. Lexington: University Press of Kentucky, 2003.

Kosser, Michael. *How Nashville Became Music City, U.S.A.: 50 Years of Music Row*. Milwaukee, WI: Hal Leonard Publishing, 2006.

Kreyling, Christine. *The Plan of Nashville: Avenues to a Great City*. Nashville, TN: Vanderbilt University Press, 2005.

Kreyling, Christine. *Nashville Past and Present*. Nashville, TN: Nashville Civic Design Center, N.D.

Kyriakoudes, Louis M. *The Social Origins of the Urban South: Race, Gender, and Migration in Nashville and Middle Tennessee, 1890–1930*. Chapel Hill: University of North Carolina Press, 2003.

Lamon, Lester C. *Black Tennesseans, 1900–1930*. Knoxville: University of Tennessee Press, 1977.

Lovett, Bobby L. *The African-American History of Nashville, Tennessee, 1780–1930: Elites and Dilemmas*. Fayetteville: University of Arkansas Press, 1999.

Lovett, Bobby L. *A Touch of Greatness: A History of Tennessee State University*. Macon, GA: Mercer University Press, 2012.

Lowry, Thomas P. *The Story the Soldiers Wouldn't Tell: Sex in the Civil War*. Mechanicsburg, PA: Stackpole Books, 1994.

Maraniss, Andrew, *Strong Inside: Perry Wallace and the Collision of Race and Sports in the South*. Nashville, TN: Vanderbilt University Press, 2016.

McDaniel, Karina. *Nashville: Then and Now*. San Diego: Thunder Bay Press, 2014.

McKee, C. William. *North Edgefield Remembered: Story of a Nashville Neighborhood*. Nashville, TN: C. William McKee, 2008.

Mohl, Raymond A. "Citizen Activism and Freeway Revolts in Memphis and Nashville: The Road to Litigation." *Journal of Urban History* 40, no. 5 (2014): 870–93.

Norman, Jack, Sr. *The Nashville I Knew*. Nashville, TN: Rutledge Hill Press, 1984.

Richardson, Joe Martin. *A History of Fisk University*. Tuscaloosa: University of Alabama Press, 2002.

Roman, Charles V. *Meharry Medical College: A History*. Nashville, TN: Sunday School Publishing Board of the National Baptist Convention, 1934.

Rothrock, Mary U. *Discovering Tennessee*. Chapel Hill: University of North Carolina Press, 1936.

Rouda, Bill. *Nashville's Lower Broad: The Street That Music Made*. Washington, DC: Smithsonian Books, 2004.

Sharp, Tim. *Nashville Music before Country*. Charleston, SC: Arcadia Publishing, 2008.

Spinney, Robert G. *World War II in Nashville: Transformation on the Homefront*. Knoxville: University of Tennessee Press, 1998.

Summerlin, Cathy, and Vernon Summerlin. *Traveling the Trace: A Complete Tour Guide to the Historic Natchez Trace from Nashville to Natchez*. Nashville, TN: Rutledge Hill Press, 1995.

Summerville, James, and Chris Adams. *Southern Epic: Nashville through Two Hundred Years*. Gloucester Point, VA: Hallmark Publishing Company, 1996.

Thomas, Jane Henry, and Leona Taylor Aiken. *Old Days in Nashville: Reminiscences*. Nashville, TN: Charles Elder, 1897.

Thompson, E. D. *More Nashville Nostalgia*. Nashville, TN: Westview Publishing Company, 2004.

Thompson, E. D. *The Nashville Nostalgia Years*. Nashville, TN: Westview Publishing Company, 2005.

Websdale, Neil. *Policing the Poor: From Slave Plantation to Public Housing*. Lebanon, NH: University Press of New England, 2001.

Wills, Ridley. *Nashville Streets and Their Stories*. Franklin, TN: Plumbline Media, 2012.

Winders, Jamie. "Nashville's New 'Sonido': Latino Migration and the Changing Politics of Race." In *New Faces, New Places: The Changing Geography of American Immigration*, edited by Douglas Massey, 249–73. New York: Russell Sage Foundation, 2008.

Winders, Jamie. "'New Americans' in a 'New-South' City? Immigrant and Refugee Politics in the Music City." *Social and Cultural Geography* 7, no. 3 (2006): 421–35.

Wooldridge, John. *History of Nashville, Tennessee*. Nashville, TN: Publishing House of the Methodist Episcopal Church, South, Barbee & Smith, Agents, 1890.

Zepp, George R. *Hidden History of Nashville*. Charleston, SC: History Press, 2009.

Zimmerman, Mark. *Guide to Civil War Nashville*. Nashville, TN: Battle of Nashville Preservation Society, 2004.

Zimmerman, Mark. *God, Guns, Guitars & Whiskey: An Illustrated Guide to Historic Nashville, Tennessee*, vol. 1. Nashville, TN: Shagbark Publishing, 2012.

NOTES